GARDEN FLOWERS

ORIENTAL POPPY
(Papaver orientale)

SCARLET RUNNER BEAN
(Phaseolus multiflorus)

PERENNIAL PHLOX
(Phlox paniculata)

CHINESE BELLFLOWER
(Platycodon grandiflorum)

LITTLE NATURE LIBRARY

GARDEN FLOWERS WORTH KNOWING

ARRANGED BY

ROBERT M. McCURDY

*Sixteen pages of black-and-white illustrations
and twenty-four pages in full color*

PUBLISHED BY
DOUBLEDAY, DORAN & COMPANY, Inc.
FOR
NELSON DOUBLEDAY, Inc.
1934

PUBLISHERS' NOTE

Any classification of flowers into seasonal subdivisions such as flowers of spring, of summer, of autumn, and of winter must necessarily be a purely arbitrary classification. A plant that blooms in April in one section of the country may bloom in June in another, or in July in another. Broadly speaking, however, the seasonal classification followed in this volume will, for the greater number of its readers, be fairly accurate. Also, the expression, "flowers of winter," is necessarily a misnomer, for the reason that in most sections of the United States in winter no garden flowers bloom, while in other sections there is no winter! The question naturally arises why a section of such a book as this should be devoted to "flowers of winter." The answer of course is that these plants may be grown indoors.

Again, the publishers believe that no reader will quibble on the ground of scientific accuracy because in this book on "Garden Flowers Worth Knowing" are included some trees and shrubs that do not flower, as well as some plants that, in the United States, are not, strictly speaking, garden plants. A picture is hardly complete without its frame; nor is a flower garden complete without its background of trees and shrubs. And if the growing of certain flowers and plants during the winter months bring to January something of the joy of June, we think this fact warrants the inclusion of "flowers of winter," even though one's "garden" is a greenhouse or a solarium.

CONTENTS

LIST OF COLORED ILLUSTRATIONS

LIST OF HALFTONE ILLUSTRATIONS

GARDEN FLOWERS

GARDEN FLOWERS

SPRING

The Pearl

Achillea Ptarmica

Achillea is better known under the name of White Tansy. White Tansy is a cousin of the weed Yarrow. There is an old superstition that if one sleeps on Midsummer Night's Eve upon a bunch of Yarrow, he or she will dream of a future wife or husband, as it may be. The Pearl is a small perennial esteemed for its profuse bloom. Double Sneeze-wort, Goose Tongue, Fair Maids of France, Seven Years' Love, are also designations of this much-named flower. In the single variety the disk flowers are yellow, the ray flowers white. In the Pearl—the double variety recommended for gardens—the disk flowers have disappeared; the flower is all a fluffy rosette of white. These rosettes have been greatly esteemed for cutting and for formal bouquets. In the garden Achillea should be kept well picked, as after the first bloom the plants turn brown and present an unsightly, rusty appearance. The Pearl grows successfully in practically all sorts of soils and spreads rapidly. In planting allow ten to twelve inches of space. The best method of propagation is to divide old plants in spring.

1

Adonis

Adonis vernalis

If you want something in early spring to give color to spots that later will be covered by growing shrubbery, get Adonis. Vernal Pheasant's-eye, Ox-eye, Bird's-eye, False Hellebore, are other names for this little bright yellow perennial. The dainty foliage forms dense tufts that die to the ground after the blooming season. The large yellow flower somewhat resembles a Buttercup. Plants range from eight inches to a foot high and may be planted in sun or half shade. A light moist or sandy soil is preferable. Adonis may be raised by seed sown in the autumn, but you must exercise patience as the seed germinates but slowly.

Mountain Lady's Mantle

Alchemilla alpina

Mountain Lady's Mantle is an inconspicuous plant of European origin often utilized in corners of rock gardens and perennial borders. The "Lady" for whom the plant was named must have been a dwarf, for her "mantle" grows no more than six inches in height. The digitate leaves have a silky and hairy under surface; the modest, quite drooping flowers should appear in late April and May. You may start this little plant from seed in either sun or shade, and it can easily be increased by division.

Gold Tuft

Alyssum saxatile

Gold Tuft or Gold Dust is the most prolific small yellow flower of spring. This old favorite forms a neat carpet of small, fragrant, golden-yellow flowers in loose panicles no more than a foot high. The leaves are small and rather slender, silvery and persistent. If the flower stems are cut back after blooming, a second crop of blossoms may be anticipated later in the fall or even after early frost. The plants thrive in the sun and in a sandy soil. Avoid heavy clay. Gold Tuft is commonly used for edging borders or as a cover in the rockery. It is best started indoors early in February and transplanted into the open in May. The variety *compactum*, growing six inches high, is an excellent plant for edging.

Love-Lies-Bleeding

Amaranthus caudatus

Love-Lies-Bleeding is a pleasant old-fashioned plant seldom seen nowadays and perhaps considered too gaudy for dainty gardens. Amaranthus, as it gets its growth (three to five feet), is inclined to become tall and straggly. The flowers are long, showy drooping panicles. The terminal spike in each cluster is longer than the others and whiplike. Red-flowered clusters are more common, but there are also yellow and white varieties. This is an annual and may be sown right out in the garden bed. If the soil be too rich, the plants are liable to rank growth and lose their bright coloring.

Shadbush

Amelanchier canadensis

The Shadbush is the most effective white-flowered tree along woodland borders before the Dogwood. All coun-

try children know the Shadbush, only quite possibly they
call it Service Berry or June Berry.   The shrub at blossoming time becomes a mass of small, white, very attractive,
plum-like flowers.   The red berries, quickly disposed of by
nesting birds, come later.   If you wish particularly to at-
tract birds to your garden, you need only plant a Shadbush
or a Mulberry.   Shadbush grows to the height of twenty
feet in the North and frequently as high as sixty in the
Southland.   The blossoms are at their height just about
the time the shad run up the rivers to spawn, and the origin
of the name is easily traced to the fishing habits of the early
American colonists.   As they whipped the streams for
shad they doubtless saw a charming and to them unknown
little tree lighting up the river banks with early color.

Poppy Anemone

Anemone coronaria

Most people never think of the Anemone except as a
wild flower, but it may be adapted as a garden plant of
beauty and value.   There are many species, some of
larger growth, of flowers of greater size, of colors more
rich and varied than those of their wild sisters.   The
Anemone has the double interest of garden beauty and
legendary association.   The litterateur remembers that
the Anemone is the flower referred to by Shakespeare in
"Venus and Adonis."

> And in his blood that on the ground lay spill'd,
> A purple flower sprung up, chequer'd with white.

An antiquarian remembers that the word comes from the
Greek *anemos* (wind) and that Pliny says the plant was

so named because "This flower hath the propertie to open but when the wind doth blow." But Pliny must have had some other plant in mind or have been incorrect in his statement, which is not at all characteristic of our common Anemone.

There are many species and varieties. *A. Coronaria* (Poppy) and *A. hortensis* (Star) represent two great sections of early bloomers. *A. nemorosa*, white tinged with purple. *A. sylvestris* is cream white, tinged with pink flowers in summer. The Japanese Anemone blooms in late summer.

The Poppy Anemone grows about a foot high and thrives in most kinds of soil. Plant in autumn for spring bloom, and in spring for summer flowering. Set the tubers two inches deep and six inches apart. Look over the tubers, pick out the incipient buds, and plant these pointing upward. Cover the bed in winter. The first flowers should appear in March and bloom should continue through April and May. After bloom is over, the tubers may be dried and stored away; or they may be cut to the ground and left as you would Tulips or Hyacinths.[1]

Rocky Mountain Columbine

Aquilegia caerulea

A. caerulea is a native Columbine growing wild from Montana to New Mexico. This spring visitor will prove itself worthy of space in the rock garden. The stem rises from one to one and a half feet high. The flowers which bloom from April to July are whitish tinged with blue and yellow, and about two inches across. The sepals fre-

---

[1] *Anemone sylvestris* and the Japanese Anemone are in the summer section.

quently are blue.   The spurs are long with knobs at the
ends.   For culture a light, moist, sandy soil is required.
Theoretically a hardy perennial, *A. caerulea* rarely blooms
more than two or three seasons and had best be treated as
a biennial.

Wild Columbine

Aquilegia canadensis

There are many glimpses of the Columbine in early
English literature and in particular the many references by
Shakespeare to the flower may be taken as a measure of its
popularity.   History narrates that our common American
Columbine, known to all New England children as the
Honeysuckle, was sent as a gift from the Virginia colony to
Tradescant, botanist to King Charles I, and by him in-
troduced to Hampton Court gardens.   The Columbine
has frequently been suggested by enthusiastic admirers for
our national American flower.

Certainly there is no lovelier wild flower to grace a home
garden.   Columbines dance on airy stems along the rocky
ledges with cheerful nods and bows or at times dignified
curtseys.   One garden writer remarks playfully that the
early wild flowers seemed to have stationed the Columbine
as a reception committee along the leafy balconies of woodland ridges to extend a hearty welcome to all strangers who
chance to come within nodding distance of their abode.
In fact, in many sections of the country the Columbine,
gathered in armfuls by the thoughtless, has been forced to
pay the penalty of its popularity and become difficult to
obtain.

Remember its habitat, and in domestic culture tuck
away in pockets of soil in the rockery.   Columbine grows

from two to four feet high and blooms from May to July.

Golden Spurred Columbine

Aquilegia chrysantha

Golden Spurred Columbine will be an attractive addition for the corner of your garden. This is almost a perfect flower in outline, as the spurs are extra long and golden. The foliage is dark and handsome and the flowers are numerous, slightly fragrant, and clear yellow, carried on graceful, branching stems three or four feet high. The Golden Spurred is considered the most hardy of the Columbines. You will have good results in any loose, well-drained soil with plenty of sun. Start from seed indoors in March and set out in April. More often you will get no bloom the first season.

Rock Cress

Arabis albida

Rock Cress is one of the easiest growing and showiest spring-blooming, white-flowered plants for carpeting the ground. Rock Cress is a hardy, courageous, low-growing perennial (six to eight inches high) which it is wise to remember when you are looking about for border plants or for some flower to cover a steep bank. The bloom begins in April and will last on through June. The flowers are pretty and somewhat fragrant. Rock Cress spreads quickly to cover considerable space and it is customary to buy a few plants and let them increase. They could be raised from seed if desired. There is also another species,

A. alpina, with smaller flowers, considered inferior by most garden writers.

Sea Thrift

Armeria maritima

Sea Thrift, or Sea Pink, flowers in dense heads above tufts of evergreen foliage. This pretty little perennial is found growing along the seacoast in England and on the continent of Europe but may easily be domesticated for our American home gardens. Start seeds indoors in February and transplant into the open in May. You had best utilize Sea Thrift as a low-growing, trim border plant to edge walks and fill out corners in the rock garden. Well-drained sandy loam is ideal. Sea Thrift will even stand a considerable amount of drought. Old plants divide easily. There are for choice white and rose-red varieties.

Chokeberry

Aronia nigra

The Black Chokeberry and its companion, *A. arbutifolia*, the Red Chokeberry, are both perfectly hardy and among the most beautiful fruiting small shrubs. Red Chokeberry grows from six to twelve feet high and the Black not generally quite so tall. The flowers are white or tinged red, in corymbs, and come from April to June. The two species look well planted together and are desirable for border planting. Chokeberry prefers moist soil but will grow also in deep rocky spots. The foliage turns a pretty red in the fall and the fruit remains all winter. You may propagate from greenwood cuttings or get young shrubs from dealers in the late summer or early spring.

Alpine Aster

Aster alpinus

The Alpine Aster is a dwarf member of a very large family. This baby Aster grows from three to ten inches in height, with large, solitary, star-shaped, bluish-purple flowers with yellow centers. The plant blooms from early May to mid-June. Effective in the border, in sun, or part shade; but should be protected from the very hot rays of midsummer. You may start this Aster from seed, but it is more customarily propagated by division of the clumps. There is a fine white-flowered variety, *alba;* and a variety *speciosus*, growing taller and stronger than type with large, rich, purple flowers.

Azalea

Azalea calendulacea, Rhododendron calendulaceum

No wonder this plant has received the popular name of Flame Azalea, for that is exactly what its flowers in varying shades of orange-red and flame-red suggest as they are seen in the undergrowth of open woodlands, fairly illuminating the May landscape. Though it is native to eastern North America, it is one of the truly popular plants of the hardy shrubbery. It has a number of almost equally showy relatives which are likely to be found in our gardens, Japanese and Chinese cousins.

The Flame Azalea grows from four to ten feet high, but the maximum is not often attained except in peculiarly favorable conditions. In common with the other mem-

bers of the family to which it belongs—the Heath family—
the Azaleas demand an acid soil and will not tolerate any
suggestion of lime. Consequently they are not often
found in healthy conditions when planted near the foun-
dation of houses where the soil is usually lime impregnated.

False Indigo
Baptista australis

With good habits and showy, well-colored flowers, the
Baptisia is one of the best plants for garden cultivation.
Blue Rattle-Bush and Blue Wild Indigo are other common
names. In early growth the plants may be mistaken for
Lupines. They grow bushy and about four feet in height;
the leaflets are sea-green in groups of three; the blossoms,
blue, in long, loose racemes. Baptisia thrives in any soil,
likes sunshine, blooms well; but as the foliage blackens
after August, it is not well to give the plant the prominent
position to which on flower merit the False Indigo would be
entitled.

B. leucantha is a native perennial with small white
blossoms found from Ontario to Texas. Grows from two
to four feet in height in any ordinary garden soil. The
seeds, started indoors, produce plants of a size to transplant to the open in May. Set them in the border a foot
apart. In choosing where they are to go, do not forget
that they are likely to turn black in the late season and
present an unsatisfactory appearance.

Begonia
Begonia hybrida

The Tuberous Begonia, as we grow it in our gardens to-
day, is an entirely modern production. There is little in-

terest of folklore or literary association in the Begonia, and it was but little esteemed until recently. In the seventies and eighties certain nurserymen in England began to become famous as growers of Begonias and now we have a magnificent array of varieties including many shapes and colors.

Begonias may be used as bedding plants in the outdoor garden if you select a shady spot. Dig your bed deep and work in plenty of manure. The tubers are roundish, bulblike affairs with a depressed side in which a growing tip may be discovered. Plant the tubers, pointed end up, indoors about the end of April. In late May or early June put the plants into the outdoor bed about a foot apart. The leaves are large, green above, and red below the surface. The flowers are large, waxy, and handsome. Bulblets appear in the axils of the leaves of some kinds after blooming is over. Begonia is an enormous family and only one, B. Evansiana, is hardy, living over winter outdoors successfully.

Daisy, English

Bellis perennis

This is the English Daisy the praise of which runs through many familiar lines of the great English poets. Our common American Daisy of the college "daisy chain" and the childish "he loves me, he loves me not" is another flower, botanically, weighed down with the formidable name of *Chrysanthemum leucanthemum*. The English Daisy is a cheerful little plant for edgings and for window boxes. You had best plan to remove the English Daisy after blooming, as it is apt to present rather an unsightly appearance. The flower stalks rise stiff and soldierly; the

GARDEN FLOWERS

flowers, generally double varieties with no yellow center in our gardens, are an inch or more across with white rays tipped with red or pink or wholly red. The English Daisy is not of difficult culture; it thrives best in cool, rich, moist soil with some sun. It is advisable to protect the plants with a light mulch over winter. Plant indoors early in boxes. The plants should go in the ground about six inches apart. Before the summer is over they will send out new offsets which should be divided in the fall, forming additional plants.

Spice Bush

Benzoin odoriferum

The Spice Bush known also as Benzoin Bush and Wild Allspice is one of the earliest flowering shrubs, with aromatic bark. This very desirable garden shrub grows from six to fifteen feet high with bright green oblong leaves that turn a pretty yellow in the fall. The small yellow flowers appear in the spring in clusters before the leaves open out. The fruit is a crimson berry, quite spicy and much relished by the birds. The Benzoin of druggists is derived from a member of this plant group. The Benzoins are quite hardy, preferring sandy, peaty soils. Propagate by green wood cuttings under glass, taking plenty of cuttings, as a large percentage are likely not to root. Propagation by planting the seeds is also possible but a very slow process.

Ashberry

Berberis aquifolium or *Mahonia aquifolium*

The glossy-leaved, blue-berried Mahonia is a fine, low-growing, ornamental evergreen shrub. The height at maturity will be no more than three feet. The compound leaves are a fine lustrous green. There are tassels of golden yellow flowers in May, and the berries come in late summer. Choose a sheltered spot with a fair amount of sun and not too moist a soil for the Ashberry, which is most often planted with other shrubs. Foliage sometimes burns in winter. A closely allied species is *M. japonica*, with broader leaflets and taller growth—a fine shrub and worthy of more extensive planting in favored places.

Japanese Barberry

Berberis Thunbergi

This shrub is a quick grower and one of the best, low, ornamental, defensive hedge plants. The branches are sufficiently spiny so they are not disturbed by animals or small boys. The foliage is dense and arching, more so than that of the common Barberry. Japanese Barberry grows from two to five feet high; there are pale yellow flowers in April and May, followed by brilliant red foliage in fall and red berries that often persist through winter. This species of Barberry is used as a border for walks and drives and, clipped close, as a dividing hedge in lawns and gardens. While the old-fashioned Common Barberry is a host to the wheat rust, and therefore should not be planted generally, the Japanese Barberry is quite free from the fungus that causes the disease.

Spring Meadow Saffron

Bulbocodium vernum

The rosy purple flowers of the spring Meadow Saffron come early on the spring scene with the Crocus, which they

somewhat resemble. The flowers, three or four to each
bulb, precede the leaves, which are broad and rather strap-
shaped. This Saffron is a prime favorite as a house bulb.
Pot in September or October, placing several bulbs in a
pot (allow an inch between bulbs) and cover with a half
inch of soil. The pots are then plunged in ashes till December or January. If they are to be planted outdoors, select
a warm, sheltered position in light, sandy soil. The bulbs
increase rapidly, and it is necessary to take them up and
separate the offsets every two or three years in July or
August. The Saffrons are natives of the mountains of
Europe and Russian Asia.

Japanese Quince

Cænomales lagenaria

If you are going to have any shrubs at all, you must have
a touch of low-growing, fiery red, Japan Quince or Fire-
bush to set off your darker evergreens. This is the earliest
bright scarlet-flowered shrub that appears in our gardens.
It should not be planted near decorative fruit trees unless systematically sprayed, as it is subject to the San
José scale. April and May are flowering time and the
flowers lie open in clusters, two to six in a cluster. The
fruit which comes later is globular and yellowish. This
Cydonia will bloom most freely in a sunny spot but will
mature in shade as well. There are also white and pink
varieties, but the red is the one most commonly seen.
Until recently this was generally known as *Cydonia
japonica*, but Cydonia is now exclusively used for the fruiting Quince.

Pot Marigold
Calendula officinalis

This is the old-fashioned herb whose dried flowers were used by our grandmothers to flavor soups. Calendula grows about a foot high and is quite hardy. The plants will bloom from spring till fall if the flowers be kept well picked and the season be not too dry. The leaves form a rosette near the ground from which the flower stalks emerge. The flowers are orange, yellow, occasionally white, Aster-like in form. The seed may be planted outdoors. Calendula grows anywhere but delights especially in warm, rich soil. There are plenty of varieties to choose from. Sulphurea has light yellow flowers; Nankeen, yellow; Meteor, orange; Prince of Orange is a very effective orange and yellow.

Strawberry Shrub
Calycanthus floridus

The group of Calycanths consists of a number of sweet, deciduous shrubs which includes several old-time garden favorites. Strawberry Shrub or Sweet Shrub grows from six to ten feet high with rather coarse leaves and deep red-brown flowers of pungent, spicy odor. In colonial days the little blossoms were often tied into the corners of handkerchiefs, but such simple tastes could not long survive the possibilities of buying perfumery in bottles. Carolina Allspice belongs also to this group. The Calycanths are all desirable because of their sweet-scented flowers. The conspicuous part of the flower is the calyx. There are no distinct petals. Plant in any good garden soil in early spring.

The Calycanths, except the California species, *occidentalis*, are quite hardy in the North.

Great Bellflower

Campanula latifolia

The Great Bellflower is a striking representative of a big family containing more than three hundred species, annual, biennial, and some perennial, The flowers grow six to fifteen in number, borne on stems three or four feet tall. The leaves are large, hairy, and heart-shaped, sometimes six inches long at the bottom and more pointed higher up. Because of its height, it is best set toward the back of the border. *C. latifolia* grows wild in England and is not difficult of culture here. Sow early in the spring indoors, plant outside in late May, spacing eight inches to a foot apart. Bellflowers grow in any well-drained soil in sun or shade. As the plants grow they may be divided for new plants. The blossom-time is May and June and the blossoms are commonly purple or dark blue. There is also a white-flowered variety.

Pea-tree

Caragana arborescens

The Pea-trees are ornamental shrubs grown for their profuse yellow, pea-shaped flowers appearing in April and May and are quite effective. The Pea-tree has the reputation of being the best yellow-flowered shrub of its season. You had best buy a young plant, as growing from seed will be a very slow process. Plant wherever needed, but a sandy soil is best and a sunny position desirable. *C. frutex* is about half as high and even more graceful than

C. arborescens, which in fact is the only one of the Pea-trees that really grows high enough to be called a tree.

Judas Tree

Cercis canadensis

As with the Magnolia and Shadbush the flowers of the Judas Tree, or Red Bud, come before the leaves appear. The peculiar small pea-like purplish pink blossoms borne along the bare wood are rather startling. Plants of this kind had best be planted in front of evergreens or against water, or wherever the effect of distance may be gained. The fruit of Cercis is a thin pod. The tree grows best in rich, moist soil and is quoted in garden manuals as reaching a height of thirty feet, though rarely seen so tall. Plants begin blossoming at four years of age. A larger-flowering species and better colored is *C. chinensis.* It seems too bad that this pretty shrub bears the somewhat heavy burden of tradition of having been the tree on which Judas Iscariot went forth and hanged himself.

White Fringe

Chionanthus virginica

The glory of this tree or shrub lies in the big, showy, drooping clusters of white flowers that appear in May and June. Sometimes staminate and sometimes pistillate flowers are to be found. Staminate flowers are handsomer but lack the beautiful dark blue pendulous fruit the pistillate bear in the autumn. This American plant with its attractive flowers makes a much-envied lawn shrub when in full bloom. The White Fringe is hardy, preferring sunny places, rather moist peaty soil, and if possible not too exposed a position.   Plants may be started from cuttings.   In Europe White Fringe is planted as a beautiful exotic from America, but here because it grows wild we have been slow to introduce the tree to cultivation.

Glory-of-the-Snow

Chionodoxa Luciliae

"After the Snowdrop comes the reign of blue and purple . . . Glory-of-the-Snow makes spots of beauty on the earth where snowdrifts lately lay, when the first bluebird shows a glint of the heavenly color, too, as he flies about the orchard looking for a nesting hole." (*Blanchan*.)

Plant these little bulbs in the fall about three inches deep and an inch apart.   They do not need any winter cover. Leaves and flowers are thrown out together, in February, March, or April, according to exposure and depth of planting.   The flowers vary in color, blue or white.   No special care is needed in preparing the soil and the bulbs may be left without disturbance for several years.   Eventually they should be taken up and separated as the bulbs increase by offsets.   *C. grandiflora* is a cherished variety of this with large violet flowers paling to white in the throat.

Clarkia

Clarkia elegans

Clarkia, named for the explorer of the Rockies, is a garden annual of the easiest culture and one of our commonest plants.   The colors run from rose through white to purple, blooming from June till after frost if you make late sowings.   Adaptable to all soils and may be planted in early spring outdoors in the sun.   Sow in rows and thin out to ten inches apart.   *C. elegans* has been known to reach a height of four feet, but the usual growth is no more than two feet.   If you wish late bloom, keep the flowers well picked so that seed does not form.

Lily-of-the-Valley

Convallaria majalis

Is there any one who does not know the Lily-of-the-Valley?   Is there any one who does not instantly recognize the white, globular, bell-like, and very fragrant flowers hanging daintily from long, graceful flower stalks?   It is of the easiest culture, and is one of the most satisfactory spring flowers.   Commonly a dweller in shady spots there is no reason why the *C. majalis* will not thrive in full sun if the ground be properly enriched.   Very characteristic is its habit of spreading through the grass and groping its way along the edge of shrubbery.   The smooth, broad leaves grow up from the base of the stalk and preserve their fresh, clean character all summer.   Old beds run out and will not bloom profusely; with a dressing of manure each fall, there should be satisfactory bloom four or five years. This Lily has a horizontal root stalk from which is produced an upright, bud-like part called a pip.   These pips may be put into cold storage and later used for indoor forcing. In the garden the pips lie dormant till spring, when they open, sending up leaves and flower stalks.

Hawthorn or May

Crataegus Oxyacantha

This is the English Hawthorn, beloved of the poets, famous as a hedge plant, and among the loveliest of flower-

ing trees. Burns sings of the Hawthorn, "wi' its lock o'
siller grey," and Shelley of the "moonlight coloured May."
The Hawthorn is a low-growing tree, quite hardy, thrives
on dry soil, stands severe pruning. In cultivated varieties
flowers may be had in various pinks and reds, single or
double, but the original single white is perhaps the most
characteristic and beautiful. The effect of the tree in
flower is not pure white but almost silvery. The air in
blossom time is filled with rare perfume. The light scarlet
fruit is much relished by the birds. The Hawthorns are
protected by sharp thorns and become very slow-growing
after reaching ten feet in height. Hawthorns are clipped
as desired to form hedges. This plant is often confusingly
referred to another species *C. monogyna*. Some desirable
red-flowering varieties are *submollis, coccinoides, punicea,*
and the popular Paul's Scarlet (double).

Crocus

Crocus susianus, sativus, and *C. aureus*

After the Snowdrop the Crocus! "Bulbs have a mission
in life," says Wilhelm Miller. "They seem to have been
divinely appointed to entertain us from the moment when
winter becomes too tedious for words until the trees leaf
out and spring strikes high C." If you have any spring
flowers at all you must have purple, lavender, white, and
yellow Crocuses.

Crocuses need to be planted two inches deep and from
four to six inches apart. When planting in the grass, take
a handful of bulbs, or rather corms, and toss them carelessly
on the lawn, and where they drop, plant them. Some gar-

deners turn back a bit of sod on the corner of their spade, drop the bulb in the opening, and replace the sod, leaving no trace of their operations behind them until the flowers push their way through in spring.

Blue, white, and yellow predominate in the Crocuses commonly purchased. Named varieties are usually more expensive than those purchased according to colour.

Excellent varieties are: Mont Blanc, white; Albion, purple and white; David Rizzio, purple; King of the Blues and Non Plus Ultra, blue edged with white.

Garland Flower

Daphne Cneorum

The Garland Flower, a prime favorite and most charming as a border plant, is a low trailing evergreen shrub with glossy dark green leaves and small pink, fragrant flowers. The flowers appear in April and May and quite frequently a second time in August. Thrives best in light, well-drained soil enriched with well-rotted manure but will succeed in half shade or even in dry spots if once well established.

The Daphne is best propagated by layering: that is, removing the earth round an old plant in spring and pegging down the branches, filling with fine compost almost to the tops. In another year, on removing the compost, a number of little buds supplied with roots will be found among the branches. These may be taken off and planted in pans or boxes. Daphne may also be raised from cuttings taken in the fall and kept in a cool greenhouse over winter.

Mezereon

Daphne Mezereum

Often in late February before a leaf is to be seen this little shrub has wrapped its stiff, thin branches in a fragrant purple scarf. The Mezereon offers the best lavender and the nearest approach to blue among the shrubs flowering before the leaves. This dwarf shrub succeeds best in a light, well-drained soil made rich with old cow manure. Garland Flower is also a popular name applied to *D. Mezereum* and *D. Cneorum.* The leaves are attractive, oblong, and gray underneath. The berry is bright scarlet. The variety *grandiflora* blooms early and sometimes later in the fall. You may propagate by seeds which germinate but slowly or by layers in the spring. Unfortunately the shrub is not hardy very far North.

Larkspur

Delphinium grandiflorum, etc.

No hardy plant gives us the splendid range of blues that we get in the Perennial Larkspur—blues as dense as Gentians, as brilliant as Sweet Peas, as clear of eye as Forget-me-nots. In the garden the Hybrid Larkspurs play a part that few other plants are fitted to fill. They make noble pictures with their tall spikes and vigorous growth. Gardeners who consider that the most striking form of flower gardening is to make a few bold groups of selected plants, seize on the Larkspur as peculiarly a plant for their purpose.

The flowers are curiously shaped, single, semi-double, or

double, from one to two inches across, borne on stately, graceful spikes, on erect branching stems, from four to eight feet high. They had best be planted against a background as they show poorly against a blue sky. Larkspur has an unfortunate habit of looking straggly and shabby in midsummer. The seeds germinate slowly and may be sown in the fall or started indoors in February. *D. Ajacis*, an annual species, blooms from July to August from spring sowing, but from May to June if sown in the fall.

Deutzia

Deutzia scabra, D. gracilis, etc.

Not the least of our numerous garden obligations to Japan is the ornamental shrub Deutzia. With arching branches, bright green foliage, and pure white blossoms in large corymbs, Deutzia will always be noticed even in the lush days of June. *D. gracilis*, a low spreader, with single white May flowers is particularly to be recommended. *D. scabra candissima* is a double-flowered Deutzia, called in the extravagant words of a dealer's catalogue, "The most desirable flowering shrub in cultivation." The flower colors of Deutzias in our gardens vary from white to white tinged with rose or purplish and straight pink. *D. Lemoinei*, a new hybrid, is considered one of the hardiest. There are many beautiful modern hybrids.

Plant this Japanese shrub in any good soil if it is well drained and a little sheltered. Give slight cover over winter. Make cuttings four to six inches in length, preferably after the leaves have fallen, and place them in little bundles of six or eight tied together in moss in a coldframe. In the spring plant the cuttings in a mixture of sand and soil indoors, transplanting to the outside only when well rooted. By fall cuttings should be fair-sized plants.

Bleeding Heart

Dicentra spectabilis

Bleeding Heart suggests the old-fashioned garden. Deep rosy-red and pink candy "hearts" on tall, graceful, wand-like stems; foliage; early bloom; all these help to account for the popularity of this excellent flower. The old-time garden never was, and the modern garden never ought to be, without at least a few roots. It is important to remember that Bleeding Heart dies to the ground after the flowering period. Rich, moist earth is to be preferred, but the plant is not fussy and will do well in any fair soil. Bleeding Heart is usually planted in the open but is also a favorite for forcing. Remember that it belongs to the small group of plants that like to be left alone year after year without division. There is a white-flowered variety, if you prefer, quite pretty, but of weak and sickly habit.

Foxglove

Digitalis purpurea

Foxglove, a flower of much history and many popular names, vies with the Larkspur and the Hollyhock in its habit of blooming in spire-like stalks. The Foxglove is a fine plant in bloom, particularly effective in masses against shrubbery, but rather unkempt in appearance at seeding time. Colors are multi-varied—black, purple, rose, white. The flowers are large and tubular, two inches long, drooping in long, pointed terminal spikes. The Foxglove is a perennial but is more usually treated as a biennial. The first year the plant sends out firm, big leaves; the second, the flower stalk shoots up. If you have a choice of soil select one that is light, rather moist, in sun or partial shade. If you intend to let the seed ripen to self-sow, arrange that your Foxgloves be concealed in midsummer by other tall-growing perennials.

Shooting Star

Dodecantheon Meadea

The pert, nodding blossoms of this native flower (also known as American Cowslip and Pride of Ohio) are found along moist cliffs in open woodlands in April and May from Pennsylvania to Georgia and west to Manitoba. The flowering stalk rises one or two feet high, and the showy flowers, rose to purple and white, are gathered loosely in clusters or tall stalks. The stamens are yellow capped and coming to a point appear to be shooting ahead with the petals streaming behind. Shooting Star may be domesticated in any well-drained garden soil, but remember its wild habitat and do not allow too much sun. The rootstock is stout and fibrous. Plants may be divided or started from seeds but this last is a slow process.

Leopard's Bane

Doronicum excelsum

Yellow daisy-like flowers are very rare before the end of May. Leopard's Bane with its mid-April bloom is a flower to be remembered. It is quite hardy, grows a foot or two in height, in any good soil and in partial shade;

the best results are said to be obtained from rich loam in full exposure to the sun. The flowers are about two inches in spread, one on a stem, carried well above the foliage, which is mostly in a crown at the base of the plant. Doronicum may be raised from seed or by division. There are about twenty species of this attractive flower.

Goumi

Eleagnus longipes

Goumi is not a very conspicuous shrub and is planted mostly, perhaps, for its showy scarlet fruit, appearing late in the year. The flowers which appear earlier are small and yellowish white. Goumi grows to be about ten feet high. The leaves are silvery on the under side, the branches red-brown. The Eleagnus family will do well in any well-drained soil and may be propagated by seeds or cuttings. *E. argentea*, blooming in July and August, is an American form called Silver-leaved Oleaster. *E. angustifolia*, the Russian Olive Oleaster, grows to the height of twenty feet with handsome foliage, silvery on the underside.

Barrenwort

Epimedium macranthum

If you wish to experiment with oddities, try Great-leaved Barrenwort, an importation from Japan. For their nine inches in height these little plants make a very brave showing. The flowers appear in May and June, rather orchid-like. The eight sepals are in two sets, the outer often bright red, the inner violet. The spur-like petals are white. The bright red of the outer sepals often persists after the other parts of the flower have fallen. Barrenwort will thrive in any soil, and if you select a well-sheltered position, the foliage is likely to remain all winter. The variety *violaceum* has violet-colored spurs.

Winter Aconite

Eranthis hyemalis

Eranthis, coming in March, is the earliest bright yellow flower of the spring. The flowers are out before the leaves, one to a stem, and the little plant, six or eight inches high, stands as stiff as a soldier. The flower has five to eight sepals and the petals are smaller. The foliage dies down in summer. Winter Aconite is propagated by division of its tuberous rootstock. Plant in the autumn in part shade, along the border with shrubs. Winter Aconite is a European and Asiatic plant. There is a dwarf species, *E. sibirica*, which grows only four inches high.

Heath

Erica carnea

This bright little member of the very numerous family of Heaths is an early bloomer and an old-time popular favorite. The colors vary from pale to a light rosy red. The plants grow no higher than six inches and bloom from late March through May. The Heaths are most successfully grown in peaty soil with full exposure to the sun. A delightful summer-blooming variety is *E. vagans*. Other commonly grown species are *E. melanthera* with black anthers and *E. fragrans* with flowers always in pairs.

Perennial Wallflower

Erysimum asperum

The genus Erysimum contains a number of yellow blooming annuals and biennials, some of which make excellent border plants. *E. asperum* is a perennial with pretty, effective yellow blossoms growing in elongated terminal racemes. You should have no garden troubles with this Wallflower. Divided plants are more frequently obtained than seeds which have been seldom kept in stock by our American dealers. If you raise from seed, plant in February, transplant to the outdoors in May, spacing about eight inches apart.

The yellow Wallflower *E. ochroleucum* or *E. helveticum*, grown mostly as an annual, is not difficult to raise and almost equals the yellow forms of English Wallflowers.

Dog's-Tooth Violet

Erythronium dens-canis

Everybody loves the Dog's-Tooth Violet, and everybody knows it by this misleading name. It is not a Violet at all. It is a Lily. Maybe the name originated from the shape of the flower parts, which have something of the outline of the long pointed teeth of a dog. The type flowers are rosy purple or lilac, the stems four to six inches in length. The mottled leaves are characteristic. Dog's-Tooth Violet is a spring flower which likes partial shade and a light soil. The club-shaped pistil of the rather large perfect flower has its tips or stigmas united. The flowers close at night. They always face toward the sun and the outer divisions recurve to their fullest extent on brightest and warmest days. The bulb is edible and when roasted used to be relished as a tidbit by the Indians. The bulb and leaves are also used as a medicine for producing nausea.

California Poppy

Eschscholtzia californica

Those who think of the California Poppy only as a yellow flower will be surprised to learn that there are now rose, scarlet, carmine, orange, and white varieties of the same original. The flower scarcely needs description. Prettiest and gayest of annuals, the California Poppies adore the sun, scorn drought, have no bad tricks of any sort. This hardy plant is quite roving in habit, makes itself comfortable in the chinks of walls and steps and all sorts of seemingly unlikely places. Poppies like the sun. Sow scatteringly and thin out to stand four inches apart. The plants will self-sow, and if the bed be covered over in the fall, the plants will come up next year. They bloom from June till frost and it is best to keep them well picked.

Pearl Bush

Exochorda grandiflora

The Pearl Bush somewhat resembles a giant-flowered Spiraea but blooms a little later. It is very much a "mass" shrub, neither flowers nor foliage boasting great individual charm; but the dazzling white blossoms, more than an inch across with large green disk, become quite radiantly effective when artfully massed with other shrubbery. This shrub grows in any soil and may be easily propagated in the usual ways. Exochorda gets into poor general condition unless kept pruned.　Only old plants produce fruits. The Pearl Bush seems not to be planted as much as formerly, which is a pity.

Golden Bell

Forsythia suspensa, etc.

Long, gracefully drooping branches of yellow bell-like flowers brusting into bloom before the leaves give the Golden Bell its name and make it the most showy of the early flowering shrubs of its color.　The leaves remain unchanged all the summer, often lingering on the branches till late fall or early winter and then assuming a chocolate purple tone.　There are several commonly grown species looking much alike.　*F. viridissima* has more flowers but rather greenish in color, and smaller, with erect branches, and holds its foliage very late in the fall.　*F. intermedia* is a hybrid of the other two and is intermediate in habit.　Forsythia is commonly planted against dark backgrounds.　At times *F. suspensa* has been very effectively trained to droop over arbors.　All the Forsythias are hardy, presenting no especial soil problems, but the buds sometimes get injured in winter in the North.

Guinea-Hen Flower

Fritillaria meleagris

One wonders sometimes where some of the flowers get their names, but one never wonders regarding this purple mottled Fritillary.　Some will know the flower better as Snake's Head and Checker Lily.　Fritillarias are mostly low growing and early blooming.　The nodding flowers are tessellated green and purple, an inch across, borne singly in six-inch stems. The flower is tulip-shaped but the drooping head gives it the appearance of a Lily. This bulb, of British origin, should be planted early in the fall in a rather sheltered spot. Sandy soil is preferable. The bulbs should be laid down three or four inches deep and a little less apart. The California *F. recurva* is brilliant red in color. The Fritillary bed should be renewed every three years. The Guinea-Hen Flower lends itself freely to naturalistic treatment in meadows and half-wild places.

Snowdrop

Galanthus nivalis

The little white Snowdrop nodding from its slender stem is dear to those watching for the first sign of spring. This is the earliest cultivated flower of the season, being contemporary with the wild Hepatica. There is also a Giant Snowdrop which blooms a little later, with the Crocus, but can never be so beloved as "the little sister of the snows."

Snowdrops have been known to appear in January and a common name for this flower in England is "The Fair Maid of February."

Plant these small bulbs in the fall two inches deep and about the same distance apart, choosing sheltered, shady, moist garden spots. The leaves are bright green, flat, and from six to nine inches long. There are two or three leaves from a bulb. The solitary flower escapes from a spathe and hangs nodding from its stem. The three concave petals are white, and a greenish tube of green stamen filaments occupies the center.

Fringed Gentian

Gentiana crinita

Gentians are notoriously fractious in the garden and the most attractive ones really belong to the rockery or Alpine garden. Everybody would love to have a Fringed Gentian—one of the most lovely and mysterious plants of our countryside—which, however, is quite capable of being handled in the garden. The thing to remember about it is that it is a biennial and the first year from seed makes a tiny rosette that is hardly perceptible. The second year, when conditions are to its liking, it holds forth in all its vigorous glory and rewards the gardener with its many flowering branches of fringed blue cups.

Gentians like full sunlight and they also like plenty of water—but it must not be stagnate. The drainage must be perfect. Neither do they like too much heat, although they like all the light and sun you can give.

Wild Geranium

Geranium maculatum

Crane's Bill is a popular name. There is no reason why the large showy rose-purple flowers of the Wild Geranium should not be more frequently domesticated in our gardens. The Wild Geranium is a perfectly hardy perennial of easy culture, preferring a moist spot but thriving almost anywhere in the rock garden or herbaceous border. The height is about one and one half feet. The leaves, divided into five or seven wedge-shaped parts, are of somewhat thinner, finer texture than the ordinary Geranium. The flowers are mostly for color effect, as

they fade very quickly when picked. Blossoming time
is May, June, and July. Wild Geranium may be transplanted from the woods or may be grown from seed. In
planting allow ten inches space between plants. Herb
Robert or *G. Robertianum* is a very handsome species from
Europe that loves rocky places and full sunshine.

Snowdrop Tree

Halesia tetraptera, or *carolina*

Of habit twiggy and pendulous, the Snowdrop or
Silver Bell Tree offers a bewildering cloud of white flowers
that appear before the leaves in May. There are three
species in the genus, which is exclusively North American.
They may be transplanted easily from the woods or the
banks of streams, preferably in the fall. Choose a straight
tree not over four feet in height and select a rich soil in
a not too exposed position. They are a success with
other shrubbery or by themselves. The Snowdrop Tree
is hardy in the New England states, but growing wild, it
is scarcely to be found north of West Virginia and Illinois.
The tendency is to grow with a rounded top and a bit
drooping. If you desire to keep the blossoms down for
close observation, prune to shrub size.

Japanese Witch Hazel

Hamamelis japonica

The Japanese Witch Hazel, unlike our well-known American Witch Hazel, which comes in late autumn, blooms
early enough to be listed among the spring blossoms. The
curiously shaped yellow flowers burst into life in February, lasting till April. There is glorious autumn foliage,

bright yellow, orange, or sometimes purple. *H. japonica*, faithful to the country of its origin, prefers plenty of sun and less moisture than our American variety. *H. arborea* is a somewhat similar shrub but with larger leaves and petals more golden yellow. Plants may be started from seeds—a slow process, as the seeds do not germinate till the second year.

Sneezewort

Helenium Hoopesii

Perhaps the most valuable species of Helenium for general planting. Sneezeworts resemble Sunflower plants and grow from one to three feet in height, blooming in May and June. The leaves are small, narrow, and toothed; the flowers large, daisy-like, with drooping orange rays and yellow center, on stout, leafy stems, one to three feet high, branching at the top.

Heleniums like rich moist soil and sun. Planted in the open from seed, they will not bloom the first year. The roots are occasionally attacked by a white aphis, in which case they must be washed with an insecticide and reset in a new place. There are about twenty-five species of Helenium.

Hellebore or Lenten Lily

Helleborus orientalis

All the Hellebores are hardy perennials with attractive foliage. *H. orientalis* has the leaves divided like a hand, with seven to nine lobes to each leaf. The stalk grows a foot high and bears two to six flowers. The sepals are distinctive, being roundish, white above and purple beneath. Some of the best varieties by color are: purple-

SPRING ADONIS
(Adonis vernalis)

POPPY ANEMONE
(Anemone Coronaria)

GOLDEN-SPURRED COLUMBINE
(Aquilegia chrysantha)

SEA THRIFT
(Armeria maritima)

ALPINE ASTER
(Aster alpinus)

FALSE INDIGO
(Baptisia australis)

POT MARIGOLD
(Calendula officinalis)

JUDAS TREE
(Cercis canadensis)

flowered, *atrorubens* and *rubro-purpureus;* white-flowered, *olympicus* and *antiquorum;* green-flowered, *caucasicus.*

They may be planted in any ordinary garden soil which has some richness and good drainage. They prefer the shade and are favorites for less exposed portions of garden borders. Old plants had best be divided in late summer or fall, not in the spring. The Hellebores may be started from seed, but it is a slow process.

Hepatica
Anemone Hepatica or Hepatica triloba

The lovely Hepatica, known to all children as the earliest of the wild flowers of the wood, is less frequently seen in gardens. It is commonly found by searchers along half-shaded patches of open woodland on rocky hillsides just as spring opens. With low, dense growth, early period of blooming and abundance of bright flowers, they would be valuable garden plants except that they cannot stand heat. They must have cool moist soil and a shady place. Hepaticas have fibrous roots and grow about six inches high. The old leaves stay on through the winter, screening the buds. After flowering, new leaves are sent up. The flowers are blue, lilac, white, or red, with lilac perhaps the most common. The blossom has no petals. Solitary flowers less than an inch broad are borne on slender, hairy stems. They exhale a delicate fragrance, although the odor is not constant. They close at night.

Hyacinth
Hyacinthus orientalis

Coming with the Crocuses before the snow is off the ground the Hyacinth is almost indispensable in any garden worthy the name. The early date at which they bloom makes them especially welcome, and once planted and left undisturbed, the bulbs increase rapidly without injury from overcrowding. Firm solid bulbs are to be selected rather than merely large ones. Flowers are single and double. In planting a formal Hyacinth bed one should take care to have colors that go well together.

Single flowers: Baron Van Thuyll, blue; Alba Maxima, white; Florence Nightingale, red; King of the Yellows, yellow. Double flowers: Charles Dickens, blue; Prince of Waterloo, white; Bouquet Tendre, red; Bouquet d' Orange, yellow. The following color combinations are suggested: red, white, and blue; light blue and yellow; light blue and rose; pink, blue, and yellow; mauve, red, and white.

Hyacinths are great lovers of water and do best in a heavy but friable soil. Some sand may be put about the bulbs when they are planted in the autumn. If the soil is light, poor, and dry, it ought to be worked deeply and given a dressing of well-rotted manure.

Evergreen Candytuft

Iberis sempervirens

By all means have in your home garden a bit of Evergreen Candytuft whose white snowy blossoms are never melted by sunshine. Candytuft planted with Moss Pink (*Phlox subulata*) form a delightful color combination for the early garden. *I. sempervirens* is hardy and of easy culture, succeeding in any soil, even in dry ground, in sun, or in partial shade. Grows from six to twelve inches high and blooms in April or May. The flowers are pure glistening white in big clusters, the outer flowers being larger and more showy than the inner. The leaves are dark green and evergreen. To start from seed, start indoors in early spring or in the fall and bed over. Candytuft is such a vigorous spreader that it sometimes becomes troublesome along borders.

Man-of-the-Earth

Ipomoea pandurata

Man-of-the-Earth, also called Wild Potato and Moon Flower, is a very hardy tuberous vine with flowers like a Morning Glory. The weight of the root (ten to fifteen pounds) gives the plant strength to live under adverse conditions. In fact, at times in the South and Middle West this vine has been more commonly regarded as a weed and a nuisance. Man-of-the-Earth is one of our best plants for covering tree stumps and old fences, and there is no reason why growth should not be kept within reasonable bounds with proper attention. The flowers are white with deep purple throat and the bloom should be steady and profuse from May to September. Man-of-the-Earth is a country flower, hardly suited to small city gardens.

Iris

Iris germanica

"The fleur-de-lys, which is the flower of chivalry," says Ruskin, "has a sword for its leaf and a lily for its heart." When that young and pious Crusader, Louis VII, adopted it for the emblem of his house, spelling was scarcely an exact science, and the fleur-de-Louis soon became corrupted into its present form. Doubtless the royal flower was the white Iris, and as *li* is the Celtic for white, there is room for another theory as to the origin of the name. It is our far more regal-looking but truly democratic blossom, jostling its fellows in the marshes, that is indeed "born in the purple." (*Blanchan.*)

The plants roughly classed as German Iris are almost all hybrids of various species and very numerous. The Iris, flowering late in May and early in June, supplies many of the most colorful and effective garden borders. The colors range from pure white to mauve and dark purple. Erect branched stems carry large showy, bearded flowers a foot or more above the clump of long, narrow sword-like leaves. Remarkably decorative, Irises may be counted on to make a fine showing banked en masse, or singly against shrubbery, or in the herbaceous border. After bloom the foliage presents a withered appearance which is difficult to conceal. Irises require plenty of room and will not stand crowding. They like best a sunny exposed situation in well-drained, rich but not freshly manured soil.

In the Japanese Iris (*I. laevigata*) the stems are more slender than in the "German" or Tall Bearded type, the flowers more delicate and wider spreading. The range of colors is fully as great but the varieties are variations of one species, not hybrids.

Sweet Jasmine

Jasminum nudiflorum

Sweet Jasmine, a native of China, is well to remember as the earliest flowering slender shrub. More frequently a greenhouse plant in the North, this Jasmine, with winter protection, is reported to be hardy as far north as the Hudson Valley. This is an erect, vigorous little bloomer with large fragrant yellow flowers which come out eagerly before the leaves. The branchlets are green and four-angled. The flowers are solitary, with calyx lobes leafy and spreading and a corolla tube that gives a graceful wavy effect. The foliage drops off quickly in autumn.

The Yellow Jasmine of our Southern states is a Gelsemium, not a Jasminum.

Mountain Laurel

Kalmia latifolia

Hardier than the Rhododendrons, smaller in blossoms and in foliage, the Laurel is in many points superior in beauty. Ordinary growth is around eight feet in height, but Kalmia has been known to reach forty feet and to form thickets that defy passage. This broad-leaved evergreen with rose-colored flowers scarcely needs botanical description. Mountain Laurel likes a well-drained situation but will be a success in any soil except a heavy clay, provided it is not alkaline. Transplant from the wild in fall or late spring, and be sure to give ground protection the first winter.

Honey made from Laurel blossoms has been found to be poisonous and the Government has classed the Kalmias among our principal poisonous plants. The foliage contains a dangerous substance which if eaten is more deadly than strychnine. The Indians were said to have been familiar with the poisonous nature of the Kalmia and to have compounded therefrom a death-dealing drink. Children have been overcome by the intoxicating effects of eating the young shoots which they have mistaken for Wintergreen.

Japanese Rose

Kerria japonica

Yellow flowers in May like single Roses, bright persistent yellowish leaves in autumn, slender, pendulous light green branches for the winter make up the unusual combination of attractions of the much-praised Kerria. Japanese Rose will do well in any garden soil, but the best color effects are commonly thought to be only obtained in half shade. There are double flowered and variegated leaved forms also. Young shrubs may be set out in early spring or propagation may be done by cuttings and root division. In a severe cold season the tips of the branches are sometimes winter killed.

The White Kerria (*Rhodotypos kerrioides*) is less profuse in bloom but very handsome and decorative and has black berries all winter. In the country of its origin the shrub grows fifteen feet in height, but in America you will scarcely see a White Kerria or Jet Bead over six feet.

Use stock about two feet high planted in the fall and you need not worry regarding soil or drainage.

Golden Chain

Laburnum vulgare

This small tree is familiar to most garden-bred folk. Bean Tree is a more common name in many sections of the country. Laburnum stands erect with gracefully drooping branches from which in May hang chains of yellow, pea-shaped blossoms sometimes nearly two feet in length. The tree is raised from seed without difficulty, grows quickly, finally reaching a customary height of twenty feet. Good results are to be obtained in sun or part shade, but farther north than southern New England the Laburnum is not reliably hardy save in sheltered places, and it requires a certain degree of moisture in soil and air. Golden Chain is considered poisonous in all parts, especially the beans that follow the flowers.

Dead Nettle

Lamium maculatum

Dead Nettle is an adaptable low carpeting plant with pretty ornamental foliage, green blotched with white along the midrib, that makes it very valuable when a filler is needed. Dead Nettle grows six to eight inches high, blooming from May to July. The flowers, purplish in color, stand up in clusters, each flower an inch long. This is the Dead Nettle of the Old World, with several varieties varying in color. The plant propagates itself by division and no especial attention is needed in cultivation. *L. album*, the White Dead Nettle, is similar, but has all-green foliage. In some sections Dead Nettle will be found running wild.

Snowflake

Leucojum vernum, L. aestivum

The Spring Snowflake has the appearance of a large Snowdrop, though on the whole not so graceful a flower. The spring species (*vernum*) blooms in March; the so-called Summer Snowflakes (*aestivum*) in April and May, and has more flowers to a stack. You should have no

trouble with these little bulbs, which may be planted
from August to October in lawns or along borders.
Plant the bulbs quite close together but not touching.
The spring species often has a delicate odor like a violet.
The flower is six-parted and the petals are tipped with a
spot of green or, less frequently, yellow or red. Summer
Snowflake is a member of the Amaryllis family and a na-
tive of the Mediterranean region.

Perennial Flax
Linum perenne

Blue-flowered plants are never too many, and the Flax
is also interesting as the source of the linen of commerce.
The plant grows a foot or two in height, with graceful little
blue flowers lasting only a short time but blooming rapidly
in succession. Flax occupies little space, gains a quick
foothold in the chinks of walls, along the edges of paths,
and anywhere in borders. It will generally flower the
first year from seeds in the open, but if you wish to make
sure of your blossoms, start indoors. Full sun in an open
spot is not too strong for this little plant. The var. *album*
is an excellent white-flowered perennial. The Narbon Flax
(*L. harbonense*) has perhaps even a more sky-like blue than
the more common *L. perenne*. *L. grandiflorum*, about
two feet in height, has flowers in varying shades of red.
The effect when planted with Delphiniums is very fine.

Bush Honeysuckle
Lonicera fragrantissima, etc.

There are many species of Bush Honeysuckle, both
early and late flowering, that are to be met with in well-

ordered gardens. *L. fragrantissima* is an early comer that
floods the cool spring garden with fragrance as well as
cheers it with creamy white blossoms. This species is
erect-growing; the leaves do not appear till after the
flowers have decorated the brown branches.

The Tartarian Honeysuckle (*L. tatarica*) averages from
eight to ten feet in height and is very handsome when in full
bloom. The flowers come in clusters in May and June,
pink, red, and occasionally white. The fruit is an excellent decorative red and a prime favorite with the birds.
This shrub is thought to be specially fragrant at dusk.
L. tatarica and *L. grandiflora* with large white flowers
make an excellent combination. Honeysuckles may best
be propagated by seeds sown in the fall.

Hall's Honeysuckle (*L. japonica*) is a vine and attains
a height of fifteen feet. The bloom is from June to
August, delicate, short-stemmed, two-lipped white and
yellow flowers with characteristic Honeysuckle fragrance.
L. Morrowi, also of Japanese origin, is of low growth
(six feet) and runs to yellowish white flowers with red
tips. The fruit is bright red or in one variety yellow,
held on the branches till late in the season.

Honesty

Lunaria annua

Honesty, or Moneywort, of which you ought to have
a sprig or two for the sake of the name at least, is a plant
of many names, and is hung about with a tradition of
magic.

Enchanting Lunarie here lies in sorceries excelling.

Honesty is a pretty little plant with large, dusty-looking leaves and flowers of shining white or various shades of purple. You may have this famous flower as an annual or as a biennial, according to conditions. *L. rediviva* is a perennial with lighter colored and smaller blossoms. Honesty grows to a foot and a half or two feet in height and becomes bushy as it grows taller. The numerous, fragrant, pink-purple flowers come in late spring and early summer. From a curious persistent inner membrane, the pods are known as "Pope's money." These pods were at one time dried and used in winter bouquets for decorative effect.

Lupine

Lupinus polyphyllus

Lupinus is derived from *lupus*, wolf, and was applied to the plant because the deeply buried roots were thought to rapidly exhaust the fertility of the soil. The fact is that Lupines are not afraid of poor soil conditions and grow well there. *L. polyphyllus*, perennial, is the best garden species, growing to be four or five feet tall. The annuals are very fast maturing, requiring but six weeks to bloom after planting.

The flowers are pea-shaped, typically deep blue, thickly borne in stately spikes rising high above the foliage. The leaves are divided like a palm, dark green and satiny, forming a very handsome persistent clump of foliage. In selecting a location for Lupines remember that after they are once well established, they will not stand transplanting. Sow where they are to remain, allow six inches of space for each plant unless you wish

to leave on all side shoots, then leave twelve inches for
spread.

Evening Campion

Lychnis alba

Evening Campion is most frequently found about old
gardens, whence it has a trick of escaping and running wild.
The flowers are in loose elongated clusters, white and quite
fragrant, opening at evening. This Lychnis may be
biennial or perennial and will grow about two feet tall,
blooming in May and June. Like its near relative the
Catchfly, the Evening Campion is coarse and hairy with
a sticky fluid along the stem. The plant will be a success
in any good light garden soil and is a good drought resister. Also will revel in full sunshine. Very similar is
the Morning Campion, *L. dioica*, having pink-centered
flowers.

Rose Campion

Lychnis Coronaria

Rose Campion or Mullein Pink is one of the best known
of the Lychnis family. The flowering season is July and
August, and the glowing rose-crimson flowers, sometimes two inches across, are borne singly on the ends of
the branches. The foliage is whitish and wooly and
the flowers show up finely by contrast. *L. Coronaria*
grows two and one half feet high and requires but little
attention. The flower structure is interesting; the five
petals have two small appendages at the base of each;
the seed vessel is a pod. Rose Campion is a native of
Europe and Asia that adapts itself easily to conditions
here.

German Catchfly

Lychnis Viscaria

This Catchfly is a fine old garden plant esteemed for its quantity of flower and its bright color. The name comes from the sticky patches below the flower clusters which often catch ants and crawling insects.

L. Viscaria grows from six to twenty inches high, likes the sun, and may be planted in almost any soil. The flowers, small, but of a brilliant scarlet, are in terminal clusters appearing in June. Some varieties have rose-colored blossoms, others are white, and one variety, *Elegans*, is striped red and white. Fine for a border, but should be placed where the foliage of other flowers will conceal the barrenness of its stems. Ragged Robin, Maltese Cross, and Mullein Pink, all old-time favorites, are also species of Lychnis.

Magnolias

Magnolia stellata, M. Soulangeana, etc.

Magnolias are of peculiar interest because they have the largest flowers of any tree in our gardens. The lustrous evergreen leaves, the big deliciously fragrant white blossoms, the cone-like fruits that flush from pale green to rose, all have helped to give the Magnolias a preëminent place in every country where ornamental planting is done. They are most commonly planted by themselves on lawns for scenic effect. Magnolias are reasonably hardy, and in sheltered positions may be planted as far north as Massachusetts. They prefer a rich moist soil. Transplanting is a difficult operation and is best done when new growth starts. The flowers show up best against a dark background of evergreens.

We can indicate only briefly here a few of the best known kinds. *M. conspicua* is the largest-blossomed white-flowered tree that is hardy farther north than Long Island. *M. Fraseri* is noted for its cream-white flowers and a peculiarly curved leaf. *M. glauca* prefers swamps. *M. macrophylla* is the largest-leaved of the Magnolias, with flowers ten to twelve inches across, white with purple center. *M. Soulangeana* is one of the most popular of the hybrids, growing to a height of thirty feet with white and pink blossoms appearing in May. Hall's Magnolia, *M. stellata*, is the showiest of the early-blooming species. This Magnolia differs from others in having star-like instead of cup-shaped flowers. The blossoms appear before the leaves and are white, sweet scented, with narrow petals. Several of the most beautiful Magnolias are Japanese, and Hall's Magnolia was so named for the Dr. Hall who brought the shrub from the East to Rhode Island many years ago.

Virginia Bluebell

Mertensia virginica

Hang-head Blue-bell,
Full of a secret that thou darsn't tell!

The Virginia Bluebell or Virginia Cowslip is one of the most familiar of early spring flowers of the Middle West. The drooping flowers are bell-shaped in loose, handsome terminal clusters, twenty or more in a cluster. Pinkish in bud, they become purplish in full bloom and finally bluish as they fade. The plants grow in clusters and should be massed in planting; remember also that the leaves die to the ground after the flowering season. Mertensia must have a sheltered position, but full sun and rich loam. A fair amount of moisture is essential. Seed should be planted very early in a place where you wish your Mertensias to stay permanently. They are among the plants which resent disturbance of the roots.

Grape Hyacinth

Muscari botryoides

This little bulb is most effective if planted in clusters. The variety known as "Heavenly Blue" has the purest color and makes patches of charming color on a shady bank near a stream. The flowers are normally blue and there is a white-flowered form. Blooms hang in little grape-like clusters on the flower stem and have the odor of musk. The bulbs will grow in any soil except one that is damp and should be placed two inches deep and only an inch or so apart. Grape Hyacinths are customarily grown in the grass, though their low height makes them an ideal border for many beds. It is well to remove the offsets of the bulbs about every three years.

Forget-me-not

Myosotis palustris

The true native Forget-me-not, "the blue and bright-eyed floweret of the brook," has blue flowers with a yellow eye. The cultivated Forget-me-nots are essentially flowers of spring. Having no liking for hot weather they get their blooming done by May; but they do not scramble through blooming time: growth is deliberate, and if the soil be fertile and moist they may even last through June. There are few plants more charming for the side of shady banks and dells in cool places.

Shade is required, but an extremely moist place is not necessary. Seeds sown in May will produce sturdy plants by October. When sowing dig deeply and make the surface soil very fine; sow no more than half-an-inch deep. Forget-me-nots are propagated so easily that one need never worry about them. Old plants may be separated or cuttings taken in the fall.

A charming Swiss species, *M. dissitiflora*, was brought into commerce in 1868. The name means scattered-flowered, the flowers being disposed more loosely on the stems than those of the older species. This fine Forget-me-not grows neatly, compactly, and is covered with dense bloom. Varieties of this are *grandiflora* and *splendens*, both blue, larger than the type; *alba*, white; *elegantissima*, the leaves of which are edged with white. There is one species, *M. alpestris*, which will grow in dry soil and may be used in the rock garden.

Daffodils

Narcissus pseudo-narcissus

Sung by the poets Spenser, Shakespeare, Keats, Tennyson, Wordsworth, whose affection for the Daffodil is particularly well known, and by a host of modern, minor poetasters, the awakening of the Daffodils announces the advent of mild and genuine spring. The Narcissus and Daffodil have long been among the most popular of all spring-flowering bulbous plants. Narcissus is the botanical title of the whole family, but in popular use the large showy forms have so dominated that the name of Daffodil has come to signify all the members of the family included in the large and the medium crown sections, embracing also the intermediate hybrid groups. The literature of the Narcissus is voluminous and the number of varieties is sufficient to stagger the amateur. In Europe and England at times the interest in Daffodils has assumed the proportions of a craze. Scores of rival enthusiasts grow and cross Daffodils, and extravagant prices ($500 to $2,000) are reported to have been paid for no more than five or six bulbs. In America we have never taken these flowers so seriously.

Daffodils are perfectly satisfactory for outdoor planting. Excellent large trumpet varieties are: Emperor, Trumpet maximus, Van Sion, Empress, and Princeps. For medium-sized trumpets try Gloria Mundi, Sir Watkin, and Barri Conspicuus.

Plant your Daffodils in early fall about four inches deep. No fresh manure should be used in or over the beds. Assuming that you have a selection of different varieties, you had best arrange them in clumps. Six bulbs make a very nice clump. Set the bulbs about six inches apart and leave a space of at least nine inches between the different clumps. The bed might be finished off with a ring of Crocuses.

Jonquil

Narcissus Jonquilla

The Daffodil is a long, trumpet-like flower on a single stalk and with broad flat leaves. The Jonquil, with

GARLAND FLOWER
(Daphne Cneorum)

FOXGLOVE
(Digitalis purpurea)

WINTER ACONITE
(Eranthis hyemalis)

GOLDEN BELL
(Forsythia suspensa)

HELLEBORE
(Helleborus orientalis)

EVERGREEN CANDYTUFT
(Iberis sempervirens)

GERMAN IRIS
(Iris germanica)

JAPANESE ROSE
(Kerria japonica)

which the Daffodil is often confused, has small flowers in clusters, bright yellow and very sweetly fragrant, and rush-like leaves. The single Jonquil is well known and highly prized, particularly for growing in pots. There is also a double variety. The flowers run from two to six in a cluster. This little flower has been so much over-shadowed by its big brother that few realize how attractive it is. The Jonquil is generally a success outdoors if planted in a sunny, protected spot in rich soil; scatter generously. However many you plant you are quite likely to wish next spring that you had planted more!

Poet's Narcissus

Narcissus poeticus

That was a fair boy certaine, but a foole
to love himself; were there not maids enough?

The poet's Narcissus or Saucer Daffodil is with the Polyanthus the leading representative of one of the three main groups into which the Narcissus family technically speaking is divided, the other two being the Large Trumpet and the Cup, commonly grouped together under the name of Daffodils. The Jonquil differs again from the recognized Daffodil in having cluster flowers like the Polyanthus Narcissus, and from the Polyanthus Narcissus itself in having rush-like leaves instead of flat.

N. poeticus should be planted about four inches deep and three apart and prefers a heavy, rich soil. They are the last of the Daffodils to bloom (late May) and are particularly to be recommended for naturalizing in groups in grass. For description we can do no better than to quote

Forbes Watson: "In its general expression the Poet's Narcissus seems a type of maiden purity and beauty, yet
warmed by a love-breathing fragrance; and yet what in-
nocence in the large soft eye, which few can rival in the
whole tribe of flowers.   The narrow yet vivid fringe of red,
so clearly seen amidst the whiteness, suggests again the
idea of purity, gushing passion—purity with a heart which
can kindle into fire."

Evening Primrose

Oenothera biennis

This is the best yellow-flowered biennial for bold effects and is easily naturalized in almost any soil.   The
stem is strong, rising to a height of from four to five feet.
The flowers four to five inches across open suddenly at
nightfall; during the day they remain crumpled up—in the
words of one garden commentator, "like a faded ballroom
beauty by daylight."   Plant in any soil except where sunshine will strike the plant.   Unfortunately, the Evening
Primrose grows weedy and shabby-looking after blooming
season.   Place the plants about a foot apart.   A form
known as *grandiflora* is better for garden use than the type
species *biennis*.   The Sundrops are allied species of Oenothera sometimes separated as Kneiffia, however.   They
have a spreading, shrub-like habit.

Pot Marjoram

Origanum vulgare

By all means set apart a corner of your garden for old-
time herbs.   Pot Marjoram is a sturdy perennial growing

about two feet high. Sow the seeds in any good garden soil in a warm spot, as the plants have a tendency to winter kill. The herb is branching, so space must be allowed for it to spread. Individual plants should stand ten inches apart in rows about a foot apart. The tender aromatic leaves should be picked just before blossoming. They are the parts used for pot herbs. The blossoms which appear in June are purplish pink in short terminal spikes or clusters. There is a pretty little dwarf Marjoram with a white blossom often used as a border plant.

Star-of-Bethlehem

Ornithogalum umbellatum

Another of the small early bulbs too inconspicuous and ineffective to be planted singly or even by dozens, but happily inexpensive enough to be used by the hundreds or, on large estates, even thousands. The lovely little Star-of-Bethlehem perhaps never looks so well as when naturalized in grass. It spreads prodigiously. A gently sloping, half-shaded bank covered with the thick mat of its white-ribbed leaves and myriads of green-ribbed stars is one of the pleasantest sights imaginable.

Star-of-Bethlehem escaped from cultivation now grows wild in swamps and meadows from New England to Virginia. The bulbs may be planted in garden borders or scattered carelessly in shaded spots. Plant in the autumn three or four inches deep and two to three inches apart. They multiply so rapidly as to become at times a nuisance, crowding out other bulbous plants.

The stalk branches at the top and bears from twelve to twenty separate flowers. The flowers are white striped

with green outside, composed of six spreading parts.
Leaves are green striped with white, carrying out the color
scheme.

Chinese Peony

Paeonia albiflora

The culture of the Peony has advanced in recent years
by leaps and bounds. Visitors to the great flower shows
gaze in wonder at Peonies as large, as brilliantly colored, as show Chrysanthemums. The modern Peony
comes from two species, the white albiflora and the red
officinalis. Botanists tell us that both were introduced
into England in 1548. The Tree or Moutan Peony,
a shrubby species, cultivated in China and Japan from
time immemorial, was not brought to England before
1789.

The Peony has to recommend it healthy hardy nature,
vigorous growth, handsome spring tints, beautiful flowers,
fragrance. Plant preferably in late summer in carefully
prepared soil, as they are heavy feeders. Dig down two
feet and work in quantities of manure, mixing thoroughly
with the soil. When Peonies are once established they
will flower for years without need of change. The colors
run from white through rose and magenta to crimson, and
the immense flowers are like glorified Roses, single or double
with handsome foliage.

There is yet another species (*tenuifolia*), known as the
Fennel or Fern-leaved Peony, with leaves finely cut and
feathery, dying down after the blooming season, which is
very early in spring. The flowers are single or double and
of a wonderful deep, glowing crimson.

JACOB'S LADDER
(Polemonium cæruleum)

FEATHERED MEADOW RUE
(Thalictrum aquilegifolium)

Tree Peony

Paeonia moutan

This Peony comes from the Far East where it was cultivated for centuries before chance brought our largest-flowered early shrub to Western gardens. Moutan is the oriental name of the flower. Dealers offer a bewildering choice of varieties with rose, magenta, pink, and white colorings. The stems grow to be from three to six feet high and the individual flowers twelve inches across and of satiny texture. The wild species has a dark, dull bloom. The improved sorts are grafted on wild roots which usually sucker and kill out the desired variety. The roots do not need winter protection; but the flower buds that cannot well be covered are sometimes nipped by late frosts. The Tree Peony will be an agreeable surprise to those familiar only with the usual herbaceous Peony.

Beard Tongue

Pentstemon barbatus

Light pink to carmine Beard Tongue is very effective in mass effect but quite a trivial little plant otherwise. The flowers, generally an inch long, are borne in a loose, slender, foxglove-like inflorescence. Too intense sun is apt to kill the plants but otherwise they have no marked peculiarities and will grow in almost all soils. The individual flower is tubular in shape, two-lipped, with the lower lip bearded. Sow indoors in February for outdoor transplanting in May. Plants should stand about fifteen inches apart. Some Pentstemons are natives; one species is Asiatic and another Mexican.

Good natives are: *P. laevigatus*, white tinged with purple, and its variety *digitalis*, purer in color, both blooming in June and July; *P. grandiflorus*, pale blue, blooming in June and July; *P. ovatus*, purplish, blooming in May and June; and *P. pubescens*, rosy purple, blooming in May and June, one and a half feet high.

Flowering Peach
Persica vulgaris

No more beautiful sight ever greets the casual garden visitor in May than a group of Double-flowered Peach trees in full bloom. This small tree will grow as high as thirty feet, but is most commonly to be met with in much smaller specimens. There is a choice of double and single flowered varieties in reds, pinks, and whites. The flowering Peach will bloom most luxuriantly in a rich soil and should be kept carefully pruned. Of named varieties Camilliaeflora will give complete satisfaction; Folius purpureis is noted for fine foliage and quick growth. Rosea plena has double rose-like flowers.

Persica vulgaris belongs to the group *Prunus* in which are to be found Almonds, Peaches, Plums, Cherries, and Apricots.

Mock Orange
Philadelphus coronarius

Mock Orange, like the Lilac, is most frequently grown near the house for its fragrance, sometimes thought too heavy and sickish. This is the most fragrant of summer-flowering white shrubs but somewhat stiff in habit and not so showy as quite a few others. The shrub grows from ten to fifteen feet in height if not kept down by pruning.

Mock Oranges are usually planted individually on lawns though they look well with other shrubs in groups. There are also lower-growing kinds to be tucked away in corners where small shrubs are needed. Plant anywhere where drainage is good. Plants may be started from cuttings, suckers, layers, and seed. There is a golden-leaved variety keeping its color the whole year through, which is very popular.

Ground Pink or Moss Pink

Phlox subulata

With its prostrate stems and dense mass of flowers, this dwarf Phlox makes a dandy little carpet for the rock garden or for sloping banks where grass will not stay. The early spring bloom is quite profuse, covering the ground with moss-like evergreen foliage. There are many charming varieties, giving much choice of color from white to rose and lilac, and all will mature in any light but not too moist soil. The flowers are flat, nearly an inch across, typically magenta, borne profusely in small clusters on leafy stems two to six inches high. Excellent varieties are: *alba*, white; *atropurpurea*, purple; and *lilacina*, light lilac; a garden form, Vivid, is pure pink.

Fetter Bush

Pieris floribunda

If an evergreen shrub which is hardy and early-flowering is desired, plant Fetter Bush. It grows from two to six feet in height and can always be distinguished by the brown hairs which cover the branches and petioles. The flowers are in dense upright clusters, but the individual flower is drooping. The bloom is white in April and May and the conspicuous flower buds make this plant all winter long particularly decorative for bordering drives, etc. A moist but not a clayey or alkaline soil is best. Fetter Bush may be propagated by cuttings of the ripe wood taken in August. Or better yet, buy young shrubs about two feet high and set out in the early spring.

Stagger Bush

Pieris Mariana

Stagger Bush will fill the demand for a pale pink or white flowered shrub blooming in April. The shrub runs from two to four feet high and the flowers are in nodding clusters, appearing on the leafless branches of last year's wood. They are most successful in moderately moist, well drained, porous soil in partial shade. Plant with Rhododendrons. Unfortunately some Pieris winterkill easily. It is said that sheep and calves, after feasting on the fresh glossy leaves, stagger about, overcome by their poisonous effect, as they do after partaking of the leaves of the shrub's near relative, the Lambkill.

Jacob's Ladder

Polemonium caeruleum

Jacob's Ladder is one of the old-fashioned flowers which the poet Maeterlinck spoke of "as having lived with us for hundreds of years and which form part of ourselves, since they reflect something of their grace and their joy of life in the soul of our ancestors." This delightful Polemonium with its spikes of light blue-lavender, grows sometimes three feet high, sometimes less. The flowers are in panicles, quite fragrant, bell-shape, five-lobed. Jacob's Ladder does its best in deep, rich soil in partial shade. Start outdoors in the fall or indoors in the early spring. If you are arranging plants in a garden bed or border, keep them twelve inches apart. Jacob's Ladder came to us from England, where it is a common cottage garden plant.

P. Richardsoni is a low-growing Alpine plant with flowers sky-blue. *P. confertum* is considered by many the best species for gardens. *P. himalaicum,* with fern-like foliage, blooms in May and June.

Greek Valerian

Polemonium reptans

The Polemonium commonly planted in gardens is *P. caeruleum* (Jacob's Ladder). Greek Valerian is said to be more often found in gardens in the West than in the East. The blossoms appear in May and June and are in clusters, a delicate pale blue. The leaves are compound, consisting of many small pointed leaflets regularly arranged along the stem, largest and most abundant at the base of the plant; very pretty and persistent. This plant grows about a foot high and is customarily seen in borders where it has best success on rich soil and partial shade. Polemoniums all find plenty of moisture essential for growth. They are commonly propagated from seeds planted in the fall.

Primrose

Primula vulgaris

In the wood where you and I
Upon faint Primrose beds were wont to lie.

The Primrose, a prime favorite of Shakespeare and Milton, is equally interesting as a wild or garden flower.

Auricula, Cowslip, Oxlip, Polyanthus, Primrose are all members of the family of Primulas. The Primulas are generally very hardy, withstanding cold as cheerfully as an Oak, and play a sort of cat-and-mouse game with Mr. Jack Frost, darting into growth if he relaxes his grip for a few days and then discreetly retiring when he renews his pressure, but they dislike hot dry soils.

The Polyanthus is the best kind for our American gardens. This is a low growing perennial that makes our gardens look gay in early May. It likes moisture and cannot stand well the full glare of the sun. The leaves, rather tough in texture and wrinkled in appearance, grow much larger after the flowering season. The flowers are red or yellow or white. Polyanthus should be protected by a light covering of leaves in winter and divided every three years. The plants separate easily; just cut the roots apart and replant. This is done after the blooming period.

Double Flowering Almond

Prunus japonica

The Almonds are fairly hardy, early flowering, and present no especial problems of soil or culture. Only the double form is generally in cultivation. The flowers are rose-colored and appear in May and June.

P. triloba is a low-growing, bushy shrub with pink or rose double flowers, mostly solitary and mostly coming out in advance of the leaves. The name *triloba* comes from the slightly three-lobed leaf about two inches long at maturity. The double flower is a dense rosette of small petals borne on stems so short that the flowers have the appearance of sitting down closely on the branch.

There is also *P. glandulosa*, the White Flowering Almond, usually with double flowers, also known in double pink low bushes.

Japanese Crab Apple

Pyrus (Malus) Halliana

Any Japanese Crab Apple is a spectacular flowering tree as a specimen on a lawn, and the fruit will remain on the branches through autumn, often into winter indeed. These small, pretty, but unpalatable yellow or red apples in miniature are produced lavishly in clusters up and down the branches. In spring the profuse blossoms of pink or white literally smother the tree. *M. Halliana* is colored deep pink and var. *Parkmanni* has double flowers.

P. floribunda is a small tree with a profusion of pink and white flowers. The May-day glory of the delicately tinted, rose-colored blossoms of this flowering Crab are to be seen and not described. The only garden trouble with it is that it will require fully as much spraying as a fruit tree. The leaf-stalks are reddish and rather thick. The small red fruits drop off before winter.

Bechtel's Crab, also called Iowa Crab (*P. ioensis*), is a double-flowered, ornamental American wild apple growing to the height of thirty feet.

Fair Maids of France

Ranunculus aconitifolius

Fair Maids of France or White Bachelors' Button belongs to the Buttercup or Crowfoot family. It is the double form of the plant that is thus known.

Fair Maids of France grows from six inches to three feet in height, blossoming the last of May and the first of June. One variety, *luteus plenus*, has double flowers of yellow gold. The plants like plenty of moisture and not too exposed a position. Ranunculus produces tubers much like those of the Dahlia, only smaller. Frost is fatal to them so they must be dug up after flowering and be replanted in the early spring. Plant two inches deep and six inches apart.

Rhododendron

Rhododendron maximum; and hybrids

It is the glory of the massed flowers against the dark evergreen leaves that has caused the Rhododendron to be generally esteemed the handsomest and most beautiful of our native flowering shrubs. The Rhododendron has been adopted as the state flower of Washington and of West Virginia. The Heath family, of which Rhododendrons are conspicuous members, delights in cool, moisty, peaty soil. Dig down about two feet and work the soil, mulching heavily. Leave twelve inches space between the roots. If the weather be dry, plenty of water is essential. In the fall mulch with their own leaves or forest leaves. The leaves are thick and leathery; the flowers, white or pink in clusters, are two inches broad, bell-shaped, five-parted, appearing in late May, June, and July. The Hybrids are much more beautiful but less hardy, especially the red-flowered ones.

Recommended varieties: Album elegans, light blush changing to white; Prometheus, deep scarlet; purpureum crispum, purple; roseum luteum, pink with yellow spots; and album grandiflorum, delicate pink, but there are so

MOUNTAIN GLOBE FLOWER
(Trollius europæus)

YUCCA
(Yucca filamentosa)

many that there is much room for individual fancy in selecting the flowers. All are showy, however.

Rosemary

Rosmarinus officinalis

There's Rosemary for remembrance
and there's Pansies, that's for thoughts.

Those who know the quotation perhaps better than they do the plant may be surprised to learn that Rosemary is a scrubby little bush growing no more than four feet high. By all means have a bit of Rosemary in your garden, if only for the sake of the pleasant name. Start the seeds in very fine soil in early May and do not anticipate too many plants. Rosemary is delicate. The leaves are linear, gray-green in color. Their sweet fragrance has often been noted. The flowers are small, blue, two-lipped, and in racemes. Be sure to cover over the little plants in winter.

Silver Sage

Salvia argentea

Salvias fall into two classes, hardy and tender. Hardy kinds, like *argentea*, are used most frequently in the garden border. The tender class includes the annuals commonly used for bedding plants, especially the Scarlet Sage *S. fulgens*. As a border plant *S. argentea* is selected for its neat, white, woolly foliage and its height of from two to four feet. The flowers are white, touched with purple, in long branched panicles. Start seeds indoors early, plant outside in May, arranging plants ten to twelve inches apart. If the soil is rich in nitrogen the plants leaf splendidly but do not flower as well. Salvias do their best in

warm weather.   *S. farinacea* has pale blue flowers, as has
S. azurea, but is useful for light flower arrangements.

Elder

Sambucus nigra, S. canadensis

The European Elder, *S. nigra*, a large shrub growing
twelve to twenty-five feet in height, is useful for mass
effects in pond borders and wild gardening.   May and
June see the Elder covered with cream-white, feathery
blossoms.   The leaves are graceful, the fruit black.   There
are cultivated varieties having fine-cut leaves, and others
golden, or variegated.

The Golden Elder is often used by landscape artists to
lighten the effect of dense masses of green shrubbery.

The Common Elder, our native shrub, will be found
particularly successful in wet soils.   It does not grow as
tall as the other.   The flowers are in broad, flat clusters in
June and July, and it is the handsomer of the two, both
having blackberries in their season.   An Elder having
attractive dark red berries that mature from August is *S.
racemosa*.

Early Saxifrage

Saxifraga virginiensis

The number of beautiful species, the charm of foliage and
flowers, the great diversity in structure and habit, certainly entitle the Saxifrages to the first place among the
rock plants.   This native early-flowering species is to be
found growing from a few inches to a foot high on moist
hill slopes and in rocky crevices.   When domesticated, it
will do well in any good loose soil but not in strong sunlight.
You had best imitate nature by covering the little plants

lightly with leaves for the winter.   The flowers are small,
white, pretty clusters on the tops of six-inch-long stems.

The thick-leaved Saxifrage (*S. crassifolia*), from Siberia,
is an early bloomer with massive coarse evergreen foliage
and rose-colored flowers in dense branching heads.

S. Huetiana has yellow flowers and makes an attractive
low border plant.   There are excellent later-flowering
Saxifrages which will be found in the summer section.

Common English Bluebell

Scilla festalis

Another of Spring's early arrivals along with the Snowdrops, Crocuses, and Grape Hyacinths is the Bluebell.
The lily-like leaves grow to be about eighteen inches high.
The stalk bears from six to fifteen blue, purple, pink, or
white hyacinth-like flowers.

These bulbs like a cool, moist spot.   Plant in the fall
two inches deep and three inches apart.   Top dressing on
the Scilla bed will keep it in good shape, and the bulbs may
stay undisturbed for years.

Dark Green Stonecrop

Sedum sexangulare

This early Sedum, also known as Love-Entangle, is a
little inconspicuous yellow flower that clings to shallow
ledges and flourishes in its small way on almost no soil at
all.   The rosettes of thick fleshy foliage cause the plant
to be preferred for carpeting purposes.   The bloom comes
in late June or July, and the plant revels in sunlight.   The
Sedums are a very big family; it seems incredible, but

there are over a hundred species catalogued by botanists.
S. Aizoon, with yellow flowers, is remarkable for a Sedum
growing eighteen inches high. *S. acre* has been called the
"Poor Man's Plant" as it is often seen in corners of city
back yards. It grows about three inches high and its
little inconspicuous yellow flowers are to be seen in May,
June, and July. The leaves are small and crowded on the
erect stem. *S. Sieboldi* is a bold member of the family with
large heads of pink flowers in late summer.

Wild Pink

Silene pennsylvanica

Considering its meager possibilities, ranging no more
than four to ten inches in height, the Wild Pink opens up
a bit of lively color in the rock crevices where it flourishes.
The beautiful pink flowers are an inch broad and several
are gathered in a flat-topped terminal cluster forming a
bright glowing mass which can be seen from a considerable
distance. The calyx tube is long and five-toothed, the
petals five. The Wild Pink resembles its cousin the Catchfly.

There is no reason why this charming Silene should not
be domesticated in all our gardens. It will flourish in a
poor soil or in the rock garden in a half-shaded spot. All
Silenes are easy of culture from seeds in autumn, or the
plant may be divided when old.

False Solomon's Seal

Smilacina racemosa

The False and True Solomon's Seal often grow sufficiently near each other in the wild to make comparison

PERENNIAL FLAX
(Linum perenne)

SOULANGE'S MAGNOLIA
(Magnolia Soulangeana)

VIRGINIA BLUE BELL
(Mertensia virginica)

DAFFODILS
(Narcissus pseudo-narcissus
bicolor)

TREE PEONY
(Paeonia moutan)

JACOB'S LADDER
(Polemonium caeruleum)

GOLDEN ELDER
(Sambucus canadensis aurea)

COMMON ENGLISH BLUEBELL
(Scilla festalis)

possible. The False has a feathery plume of blossoms crowning a zigzaggy stem, while the True has nodding, bell-shaped flowers usually in pairs along the stem. Both are well known and beloved wild flowers which will many times repay the effort and care of establishment in domestic surroundings, selecting a moist, half-shaded spot in the garden. The thick root stock may be divided for new plants.

The False Solomon's Seal flowers from May to July; the flowers are white, or greenish white, with some fragrance. Later come clusters of speckled purplish berries.

The True Solomon's Seal (*Polygonatum biflorum*) has white flowers in arching sprays coming with the leaves. There is also a smooth Solomon's Seal, a very capricious plant, growing sometimes only a foot high and then again many times higher.

Bridal Wreath

Spiraea Thunbergi, S. prunifolia

Before Spring has gone very far along her flowery path, the members of the great Spiraea family begin to deck themselves in festal array. First comes *Thunbergi*, the baby of the family, and then quickly *arguta*, *prunifolia* and others. These are among the hardiest early-flowering shrubs and some of the most commonly planted because they will even endure some shade. Any good garden soil is satisfactory, and the usual method of propagation is by cuttings.

Bridal Wreath with its pure white flowers in branched umbels was a prime favorite in the quiet tangle of grandmother's garden. *S. Thunbergi* is the first of the Spiraeas to bloom in April. The leaves are small and bright green; when they turn scarlet ir the fall the effect is very striking.

Though quite hardy, occasionally, in a very cold winter, the extreme tips will become killed. When in full bloom the branches of swaying white look like flowered wreaths.

Van Houtte's Spiraea (*S. Van Houttei*) is the showiest of all the shrubby Spiraeas and should be planted in a conspicuous place with ample room. The growth is about six feet and the flowers are in white umbels two inches across. The foliage is handsome all summer. Plant in early fall or spring, digging deep and working a little well-rotted manure into the soil.

S. prunifolia is early May blooming. The double form is the variety most commonly grown. The shrub grows about six feet high and the flowers are pure white in umbels close to the branches. *S. Reevesiana* blooms in May and has flat clusters of flowers. The leaves remain green till winter time. Most Spiraeas love moisture and well-drained soils.

Bladder Nut

Staphylea trifolia

This is an attractive, straight-growing shrub with stout branches, quite pretty with its three-foliate leaves and greenish white flowers in nodding panicles. Our American Bladder Nut grows from six to fifteen feet high and the bloom is in May and June. This shrub is not difficult of culture but will produce most vigorous growth in a moist soil and a half-shaded position. Unfortunately, Bladder Nut is not a good specimen plant and the base had best be concealed amidst other shrubbery. There is another species, *S. colchica*, taller growing; leaves five to seven foliate, pale yellow-green; flowers white, greenish at the base.

Lilacs

Syringa vulgaris

It seems impossible that any bush can be more beautiful than the old-fashioned, fleecy-plumed, white Lilac. Lilacs are known wherever flowers are. Whether right or wrong, the story goes that the first Lilacs seen in New England were imported by a gay young scapegrace, Sir Harry Frankland, for Agnes Surriage's garden. The modern varieties, however, date from the time of the Franco-Prussian War and offer a choice in flowers of lilac, blue, purple, and white, with sweet, heavy odor.

Lilacs grow to the height of twenty feet and should be pruned for form only. The shrub will grow anywhere, but best results are generally obtained in a rich, slightly moist soil. Although there are many modern named varieties, the old *S. vulgaris* is recommended because of its early bloom and ease of culture. The leaves are a bright green, two to four inches long. Transplanting is generally done in autumn. The easiest means of propagation is by division.

Feathered Meadow-Rue

Thalictrum aguilegifolium

More of the Meadow-rues ought to be domesticated in our gardens. The Feathered Columbine, as this is also sometimes called, grows from one to three feet high with leaves decompounded, somewhat resembling the Maidenhair Fern. The flowers are in white panicles. Meadow-rue is often naturalized in front of shrubbery. Any good soil will suit. They grow vigorously in strong loam and

clay, but will make surprisingly good growth and flower
profusely in comparatively poor soil overlying limestone.
Plants may be started from seeds, but later division of old
plants is the easier way.   The flowers are excellent for
cutting to lighten up a bunch of hardy flowers.   Another
fine addition to the garden is *T. dipterocarpum*, growing
sometimes five feet high with rose-like flowers.

Common Spiderwort

Tradescantia virginiana

The three-cornered blossoms of the Spiderwort grew
alongside Honesty and Jacob's Ladder in more than one
old-fashioned garden.   A perennial, averaging about two
feet in height, this Iris-like little flowered plant is esteemed
greatly as a carpeting plant.   The rich green foliage does
not fade till late, and the Spiderwort makes no protest over
poor, wet soils or over shady slopes.   The flowers are blue
or purple and appear in May.   There is also a white-
flowered variety, *alba*.   The Spiderwort will form large
clumps after a few years.   Propagation is by division of
the clumps.

Mountain Globe Flower

Trollius europaeus

The Globe Flower looks like a big, half-open Buttercup.
Large, globular, lemon-yellow flowers, one or two inches
across, borne singly or in twos, bring a dash of unusual
color to the garden in May and June.   Trollius likes moist,
heavy loam and a half shady position. Fine foliage,
beautiful form and color gain for this flower a prominent
place in the garden border.   Trollius frequently surprises

the visitor with a second crop of blossoms in the fall.
Plants started from seed bloom the second season. Seedlings should stand six inches apart. *T. asiaticus* has a
deep orange blossom.

Cottage and Parrot Tulips

Tulipa Gesneriana, and others

The Tulip comes from the Near East. "The rich and
glowing colors [of the Tulip], the large size and massive
substance of the great floral urns, the dusky sheen of some
varieties, the metallic sparkle of others, have a truly Oriental magnificence." (*Wright*). Tulips were grown in Holland as early as 1590, and the period of the Great Mania,
amusingly satirized by Alexandre Dumas in "La Tulipe
Noire," was roughly 1634 to 1637. The exact origin of the
popular varieties is quite unknown.

The Tulip is so well known as to make detailed description needless. Any one who possesses only a few feet of
exposed ground should have a bed of Tulips. Requirements of soil are very simple, and none need hesitate on the
ground of expense. Tulips are prim formal flowers and
best adapted to rigid beds. Care should be taken to keep
early-flowering kinds together and late-flowering kinds together. Among true Tulip lovers the double forms labori-
ously obtained by the hybridizer obtain little favor. Only
single Tulips can ever be fittingly naturalized—Tulips
whose clear color, painted petals, and dark spot at their
base indicate nearness to the beautiful wild type. Unfortunately, one sees more frequently, especially in public
parks, amazing Tulip beds of sharply contrasted colors
laid out in patterns as decorative as patches of oil cloth.

Tulips may be divided into two groups: those that flower in April, and those that flower in May and June. In purchasing, one may select by colors or by named varieties. the latter way is generally more satisfactory. The *Duc van Thol* kinds are dwarf and early-flowering varieties of *T. suaveolens*, and the different colors come to bloom simultaneously. The May-flowering Tulips are the *gesneriana* type. There are both single and double forms. If you like freaks and novelties try Parrot Tulips.

Tulips may be dug up as soon as the leaves turn yellow and the bulbs dried and stored away for next year's planting, but you must buy new bulbs annually to obtain the largest flowers.

DARWIN TULIPS

Darwin Tulips are a tall, aristocratic race of late "Breeder" Tulips, mostly self-colored, with no trace of yellow, and are great favorites both in this country and in England. They are all May-flowering varieties. Plant five inches deep and the same distance apart. Prepare the bulb bed as for other Tulips, place a little sand at the base of each bulb for drainage, and at frost time cover the bed. After a few years, they should be taken up, separated, and renewed. The many varieties cover a good range of self- or solid-colored, daintily formed flowers in the following shades: slate, heliotrope, mahogany, claret, cherry.

Verbena

Verbena hybrida

Sweet-scented Verbenas are old-fashioned stand-bys long in disfavor, but now slowly coming back to deserved popularity. They are exclusive plants, producing fine bold effects when planted in masses but not appearing at their best when closely associated with other flowers. In full bloom the gay-colored heads remind one a little of Phlox. The plant is quite low-growing (six inches), and the bloom is from May on through midsummer. Seeds may be planted in the open in a sunny spot; or, better, may be started indoors in March and thinned out. The best method of propagation is to cut back a few of the finest plants in September. These will quickly throw off young growth from which cuttings may be made.

Cornel and Snowball

Species of Viburnum

The Viburnums are among our best ornamental shrubs for garden planting. They are mostly medium sized, growing about fifteen feet high; they like sun and moisture and are not fussy about soil. There are about one hundred species in America, Europe, and Asia.

V. dentatum is commonly known as Arrow-wood and can be used as a hedge plant. The leaves are heart-shaped, opposite, and dentated, turning a rich purple in the autumn. The flowers are in great cymes, greenish white, and the berries blue-black.

Dockmackie or Maple-leaved Viburnum (*V. acerifolium*) grows only about five feet high with slender, straight branches. The flowers are yellow-white in big, flat clusters, and in the autumn the fruit is an almost black, round berry. This Viburnum will thrive in dryish soil under trees.

V. Carlesi belongs to the family of Japanese Snowballs,

with pure white flowers possessing a fragrance like a Gardenia. They should be used with other shrubbery as a foreground or else massed or planted as a specimen shrub.

The Sheepberry or the Nannyberry (*V. lentago*) is the tallest of the Viburnums, growing nearly thirty feet high. The fragrant yellowish white flowers light up the tree from May to June, and the bluish black berries are loved by the birds.

The Cranberry Bush (*V. opulus*) is a fine native species with smooth, light gray bark. The light scarlet fruit which appears in July will remain all winter untouched by the birds. The sterile variety is the Snowball, a familiar feature of most old-fashioned gardens.

Periwinkle

Vinca major, V. minor

Any garden troubles you have with the little common Periwinkle, Blue Myrtle, or Flower of Mystery will be all at the start. This little visitor creeps cheerfully along, throwing off glossy leaves, rooting here and there in the thinnest of soils. Once firmly established the common Periwinkle (*Vinca minor*) is almost unconquerable, will catch a sure foothold in the shadiest spots and spread in astonishing fashion. The May and June flowers are deep blue, pink, white. The leaves are oval, an inch long and a deep lustrous green. Periwinkle will hold steep terraces and is often found running wild along the edges of gardens in old settlements.

The Larger Periwinkle—larger in leaf and bloom—is not so vigorous and persistent a flower. This (*V. major*) grows about a foot high and offers continuous bloom throughout

the summer. Start in heat in February, preferably in a
slightly sandy soil. They had best be thinned and transplanted several times before reaching outdoors in May.
Remember that the plants need a plentiful supply of water.
The Larger Periwinkle is a great favorite for window boxes
and hanging baskets. Cuttings taken in the fall will be
fair-sized plants by springtime. It is not hardy.

Violets

Viola odorata, cornuta, etc.

> They are as gentle
> As zephyrs blowing below the Violet,
> Not wagging his sweet head.
>
> —*Cymbeline.*

> If music be the food of love, play on;
> Give me excess of it, that, surfeiting,
> The appetite may sicken, and so die.
> That strain again! it had a dying fall:
> O! it came o'er my ear like the sweet sound
> That breathes upon a bank of Violets,
> Stealing and giving odour.
>
> —*Twelfth Night.*

In the Sonnets, in "Venus and Adonis," and many times
through comedy and tragedy, Shakespeare sings the
praises of his favorite posy. No flower figures more prom-
inently in European literature. General description is
unnecessary. Everybody knows the Violet.

V. odorata, the Russian or Sweet Violet, a native of
Europe and Asia, is the parent of our florist's Violet of to-
day. *V. cornuta,* one of the best known species, flowers
like a small Pansy and blooms from April till frost. *V.*

cucullata has perhaps the largest flowers, violet blue or purple in shade.

If you wish to be sure of success with Violets in your home garden, select shady spots enriched with rich woodsy leaf mold, imitating wild conditions. The Violet determines for you the method of propagation. Some send out runners which you must peg to the ground with a bit of soil about them. Others with thick rootstocks are to be subdivided. It is possible to raise from seed but this is infrequently done. Certainly no spring garden, however small, can call itself complete without a few Violets.

Wisteria

Wisteria chinensis and *W. floribunda*

More commonly trained round piazza pillars, arches, fences, and walls, this brightest, healthiest of the many floral treasures brought to America from the Far East seems to be as well content merely to trail at will among trees wherever planted. "To complete a picture of mellow age there is nothing comparable to a fine old vine." (*Blanchan*.) The best results are obtained when the vine is left severely alone, but if pruning be done at all, prune for Spurs just as in an Apple tree.

The Chinese Wisteria is one of our best early-flowering, permanent vines. The unscented flowers are pea-like, in foot-long racemes of blue-violet. The foliage is smooth at maturity, graceful, and not too dense, the branches grotesque and in old trees many times twisted. A sight of sights is the Wisteria in full bloom.

The Japanese Wisteria, *W. floribunda*, is the one more commonly seen and is scented. The flowers come earlier, too, and the leaves fall sooner, the blossoms hanging in wonderful festoons. The white variety is called *multijuga*.

Rich soil and plenty of sun are considered to produce the best results. Wisteria is a heavy feeder. It is thought a good plan to provide a full three feet of good garden soil mixed with well-rotted manure beneath the roots.

Yucca

Yucca filamentosa, and others

In the Southland the children play mimic warfare with the spears of the Yucca. Adam's Needle, Spanish Bayonet, Bear Grass, Silk Grass, and Threading Yucca are all picturesque names for this ornamental plant of the desert. In June the stiff, erect stems bear cream-white, bell-like flowers on long loose spikes towering above the rosette of leaves. Being a desert plant the Yucca is not afraid of barren places, and indeed prefers a sandy soil. Yucca is a member of the Lily family, grows wild in the South, and can easily be propagated by offsets.

SUMMER

SUMMER

Millfoil

Achillea Millefolium

This Yarrow is a favorite for open meadows and all sunny places. The white summer blossoms have a very pungent odor. They appear in flat heads of very small, composite flowers on erect stalks rising from a tuft of very finely cut, feathery leaves. This makes a very showy plant for wide open spaces. Millfoil will grow practically anywhere in sunshine. There are pink-flowered and red-flowered varieties also cultivated, and a dwarf species with gray foliage (*A. tomentosa*), a fine carpet plant. Propagated without difficulty in the spring by division of the creeping rootstock. A few sprigs of this plant sometimes seen as a roadside weed come as rather a pleasant surprise if chanced upon in the home garden.

Aconite

Aconitum Napellus

True Monkshood, or Aconite, is a fine, tall plant with clean blue-and-white flowers, an ancient plant on which old-time gardeners exhausted their vocabulary of praise, always ending up with the injunction that the root must on no account be eaten. Monkshood is dangerous in all its parts for children and pets and on this account is less seen in gardens than formerly. The flower is hood or helmet shaped (hence the name), and the bloom runs through midsummer.

All the Aconites are impatient of a dry soil, so their corner of the garden had best be rich and retentive of moisture. Planted in full sunlight, they will thrive better than in part shade but the blossoms will not last as long. Their maximum of six feet in height makes them good plants for the back of a border. Monkshood is sometimes rather slow in becoming established, but when it once gets a footing will flourish for years. Old plants had best be divided. In northern latitudes the plant grows taller than in the South.

Alleghany Vine

Adlumia fungosa

The Alleghany Vine, or Climbing Fumitory, or Mountain Fringe, has finely divided flowers and finely cut foliage. Flowers, delicately pink; foliage, as finely cut as Maidenhair Fern. For the shady side of a house this vine is "the one choice." The Alleghany Vine is a native and is to be searched for in moist woods, where it will be found climbing over brush and bushes. The vine does not flower the first season and remains low and bushy; it then climbs vigorously to a height of ten or fifteen feet, advancing by the young leaf stalks. Seeds should be sown in the spring in a damp, cool place. Plenty of moisture is very desirable. This, the daintiest of our vines, is not so commonly planted, perhaps, because it does not make as dense a covering as others. Often listed as *A. cirrhosa.*

ACONITE
(Aconitum Napellus)

AGAPANTHUS
(Agapanthus umbellatus)

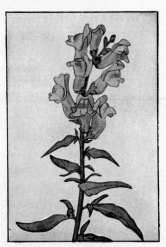

SNAPDRAGON
(Antirrhinum majus)

SWAN RIVER DAISY
(Brachycome iberidifolia)

CANTERBURY BELL
(Campanula Medium)

CORNFLOWER
(Centaurea cyanus)

COLEUS
(Coleus hybrida)

HARDY DELPHINIUM
(Delphinium formosum)

Agapanthus

Agapanthus umbellatus

The African Lily, or the Lily of the Nile, has characteristically Lily-like flowers of a fine, very rare deep blue in umbels on a long stalk. Agapanthus is best as a tub plant, and in old-fashioned gardens used often to be seen in green tubs on lawns or by piazzas In the early autumn it should be taken into the cellar, where it will remain semi-dormant all winter. Roots may be divided in early spring and new plants started in pots or small tubs. Make divisions with a sharp knife, and if the roots are mature, they had best be soaked in water before dividing. The young plants grow vigorously and are apt to break pots. This bulb has no special soil requirements but must have plenty of water while in bloom. The foliage is evergreen.

Ageratum

Ageratum conyzoides

Ageratum is one of "the annuals that everybody can grow" and is very satisfactory for edges and borders. The dwarf varieties grow no more than six or eight inches high and the taller varieties, used largely for cutting, around two feet. The Ageratum commonly seen is blue, but there are also white and rose-colored variations. The blue is purplish or lavender and the general effect is of a fuzz over the flower head. It will be necessary to plant the seeds indoors in February unless you are content to put up with only very late bloom. Ageratum does well in full sunlight in almost any garden soil. Set out the plants ten or twelve inches apart, using the dwarf varieties for

edgings and the tall varieties in a clump for cutting.   Little
Blue Star, the smallest of the Group, grows only four inches
high, and tall Lavender Blue, at the other extreme, about
two feet.

Sweet Alyssum

Alyssum maritimum

Sweet Alyssum is the easiest white flower to grow for
edges and borders and a great favorite with amateur gardeners.   *A. maritimum* will grow in all sorts of soils, even
in cold regions and in heavy clay.   You may have these
pretty little white blossoms from July till frost by cutting
back or by successive sowings.   This quick-growing annual is often in bloom six weeks after planting.   The
flowers are small, fragrant, white, in solid clusters profusely borne on low spreading stems less than a foot
high.   The leaves are small, silvery green, forming a compact spreading mat.   Sweet Alyssum is often potted for
winter bloom.   Cut the plants back to no more than three
inches and presently you will have another fine head of
bloom.   There is a variety with lavender flowers, and a
little dwarf, Carpet of Snow, only four inches high.

Bastard Indigo

Amorpha fruticosa

The purple June flowers on finger-like spikes are quite
effective, and altogether Bastard Indigo is a happy selection for a small shrubbery.   This native shrub with fine
feathery foliage and spreading habit has been known to
reach a height of twenty feet but grows commonly no more
than half that.   The fruit is a pod, one- or two-seeded.
Bastard Indigo is one of the none too extensive number of

flowers that do well in dry sunny spots. Hardwood cuttings are the most usual method of propagation, though it is sometimes started from seed. *A. canescens,* the Lead Plant, excellent for the rockery, grows from one to three feet high and bears panicles of blue flowers in June.

Virginia Creeper
Ampelopsis quinquefolia

Virginia Creeper is a graceful, headlong vine draping loosely and hanging in great festoons, always impatient of restraint. It is not a self-climber. Of lighter, more graceful habit than the Boston or Japanese Ivy, the Virginia Creeper delights to scramble over rocks, banks, bushes, and up trees living or dead. The leaves are large, five-partite, the flowers greenish and inconspicuous. The vine is perfectly hardy, thriving in any soil. The smallish dark blue fruit comes in clusters. The autumn colorings of the leaves, scarlets and deep crimsons, are marvelous.

This Ampelopsis may best be established from young plants a year or two old, which should be carefully protected over winter till the vine attains fair growth. *A. Engelmanni* clings better, having suckers and has even more vivid autumnal color; but is otherwise very much like the Virginia Creeper.

Golden Marguerite
Anthemis tinctoria

These large daisy-like flowers are fine for cutting and if planted in sufficiently large masses will make an attractive showing in a border. The thin stems and delicate leaves are apt to appear straggly if not framed by plants of more vigorous foliage. Golden Marguerite grows two feet tall and starts blooming in May and June, continuing till October. Ray and disk flowers are both yellow. This Marguerite is a hardy perennial of easy culture, not fussy as to soil, but doing best in full exposure to the sun. The rarer *A. Kelwayi* has finer cut foliage and flowers of a deeper yellow. There is also *A. montana*, with white flowers, from June to October, which can be depended upon for good behavior and almost constant bloom.

Snapdragon
Antirrhinum majus

The Snapdragon is an invaluable annual (in mild climates and often in sheltered spots and joints of walls a perennial), particularly attractive for its wide range of color. Besides the clear whites and yellows there are flame color, apricot, chamois-rose, coral pink and a host of delicate shades to tempt the purchaser. The flowers are an inch long, borne on spikes blooming from the bottom over a period of several weeks. There are tall and dwarf strains offered, the range of height being one to three feet. Sow outdoors in May or, for early bloom, in frames in February. In northern latitudes the plants had best be covered over winter. When cut back after blooming a second crop of flowers develops, but the first crop of bloom is always the best. Soil should be well cultivated and kept well watered.

Prickly Poppy
Argemone grandiflora

This Mexican Poppy has striking white crêpe flowers with conspicuous golden stamens. The general effect of the plant is coarse, but it could well be more frequently employed where masses of color or bold and striking effects are desired. It ranges from eighteen inches to three feet in height and is curiously destitute of the prickles of other species. This Poppy is too free a seeder to be admitted to choice situations, but is splendid for waste places where it may be allowed to perpetuate itself freely. Soil should be light and exposure sunny. When the flowers fully open they show a yellow center.

Dutchman's Pipe

Aristolochia macrophylla

Dutchman's Pipe is an unusually large-leaved vine and a fine climber, best selected for spots where dense shade is desired, such as screens and arbors. The almost round leaves measure ten or twelve inches across and often over-lap. The Pipe Vine is rather slow in getting well rooted but after that one is not likely to complain that it is not a sufficiently vigorous climber and spreader. The May and June flowers are rather surprising, goose-neck-shaped, yellowish-purple, not very conspicuous. The large Aristo-lochia family of which the Pipe Vine is a member is mostly tropical and has generally an unenvied reputation for flowers of evil odor.

Giant Reed

Arundo donax

The Giant Reed and its variations are the tallest and most stately of the ornamental Grasses. Arundo has been known to grow as high as twenty feet, but will hardly average over fifteen. The leaves are broad and light green, the general effect something like a cornstalk. The long plumes are reddish and lasting. Practically all this Grass requires in the way of culture is sunlight. Several forms are grown: *variegata* is a dwarf growing rarely over seven feet high; *macrophylla* has very effective bluish foliage, but is none too hardy. The Giant Reed may be propagated by ripe canes laid on wet moss in winter. If you wish a semi-tropical corner in your garden, try a clump of Giant Reed.

Astilbe

Astilbe Davidi, A. japonica

Both species are more or less frequently confused with the Spiraeas. The Chinese Astible, *A. Davidi* or False Goat's Beard, is a hardy perennial with small, rosy-violet blossoms in long, showy, feathery clusters, borne on branching leafy stems four to seven feet high. The general effect at the back of a border is of great white pointed plumes. Plant the roots in any good garden soil. A new type, *A. Arendsi*, with flower heads of many colors but mostly in shades of pinks, is a hybrid group.

The Japanese Astilbe grows two feet high and the mid-summer flowers are pure white and feathery. This Astilbe is often used for indoor forcing for Easter but neither in growth nor in expanse of bloom outdoors ever seems to measure up to the corresponding outdoor varieties. For indoor forcing pot so that a little of the root protrudes above the soil. Leave in a cool light place till growth starts, then expose to heat and light. The plants need plenty of water at all times.

Plume Poppy

Bocconia cordata

The Plume Poppy or Tree Celandine, will make a rich subtropical effect along the edge of a border or of shrubbery, and generally is best planted where height and size rather than close inspection are desired. The plant grows so rapidly and gives off suckers so fast that it is likely to become embarrassing for the small garden. This Poppy ally seems strangely named, for it does not look like a Poppy at all, grows five to eight feet tall and has small pinkish-white flowers borne in plumy, terminal masses high above the foliage. The leaves are large, dull green with white reverse, heart shaped. The plumes of the seeds which follow the flowers are feathery and decorative. Bocconia is a gross feeder and spreads so fast in a rich moist soil as sometimes to become a weed. Suckers, of which there are always a plentiful supply, may be detached and will make a vigorous young plant in a single season.

Swan River Daisy

Brachycome iberidifolia

The Swan River Daisy from Australia is a free-flowering, refined little plant that will make a very pretty edging for a summer border. The flowers are clear lavender or blue with black and white central disk. The leaves are small and divided. This Daisy grows six inches or a foot high and is in appearance something like an Aster, but flowers earlier. Sow in May in any good garden soil in a sunny exposure for August bloom, or start in heat if you wish for bloom earlier. In either case they should remain in flower

till frost.   Allow twelve inches space between plants.   The
Swan River Daisy, praised by all who have tried it, is being
each year planted more and more in our American gardens.

Amethyst
Browallia demissa

Browallia, of South American origin and named by
Linnaeus for a friend with whom he later quarreled, is a
low-growing, half-hardy annual with clustered blue, violet,
and white flowers.   The leaves are single and alternate.
The flower flourishes in poorer soil than most others of a
tender nature and had best be planted outdoors by the
middle of May from seed started indoors and should bloom
till frost.   If the plants are potted in the fall, they are
likely to surprise you with bloom all winter.   Browallia,
still somewhat of a novelty, is to be seen chiefly in borders
or as a bedding plant.

Summer Lilac
Buddleia Davidi

The newcomer, also called Butterfly-bush, grows to be
a fair-sized bush with wand-like, drooping branches bearing flowers not unlike the Lilac in form and of a charming
rosy-lilac color, but of various shades.   The bush grows
from three to eight feet tall with large, coarsely notched
leaves, whitish beneath and almost without stems.   Provide light, well-drained soil and a position in the sun.   This
Buddleia is not quite hardy in the North but will flower on
new growth from the root.   Propagate by greenwood cuttings in spring or hardwood cuttings in the autumn, kept
away from frost.   It also self sows in favorable locations.

There are several varieties listed in catalogues such as Wilsoni, variabilis, etc., which differ in coloring only.

Carpathian Bellflower

Campanula carpatica

Most of the Bellflowers are blue and if it is true that blue is Nature's most difficult color, the Bellflowers must have appeared late in floral history. Carpathian is the easiest to grow and the most permanent low-growing member of the large family. This one blooms in June and July and scatteringly later on. The flowers are large, erect, purple-blue, or white cup-shaped, on delicate stems six to twelve inches high. The leaves make very neat, dainty clumps of foliage four to six inches high and show up well along a border. Bellflowers are hardy perennials or biennials, and should flourish in any rich, well-drained, sunny, garden soil. They are most commonly grown from seed started indoors in March. Transplant to the open about May 15th, allowing nine inches of space between plants.

The oft planted dwarf variety *turbinata* is more compact than type, has larger leaves and less erect habit. The white variety is also much admired.

The Peach-leaved Bellflower (*C. persicifolia*) with blue or white blossoms is one of the most beautiful of these old-time perennials and next to the biennial Canterbury Bells in size of flower.

Canterbury Bell

Campanula Medium

"Canterbury Bell" has an old English sound and it is not surprising to hear that the "Canterburie bels" was

included in the garden of the *Maison Rustique*, published
by Stevens and Loebault in 1600. The Canterbury Bells
are tubular, bell-shaped flowers, blue, purple, pink, or
white, in a loose-spreading spike blooming from early
June to mid-July. They belong to the much planted
Bellflower family and are commonly hardy biennials
flowering the second year from seed sown in the open; or
the plant may be treated as a tender annual, with seed
sown indoors and young plants set out early in May. As an
annual, flowers may be obtained the first season, but they
are larger and finer the second year. Campanulas are all
early growers, and splendid results should be obtained on
any good well-drained loam soil. They like the sun and
make a fine showing at the back of a garden border.
There is a very attractive double form, *calycanthema*,
popularly called Cup and Saucer, or Hose-in-hose, in
which the sepals have grown together, forming a saucer
similar in color and texture to the corolla.

Creeping Bellflower

Campanula rapunculoides

The Creeping Bellflower has become so much at home
in parts of the East that it may often be found in riotous
control of roadsides and tumbledown fences, particularly
about old abandoned farmhouses. Yet it is a typical Bellflower with the drooping, bell-shaped blossoms. This
Campanula is a sturdy, reliable midsummer bloomer, but
had best be restrained a little in its spreading habit. The
flowers are a fine violet-blue and bloom from July to
September. The plant grows from two to four feet high
and will give a nice background effect where a blue is

wanted. Transplant indoor seedlings outdoors in May and be careful to allow plenty of space—as much as a foot and a half is recommended—between plants.

Hemp

Cannabis sativa

Hemp is a rough-looking plant with greenish flowers and is occasionally used as a screen or where bold foliage effects are desired. The height will be a good ten feet, high enough for screening purposes, and the bloom is in August. This is an Asiatic plant and of the several varieties *gigantea* is the most satisfactory for garden use. It is best to sow Hemp where wanted, but it might be started in heat and transplanted if desired. A rich, moderately moist soil is best. The common Hemp is a coarser-growing plant that one would not ordinarily care to cultivate in gardens. An odd corner might be filled in very nicely with garden Hemp, but one is hardly likely to overplant it.

Wild Senna

Cassia marylandica

Wild Senna is a perennial native herb with a pretty little midsummer yellow flower that is very attractive in clumps in its preferred habitat, moist open situations and swamps. The flowers are bright yellow, with chocolate-colored anthers in clusters near the top of a handsome shrub-like plant three to five feet high. Foliage is light green, compound and finely cut, and dies away after blooming season. Wild Senna loves the sun and looks handsome amongst shrubbery, or may be naturalized in waste spots. It propagates easily from seed; eventually allow eighteen

inches of space between plants. This Wild Senna will do well in all soils but should be planted where other plants or shrubbery will hide its bareness after the flowering season.

Basket Flower

Centaurea americana

The Basket Flower is a charming little annual that ought to be seen in our gardens more frequently than it is. The Centaurea family presents no difficult problems of culture, preferring sun and good soil but doing at times astonishingly well on thin, meager sustenance and in half shade. This species grows from two to five feet high with tall stems, single or only slightly branched. The flowers have purple or rose-colored heads; disk flowers are one to three inches long and ray flowers no more than an inch. Seeds for the Basket Flower need be placed no more than half an inch deep in the garden in early May. Thin the little plants to stand twelve inches apart.

Cornflower

Centaurea Cyanus

The Cornflower is a friendly little plant that once suitably installed in your garden will self-sow and appear year after year to greet you with fresh blossoms. The lovely blues are the best: the pinks and whites seem always a little faded. Bachelor's Button (applied to many other flowers as well), Bluet, Blue Bottle, Ragged Sailor, are all popular names for this Centaurea. The flowers are singularly fringed trumpets borne in thistle-like heads. Planted outdoors in April, the Cornflower should be blooming in July;

when the plants begin to look straggly cut them back for fresh later bloom.

Centaurea is a very large family, some five hundred species in all. The Mountain Cornflower (*C. montana*) has large, flat, blue flowers which turn purple as they grow old. This is a compact dwarf often planted either in the type flower or in the excellent white, rosy, and citron variations. *C. macrocephala* with unusually large, globular, bright yellow flowers, is especially recommended for cutting, the flowers preserving their freshness longer than other varieties.

Sweet Sultan

Centaurea imperialis

The long-stemmed, musk-scented mauve, purple, or white Sweet Sultan is the most charming of annuals and a prime favorite for cutting. It grows about two feet tall with large heads like giant Cornflowers. It likes a sunny situation which you must select with care, for the Sweet Sultan is one of the plants that do not like to be moved here and there about the garden. The flowers are in clumps and bloom from July till time of frost. Plant outdoors in May, in drills a half inch in depth, and thin to stand a foot apart. *C. Margaritae,* a pure white and a famous modern strain, and *C. moschata,* not so beautiful, but hardier, are considered to be the progenitors of the Sweet Sultan.

Wallflower

Cheiranthus Cheiri

Wallflowers, popular favorites in England, but not so much planted here because of the hotter, drier climate, have to recommend them: evergreen foliage, plenteous bloom, mild pervasive fragrance. This perennial grows twelve to eighteen inches high, but as it runs out after two or three seasons, the Wallflower cannot in common use be called a perennial. It is best treated as a biennial. The colors are very fine, red-browns to deep yellows and purplish browns. The Wallflower is easily grown in cool rich soil in partial shade, but is not quite hardy in the North and will need winter protection. Some early-blooming forms are customarily grown as annuals. Sow indoors in March, or better in August for wintering in frames. If sown in August there will be bloom the second year. Attractive as it is, gardeners in this country have never had the success with the Wallflower that it seems as if they ought to have.

Turtle Head

Chelone Lyonii

Turtle Head, so named, as you might suspect, from the form of flower, rejoices also in the curious names of Cod Head, Fish Mouth, and Snake Head. This flower grows wild from Newfoundland to Florida and has many good points for domestic use. The flowers are rosy purple in dense, showy terminal spikes, and the leaves handsome, deep green, heart-shaped. Turtle Head is a plant particularly desiring rich ground and moisture, and given these conditions will bloom profusely. The roots lie near the surface and in a garden border during the growing season must be covered with a heavy mulch four or five inches thick of well-rotted manure both as nourishment and as a preventive against drought. Turtle Head may be propagated in all the usual ways. If you can provide the necessary conditions of soil, by all means try this lover of damp spots.

largely used for cutting are double-flowered. Feverfew is quite accommodating, will grow in any soil, and give generous bloom all summer. Golden Feather is a yellow-leaved variety of this plant.

Coleus

Coleus hybrida

Coleus with its bright-colored leaves—red-browns to yellows—is a popular foliage plant for bedding and for greenhouses. The flowers are quite negligible and to improve the foliage are best snipped off before they come to maturity. Coleus came originally from Java the early true species have been lost in the brilliancy of the products of hybridization. Take four-inch cuttings in the autumn and put them into a moist bed of sand. When they are well rooted transfer to small pots in a mixture of half sand and half garden soil. Any soil condition that will suit the Canna or other ornamental foliage plant will do for the ... Light sandy loam enriched with manure is as ... anything. Leaf mold answers admirably. Plant ... unlight, allowing about ten inches of space for a ... Coleus had best be dug out of the garden in the fall; ... es wither with the first frost.

Elephant's Ear

Colocasia antiquorum esculenta

The Elephant's Ear, most often seen with Cannas in the much-abused circular beds on lawns, has the distinction of being the most massive, subtropical foliage plant for summer bedding. The leaves grow from two and a half to three feet in length and sometimes twenty inches across.

The plant itself grows about four feet tall and is not hardy, though it will winter indoors if kept dry. Make the soil rather fine, mixing in plenty of bone meal. Plant the tuber with the end just emerging. in a half-shaded position. These plants are somewhat of a problem in arrangement, as their semi-tropical appearance is hard to reconcile with most of the vegetation of Northern gardens. It is often listed in catalogues as "Caladium esculentum."

Bladder Senna

Colutea arborescens

Among garden shrubs the Bladder Senna is distinguished for rapid, compact growth and for free flowering. Its pale greenish foliage is valuable as a foil against the much more frequent darker greens. The flowers, pea-shaped and yellowish or yellowish-red, appear in June and July and are followed by reddish ornamental pods. The shrub grows frequently fifteen feet high and in general appearance minds one of the Locust. The Bladder Senna, un nately, is not quite hardy in the North. A fairly sunny soil seems to be what is desired. The your preferably one about two feet high, should be s September and must be kept well watered during tumn. The Colutea family, natives of the Mediterra region, have seven or eight species, among which arbore cens is the best for garden use.

Hardy Delphinium

Delphinium formosum

The Perennial Larkspur, pride of the late June garden, has perhaps in recent years been somewhat overdone by

zealous hybridists. *D. formosum* has curiously shaped
flowers of brilliant deep blue with white centers and long
violet spurs in loose spikes about twelve inches long. The
foliage is rich dark green, finely divided and handsome.
This is thought to be the best of all tall-growing blue
perennials. Start indoors in February and transplant
into good soil and full sunshine. Copious watering in
June will ensure better spikes and longer bloom. After the
first blossoms, cut down the stalk and you will get a second
flowering season in September. Delphiniums shifted
every two or three years will do better than those that remain steadily in one spot. Delphiniums against a trellis
of climbing Roses make a wonderful picture.

Sweet William

Dianthus barbatus

Sweet William is an old-time favorite popular at the
present day fully as much for historical association as on
real garden merit. Many years ago florists divided the
fragrant Bearded Pinks, calling the narrow-leaved varieties
Sweet Johns and the broad-leaved varieties Sweet
Williams. The name Sweet John has disappeared. Sweet
Williams are still with us and show no signs of extinction.

Sweet William, or Bunch Pink, bears flowers in dense
rounded terminal heads of twenty to thirty flowers each.
The general appearance is stiff and somewhat gaudy.
The plain whites, true pinks and dark crimsons make pretty
dashes of color, but many of the parti-colored varieties are
quite ugly and undesirable. Foliage is simple and, while
the plant is young, clean looking. Sweet William grows
from twelve to eighteen inches high and the bloom is

generally in mid-May through June. The flower seeds itself, but does not always "come true," and increases from old stock. Seeds must be started very early in the greenhouse to get bloom the first season. If the seeds are sown outdoors in early spring, thin by autumn to stand six inches apart. The following spring they should bloom.

Carnations

Dianthus Caryophyllus, etc.

"Pinks belong to June and are, of all her belongings the sweetest." (*Wilder.*) Pinks are plants for sunny nooks, "of a most fragrant scent comforting the spirits and senses afar off." (*Parkinson.*)

The Clove Pink (*D. Caryophyllus*) is the ancestor of our florist's Carnation of today. The spicy odor of the Pink is so well known that most people are disappointed not to find it in other members of the Dianthus family. The modern Carnation, almost entirely a florist's flower, is generally cultivated under glass, though plants of course may be transplanted to the open for the warm weather. Clove Pink is a native of the Mediterranean regions and was originally pale lilac in color.

China Pink (*D. chinensis*) is a much more satisfactory Pink for gardens. The flowers are jewel-like in brilliance with the charm common to all Pinks but are not fragrant. They are easy of culture in any good garden soils. The flowers will be reds, pinks, lilacs, solitary or clustered, about ten to sixteen inches high. They are cheerful, persistent, with blossoms from August till frost.

Garden Pink (*D. plumarius*), another flower of many names, including Garden Pink, Scotch Pink, Pheasant's

Eye Pink, has in its favor fragrance and early May bloom. This is a low-growing (twelve inches) perennial, with pink-and-white flowers and neat, persistent foliage. Propagation is by seed or by division. There are many excellent recommended varieties.

Gas Plant

Dictamnus albus

Burning Bush, Dittany, and Fraxinella are other names for this hardy perennial. Fraxinella in old New England gardens has outlived great-grandmother, grandmother, mother, and daughter. The Gas Plant has rich, dark leathery green foliage and fragrant white flowers in June and July. The plant grows about two feet high and in still hot weather gives off a volatile, lemon-scented oil which, if a match be held near, will ignite in a puff of flame. Fraxinella, as it is also called, prefers a strong, rather heavy, rich soil and once settled in its new home had best remain undisturbed for years. Sow outdoors in the early autumn an inch deep; they will germinate in the spring.

A variety with rose-pink flowers is also quite commonly grown, and is often thought to be its type plant.

Weigela

Diervilla florida

After Lilac time in June the Weigela shrub takes up the story. Weigela flowers are trumpet-like, pink, white, red, claret-crimson to magenta. Weigelas are among the showiest shrubs of midsummer, and the best flowering shrub to place under big trees. The bloom is profuse and

continues well through the hot season. Weigelas are a
good combination shrub and are more often seen in groups
with others than as specimen shrubs on laws. Little pruning is required except to keep the sturdy bushes free from
old and useless wood. If possible, buy a young shrub two
or three feet in height and set out in autumn or spring.
There are many named varieties in catalogues: Eva
Rathke, deep crimson red, is a very fine variety. Conquête,
deep rose; Perle, creamy white with pink-bordered petals;
and Saturne, carmine red.

African Daisy

Dimorphotheca aurantiaca

Plants from all over the world come to our gardens nowadays, and the African Daisy, a newcomer recently introduced, is certain to become very popular. This is a
neat small perennial, usually treated as an annual (twelve
to fifteen inches high), with foliage nestling quite close to
the ground and gay, Daisy-like flowers that offer long,
sustained summer bloom. The flowers are orange and
yellow. The petals curve upward. The flowers close at
evening. Sow outdoors as early as weather permits in
bright sunshine, thinning to stand ten inches apart.
There is also a white-flowered species (*D. annua*). African
Daisy will introduce a bit of novelty amid the familiar
picture of the small garden.

Oleaster

Elaeagnus angustifolia

Oleaster, or Russian Olive, is a handsome shrub reaching a height of twenty feet, with foliage grayish green

above, silvery white below. The yellow June flowers are
fragrant but rather inconspicuous. After the flowers
appear small yellow berries. Oleaster is a fine seashore
shrub and will do well in any well-drained soil including
limestone. Propagated by seeds, cuttings and layers, but
it is much easier to buy a small shrub and set out in autumn
or early spring. Allied species are: *E. argentea* with silvery
foliage; *E. umbellata* ripening its fruit late and holding it till
midwinter; *E. multiflora* also known as *E. longipes*, having
dense clusters of bright red acid fruits late in the season.

Crown Imperial

Fritillaria imperialis

Quaint old Gerarde praised the "stately beautifulness"
of the Crown Imperial and in every old-fashioned garden
could be seen the familiar tall stem bearing near the top a
graceful umbel of red, yellow, or orange bell-shaped flowers
with a tuft of foliage above them. Modern gardeners,
more sensitive than the old, find the flower has too rank and
heavy an odor for modern taste. Crown Imperial grows
about three feet high and the flowering time is May. The
impressive flowers with their pearly drops of nectar that
seem never to drop off have everything to recommend
them except fragrance. Certainly we should have a re-
vival of the Crown Imperial. The bulb should be planted
six inches deep in rich soil with manure below: set them
a foot apart in a spot where they will not receive the
heavy noonday sunshine. Too much strong sunlight
seems to hurt the growth and make the blossoms shorter-
lived.

Day Lily

Hosta plantaginea

The names Day Lily, Plantain Lily, and Funkia are rather loosely used for the familiar clumps of large-leaved Lilies, a common sight in most old gardens and less frequently in new ones. The Lilies themselves, late summer flowers, are large, white, waxy, and very fragrant, four to six inches long, borne above clumps of large heart-shaped, shiny, light green leaves. The combination is very attractive either as solid mass or as so often in olden style along the edges of walks.

Day Lilies are easy to cultivate and when once well established had best be left severely alone. Half shade is the preference and the leaves are likely to burn at the ends in midsummer unless the roots be kept well watered. Give deep rich soil and propagate by setting out young plants in the spring.

H. lancifolia has lilac-blue flowers growing about ten inches in height and often used in borders.

Fuchsia

Fuchsia speciosa

This South American plant, now as well known as a native, is accommodating, easily cultivated, and unrivalled for decorative purposes. The flower is funnel shaped and drooping, red-pink, purple, white, in combinations of color. The plant itself, a foot and a half high with opposite shiny leaves, has rather a formal appearance. Fuchsia is a popular favorite in window boxes and pots.

Cuttings are customarily made about three inches in length. If started in the autumn, these little plants should be ten inches high when it comes time to put them outdoors in the spring garden. They may be arranged outdoors for the summer season in any good garden soil in sun or part shade. There are seventy different species of Fuchsia, most of which are natives of tropical America. Some are merely shrubby plants like our best-known variety; there are others that are climbers and some even small trees.

Giant Summer Hyacinth

Galtonia candicans

The Giant Summer or Cape Hyacinth has large, expanded, fragrant white August flowers on long arching stems. Except that it is much larger, the foliage is hyacinth-like, clean, and strong. The bulb is considered hardy in the northern United States but had best be protected by a heavy mulch in winter. It is better to do this leaving the bulbs undisturbed than to take them up during the cold season. Plant in the fall about five inches deep. They grow well in front of shubbery if the soil be rich, and may be counted on to produce striking effects toward the back of a mixed border.

Long Plumed Avens

Geum triflorum

The common Avens, growing about eighteen inches high and preferring moist, shady places, grows wild on a wide range of country from Canada south to Missouri and Georgia. The long-plumed Avens, growing two and a half feet high, is really handsomer in fruit than in flower. The fruit is in feathery clusters with long silver hairs. *G. chiloense* is the best known species in gardens, and has wide-open, five-petaled flowers of a brilliant red-orange with bright yellow stamens and leaves mostly close to the ground and somewhat the shape of Dandelion leaves. The bloom is in late May through June. Geum may be raised from seed or the plants bought and spaced about ten inches apart. The Geums might profitably be used more frequently than they are in rock gardens and borders.

Sword Flower

Gladiolus hybridus

The Gladiolus, native of South Africa, improved in France and Holland and now domesticated in America, can well lay claim to be a world flower. The long bright spikes —hence the name Sword Flower—rush successfully to the aid of the late midsummer garden that often needs a bit of freshening before the anticipated burst of autumn splendor. Fine as are many of the current offerings, the hybridizers keep producing larger and larger strains, newer and newer shades of color, so that the amateur is likely to become bewildered with the variety of choice offered in seedsmen's catalogues.

Grace of form and beauty of blossom distinguish the Gladiolus. For cutting the flower is unique. If the budded spike is cut and taken indoors to adorn a tall vase, it will for the next three or four weeks unfold a succession of beautiful flowers.

The bulbs should be planted in May after the ground is

warm and at regular intervals for five or six weeks to provide a succession of bloom. Bulbs should be lifted after frost and stored dry till spring. A fairly light, loose, well-drained soil is considered best and the Sword Flower should be planted about four inches deep. "America," the pink Gladiolus of the florists' shops, is a fine, vigorous, large-sized flower.

Everlasting

Gnaphalium Leontopodium

This little plant with a very long name sends out runners and creeps along after the fashion of Edelweiss. The leaves are white, hairy on the under surface; the flowers are from seven to nine in a cluster, from four to twelve inches high; the flower remains almost undimmed if gathered just before fully expanded and hung head downward in a dry cool place. A well-drained, medium-light soil in full sun is considered best, and this Everlasting is often selected for high, exposed spots in rockeries. Set out the plants early in May from seed planted indoors in February. If the winter be severe, the plants had best have light protection.

Baby's Breath

Gypsophila paniculata

This perennial forms an exquisite accompaniment to many others and for that reason is often used by florists in making up bouquets. Baby's Breath grows from one to three feet high with continually dividing branches. The leaves are smooth, sharp-pointed, light green. The white flowers are numerous and minute, borne on a gracefully branched feathery stalk. Some gardeners are fond of using this plant for mist-like effects on borders, but mostly it is grown for cutting. The Annual Baby's Breath (*G. elegans*) blooms within six weeks of sowing: and it is well to arrange for several sowings as the blossoms run out in a few weeks. carrying out its appointed plan of existence oblivious to scorching sun or prolonged drought. Baby's Breath with Heliotrope or Poppies make a charming combination.

G. repens is another misty-flowered perennial Gypsophila useful in combinations. The linear leaves are sharp-pointed, the white to rose flowers larger than one would expect. Useful in rockeries.

Globe Amaranth

Gomphrena globosa

The Globe Amaranth, a round, bright flower, also called Bachelor's Button, blooms all summer and is quite cheerful company. The blossoms are purplish, pinkish, white, or golden, borne well above the bush. Historical students will be interested to learn that this Bachelor's Button (the name is confusingly given to many flowers) is a native of India introduced to England as early as 1714. The leaves are downy and the colored bracts persist, hiding the true flowers. If the flower heads are picked and dried, they become everlasting. Globe Amaranth may be sown out-doors in May in almost any soil, preferably in full sunlight. Thin the young plants to stand eight inches apart. There is also a dwarf (six inches) for pot culture and border planting, with a choice of two shades, white or red-purple.

False Sunflower

Heliopsis helianthoides Pitcheriana

The False Sunflower is a vigorous, wild-blooming composite that would be planted more frequently were its merits better known. The flowers are slightly cup-shaped, thick, and daisy-like sometimes two inches across with bright orange rays and deeper orange centers profusely borne on much-branching bushy plants, two to four feet high. The leaves are smooth, thin, pointed, and saw-edged. The False Sunflower is handy for the garden as it has no objection to dry soil and thrives well in full sunlight. The flower is also good to bear in mind for bouquets. Sow outdoors about a half-inch deep and allow a space of two feet between plants.

Heliotrope

Heliotropium peruvianum

Heliotrope is chiefly used as a bedding and window plant. The growth will be about two feet and the flowers purple and deliciously fragrant. A very desirable feature of this old-time favorite is the fact that the more persistently it is cut back, the better will be the bloom. In the garden Heliotropes must have plenty of sun but are not so particular regarding soil. If set out in May, the plants should be in bloom in July. Heliotropes are best as a combination flower. Candytuft or Sweet Alyssum goes well with them or they may be used to replace the Pansies after the day of the Pansies is past. There are white-flowered Heliotropes not so commonly seen.

Lemon Lily

Hemerocallis flava

The Lemon Lily, or Yellow Day Lily, is an old favorite, and no garden can be considered complete without its corner of lemon-yellow, lily-like flowers borne loosely along upright stems and well above the foliage. The leaves are a foot and a half to two feet long, narrow and grasslike, the individual flowers short-lived but borne in good succession. The roots are bundles of fleshy tubers easily divided, which is the best method of propagation. The Lemon Lily is a lover of half shade and moist spots along the edges of ponds, but will do well in practically all sorts of soils. There is also an orange species (*H. aurantiaca*), with flowers in July and August, that is quite hardy, and a coppery red, *H. fulva*. The generic name Hemerocallis refers to the closing of the flowers at night. The blue and white Day Lilies or Funkias belong to another family, Hosta.

Sweet Rocket

Hesperus matronalis

Long spikes of small, four-petaled flowers, most fragrant at evening, are the attractions of the Sweet Rocket, the Dame's Rocket, or the Damask Violet. The colors are magenta, mauve, and white, and the time of bloom from June to August. Sweet Rocket is a hardy perennial that will grow three feet high or more in a rich soil. The double varieties are better for garden use. Plant indoors rather early and transfer outside as soon as weather permits. The Rocket will grow easily in all soils and will form large and striking clumps, or may be used effectively along a border. A good plan is to select a plant with desirable lavender color and propagate from seed.

Coral Bells

Heuchera sanguinea

If you are casting about for a small red flower for a border, you will be glad to be reminded of Coral Bells. The long Lily-of-the-valley-like spikes of dainty coral-red appear in July and intermittently all the rest of the season. The plant grows a foot and a foot and a half high and the foliage, rich green with scalloped edges, is quite decorative. Coral Bells are also known as Crimson Bells and Alum Root. If the plant has any preference, it is for sandy, well-drained but not necessarily dry soil. Propagation is by seed or by dividing roots after flowering season. There are a number of hybrids in various shades of red and pink, the darker colors being usually thought the most successful.

Rose of Sharon

Hibiscus syriacus

The Rose of Sharon, or Shrubby Althea, one of the commonest of garden shrubs, has some of the loveliest and some of the harshest-hued blossoms of any well-known shrub. This Hibiscus grows to a height of twelve feet, blooming in late summer which makes it valuable as a screen. The leaves seem small for the size of the shrub and the flowers resemble those of the Hollyhock. There are many varieties with single and double flowers ranging from white through pink to magenta and purple. The single whites and pure pinks are very lovely, but some of the darker shades are quite coarse and ugly. Prune in winter for profusion of flowers. It is advisable not to permit the plants to run up leaving the base bare. Rose of Sharon will do well in any average garden soil. Propagate by seeds or cuttings. Plant in spring, allowing plenty of space for the roots to develop.

Japanese Hop

Humulus japonicus

The Japanese Hop is a rapid-climbing vine and its large, handsome leaves splashed with white are more decorative than many flowers commonly planted for decorative purposes. The leaf is deeply lobed, the flowers are in catkins. It has everything to recommend it except the charm of the hanging Hops which it does not bear at all. The vine may be raised from seed planted outdoors in May and will grow twenty feet during the summer. Any soil, but preferably plenty of sunshine will do, as you can train the vines without difficulty where you wish them to grow.

H. lupulus is the common Hop with heavy hanging flowers quite ornamental enough to be planted for their own sakes. Hops grow rapidly in almost any soil and like the sunlight. The Wild Hop grows in thickets and along the riverside.

Hydrangea

Hydrangea paniculata grandiflora

In August and September when it has the shrubbery stage almost to itself, the large white-flowered Hydrangea

SWEET WILLIAM
(Dianthus barbatus)

CROWN IMPERIAL
(Fritillaria imperialis)

FUCHSIA
(Fuchsia speciosa)

GLOBE AMARANTH
(Gomphrena globosa)

LEMON LILY
(Hemerocallis flava)

CORAL BELLS
(Heuchera sanguinea)

ROSE OF SHARON
(Hibiscus syriacus)

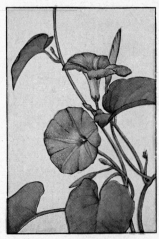

MORNING GLORY
(Ipomoea purpurea)

bursts into life with great drooping heads of snowy bloom. The only trouble with this shrub is that it has been so much overplanted. One well-known garden writer complains that "everyone who owns a twenty-foot lot" plants a Hydrangea. "Certainly the way not to plant it, or any other startling bush, is to dot it around a lawn—the usual practice. . . . A purple, golden or variegated shrub, if isolated on a fair green lawn, detached from all connection with the composition line of planting, is all the more a distracting sight because so common. Such special purpose shrubs fulfill a distinct destiny in enlivening masses of shrubbery which, without them, might easily be monotonous." (*Blanchan.*)

The Hydrangea grows in practically any soil, even one bare and thin. It is important to remember that the harder the pruning, the fewer will be the flower heads; but they will be larger and more vigorous. The shrub may be pruned in the spring because the flowers are produced on the new wood.

Garden Balsam

Impatiens Balsamina

The double camellia-flowered sorts in clear colors, salmon-rose, scarlet, and pure white are nowadays more often to be seen than the single varieties that were the favorites of earlier days. The flowers are borne in the axils of the leaves all along the stalk from July to October. Garden Balsam was brought from India to England in 1596 and is called Impatiens because the seed part irritably bursts open when touched. The individual flowers are often overshadowed by the leaves so that they become unduly inconspicuous. This Balsam dotes on rich, sandy loam in full sun and abundant moisture. Sow outdoors in May or indoors earlier. Little self-sown seedlings should be snuffed out as they almost invariably revert to the unattractive magenta type.

Morning Glory

Ipomoea purpurea

Morning Glory is another popular favorite a little common in the eyes of the fastidious expert but possessing a simple beauty that his expensive varieties seldom equal. As with most of the "very popular" flowers, culture takes care of itself. Indeed, Morning Glory resows, and years after a first planting each spring will see here and there fresh new shoots.

This rapid-growing vine simply must twine about something! If strings or wire be provided, well and good. If not, Morning Glory twines on whatever is nearest, regardless of what it is. Plant outdoors in May, after the ground is warm, half an inch deep and not necessarily more than eight inches apart. The plant climbs, but it does not spread. Morning Glory is a great success in a window box. With light support they should reach the ceiling by midsummer, blooming every foot of the way. There is a Japanese variety with large leaves and huge blossoms.

The Ivy-leaved Morning Glory is often mistaken for the Moon Flower vine. Careful inspection should show smaller leaves, smaller flowers, and a stem covered with sharp points. Propagation is the same as for the Moon Flower. Start indoors in fine soil in February; set outdoors not before the middle of May. This Morning Glory is commonly seen covering trellises and arbors.

Perennial Pea

Lathyrus latifolius

The perennial Pea is a sprawling, rampant vine that thrives on any deep fairly good soil. The blossoms are large, generally white, Sweet-pea-like except that they have no fragrance, borne in dense clusters on sturdy climbing stems four to eight feet long. The size of the large, fleshy roots makes it desirable to leave this Lathyrus undisturbed for a number of years. The perennial Pea is most commonly seen running riot on banks and on trellises, even among bushes and stones. Start from seeds. White, dark purple, and striped varieties are offered. *L. grandiflorus*, another species, has even larger flowers, two together but less vigorous in growth.

Sweet Peas

Lathyrus odoratus

If you see a half-dozen sorts of flowers blooming before a low cottage door in midsummer, one of the half-dozen will certainly be a Sweet Pea. Vigorous habit, delicately tinted blossoms, exquisite fragrance have combined to make the Sweet Pea among the best known of summer flowers. Gardeners have been steadily improving the types and the Spencer, often spoken of as the Orchid, Sweet Pea is the best of all, having big wide flowers. Culture is quite simple. If you prepare the bed in the autumn, you will have the best of results. Spade the dirt eighteen inches deep, and below this, place light manure, which will draw the roots downward. You may plant early, as slight frost will do no harm, and often sowing in the fall is very successful for early bloom. Make three sowings for succession, the last between the other two for shade. It is not advisable to grow Sweet Peas on the same soil for successive years.

Lavender

Lavandula vera

"Lavender walks" are a famous feature of English gardens and Sweet Lavender is sold everywhere on London streets. In America Lavender is not hardy very far north and such "Lavender walks" as we have are generally merely summer borders. Lavender is a perennial shrub from the Mediterranean region with blue flowers in long spikes that have in quite marked fashion the sweet scent known as lavender. In its native habit this blue flower grows on dry, hilly, open wastes. Care should be taken to plant in similar conditions in domestic gardens as far as possible; particularly should excessive moisture be avoided, but it likes a soil with lime in it. The young plants may be raised without difficulty from cuttings. It is necessary to protect Lavender over winter.

Blazing Star

Liatris pycnostachya

Blazing Star, a favorite for the wild garden, blooms in early July through August. Gay Feather, Kansas Gay Feather, and Button Snakeroot are also popular designations, the second of which indicates that the flower has its

habitat along the central plains. Blazing Star blooms in
small purple heads in showy, dense spikes five to eighteen
inches long, which begin to flower at the top. The leaves
are slender and grass-like, thickly clothing the stem. It
grows in all soils and looks best in masses. Crowd the
plants, allowing no more than eight or ten inches per
plant. If to be grown from seed, start in late August and
September and cover carefully in winter. There is also
another species *L. scariosa*, growing to a height of from
two to four feet with bluish purple flowers in August and
September.

Gold-banded Lily

Lilium auratum

Even in a garden made of Lilies alone the superb Gold-
banded Lily of Japan would certainly be king. The flower
is large, showy, fragrant, borne in heads of two to five on
leafy stems two to four feet high. The blossoms are the
largest of all Lilies, sometimes measuring a foot across; the
color is creamy white, with a golden band down the center
of each petal and thickly mottled with purple. This most
gorgeous of Lilies, while theoretically hardy, seldom lasts
more than two or three years. Well-drained soil is essential and manure should never be allowed to come in
direct contact with the bulb. The preference seems to be
for moist loam with a mixture of sand and leaf mold, but
sometimes even under the most approved conditions the
Gold-banded Lily will unaccountably quite fail to come up
to anticipations. Lily bulbs should be deeply planted,
with the top of the bulb never less than six inches below
the ground. These Lilies are propagated by means of
offsets or small bulbs and scales which, planted in spring,

and kept moist and warm, produce bulblets before fall.[71]
Raising by seed will be too slow a process for most people.

Lilies

Lilium tigrinum, *L. speciosum*, etc.

The old standard Tiger Lily is less capricious than
many others and will seldom disappoint the grower. The
Tiger has perhaps a somewhat stiff and coarse look, at
least for a Lily. The pale, whitish stems grow to a height
of five feet or so with scattered rich green leaves becoming
shorter toward the top of the stem. The flowers are bright
to orange red, thickly spotted with purple in nodding clusters of three to ten or more. The Tiger Lily will thrive in
sun or half shade, but does best if the ground be kept cool
and moist either by shade or by a top dressing of peat and
leaf mold.

The *L. lancifolium* or *speciosum* is a fine Lily for general
cultivation especially along borders, and a favorite with
florists for cutting. It is white and rose, in various shadings. The American Turk's Cap Lily (*L. superbum*), with
orange turban-like flowers, is a gross feeder and must be
provided with heavy moist soil. The Siberian Coral Lily
(*L. tenuifolium*) is very showy with rich scarlet flowers
with darker shadings and recurving petals. *L. Henryi* has
dark salmon-orange flowers sparingly spotted with red-
brown and will make a superb showing in clumps or massed
against shrubbery. The well-known Madonna Lily (*L.
candidum*) has very fragrant, pure white, trumpet-shaped
flowers. The Regal Lily (*L. regale*) is like the popular
Easter Lily but having a clear yellow throat. It is quite
hardy.

Cardinal Flower

Lobelia cardinalis

"Another special purpose plant is the Cardinal Flower, now tamed by the commercial dealer who sells its easily grown seed. Pitifully out of place among the host of garden flowers, its vivid beauty is best displayed in nature's garden where it rises beside a stream that reflects it like a mirror." (*Blanchan.*)

Brilliant carmine, the brightest flower of its kind, the Cardinal Flower flashes like a beacon along the banks of shady streams. The flowers are about an inch long, borne in spikes on erect unbranching leafy stems, two to four feet tall. The leaves are narrow and inconspicuous, dying down after blooming season. In the home garden the Cardinal Flower quickly adapts itself to a moist soil and a half-shaded situation. Start indoors in March and transplant to the open in May. Each plant needs about a foot of space.

Lobelia

Lobelia Erinus

Lobelia vies with Sweet Alyssum and Candytuft as a popular edging plant. Blue is the most frequent color, but there are rose varieties and an occasional white. Lobelia is a prolific bloomer from July forward. The little plant ranges from six to twelve inches high and is chiefly utilized for borders and edges, presenting no especial problems of culture. Sow outdoors no more than a quarter of an inch deep and thin to about six inches apart. There are some half trailing sorts that look very well in window boxes.

Crystal Palace, growing six inches high, with dark blue flowers is one of the best-known varieties in our gardens.

Maltese Cross

Lychnis chalcedonica

Maltese Cross, Scarlet Lightning, Jerusalem Cross— these names suggest an Old-World plant, which indeed the Maltese Cross is and a great favorite. The four petals of the vivid scarlet flower have squared ends like a Maltese Cross. The leaves are small, pointed, hairy, and not ornamental. The stems grow rather bare, which requires that this Lychnis, if used in the border, be placed amid flowers with more spreading foliage. Maltese Cross grows about three feet high with June to mid-July bloom. The plants require no special care and may be propagated by seed or division. Plant in a sunny spot, the sunnier the better, and thin to stand a foot apart. There are also a white variety and one double-flowered, as good as the type.

Loosestrife

Lythrum Salicaria

Spiked or Purple Loosestrife, a beautiful and little-used plant for late July, has large rose-colored flowers in a tall spike borne on a graceful leafy stem two to five feet high. This Loosestrife is well known in Old-World gardens with many picturesque names, and is one of the best bright-colored, late summer flowers for swamps and moist meadows. The height range is from three to five feet and the flowers bloom from June to August. They may be started best outdoors in late August to be covered over for the following spring. There are many named varieties such as *L. roseum*, with beautiful cherry-colored blossoms from July to September, and Perry's Variety, with cherry-red flowers.

Peppermint

Menta piperita

The Mint Family, distributed over almost all parts of the world, is characterized by creeping rootstocks, square stems bearing opposite, pleasant-smelling leaves and spikes of small two-lipped blossoms. If you want a sample of the Mints in your garden, set out a few plants of Peppermint. Peppermint grows from one to three feet high. The leaves are two or three inches long, crimpy, and covered with oil glands. If these leaves are crushed in one's hand, the familiar Peppermint odor is unmistakable. The flowers are small, purple or white, not very conspicuous. Peppermint grows along the sides of the streams or in moist places and is propagated by runners or by its persistent rootstocks.

Sensitive Plant

Mimosa pudica

The little Sensitive Plant, half-hardy and growing twelve or eighteen inches high, is often planted as a curiosity. The peculiarity of the plant, the exact nature of the mechanism of which is not thoroughly understood, is that when touched ever so lightly, the leaflets close up and the petiole falls down to reopen slowly a few minutes later. The younger the plant the more sensitive seems to be the foliage and the quicker the movements. The compound leaves are a tender green, the flowers a small ball of pink filaments. The Sensitive Plant is easily grown from seed, sown outdoors in May; the seed need be planted only a quarter of an inch deep in fine, loose soil in a sunny spot. Children should be interested to raise Sensitive Plant in window boxes. It is not hardy, but runs wild in the Gulf states.

Monkey Flower

Mimulus luteus

This somewhat grotesquely named flower—the name comes from the gaping appearance of the corolla—is a perennial, mostly treated as an annual, as it is not hardy very far north. Except that the throat is open, the Monkey Flower is in appearance somewhat like the Snapdragon. Mimulus grows three to four feet tall and should bloom gayly all summer. The plants need plenty of water but appear to have no other soil requirement. They will self-sow. *M. luteus* is yellow flowered. *M. cardinalis*, an allied species, has red-and-yellow flowers and is hardy in Massachusetts with slight protection in moist soil and shady places. The old-fashioned musk is *M. moschatus*, but the fragrant form of this is almost lost to cultivation nowadays.

Four o'Clock

Mirabilis Jalapa

Four o'Clock, also Marvel-of-Peru, earned its name from the curious fact that the flowers bloom only from about four o'clock in the afternoon until the next morning. This is a tuberous, tender perennial, more often grown as an annual, although the old roots may be taken indoors and kept from frost for the winter if dried off. Four o'Clock grows two and one-half feet high and becomes quite bush-like. The flowers are Morning Gloryish in shape but very much smaller, in bright shades of red, yellow, striped, and white. Start indoors in March for early bloom. Outdoors they should stand about a foot apart for spread. They make desirable bedding plants and are often seen in old-fashioned gardens. If you are making a selection of the old-time garden flowers, you will appreciate Four o'Clock, especially as it is not so fastidious as to soil.

Eulalia
Miscanthus sinensis

Plume Grass, or Eulalia, is our prettiest specimen Grass for lawns, growing under favorable circumstances as high as nine feet, with long narrow leaves that droop very gracefully. When old and well-established a clump may spread to be five or six feet through. Buy started plants, and set them out in the spring where they are to remain. Arrange for bold effect in an ornamental bed or amongst shrubbery. The effect along the edge of a small pond is very fine. Zebra Grass, a popular variety has striking, banded yellow leaves but is not quite hardy. The Japanese Rush (var. *gracillimus*) is very effective in small gardens. The light green foliage is as narrow as half an inch and the Rush will grow four feet high. All these Grasses require only to be planted to become permanent additions to the home garden.

Bee Balm
Monarda didyma

Only the Cardinal Flower surpasses the Bee Balm in brilliant color. Oswego Tea, Horse Mint, Rose Balm,

Fragrant Balm are a few of the numerous names of this very charming native wild flower. Monarda is too coarse to be an attractive plant in detail, but seen in masses a little distance away is very effective. The flowers are wide-mouthed, brilliant scarlet and very fragrant, borne in large heads on stalks two to four feet high. Monarda increases so rapidly as to become troublesome in a border and, as the name Bee Balm implies, is one of the numerous joys of bees and humming-birds. Along streams and moist spots generally is its habitat but it does better in ordinary dryish garden soil than do most of the flowers of its type. Blooming period is during the summer months, and Monarda should be planted preferably against a dark background to bring out the full color effect. Variations from type are well worth trying. There are a white and a rose color: also the variety *fistulosa*, growing three feet high with striking purple effects.

Flowering Tobacco

Nicotiana alata grandiflora

The white Flowering Tobacco, which was formerly known as *N. affinis*, is a fine plant for dry spots and striking enough to fill in well at the back of a border. The tubular blossoms open toward night and continue open till sunrise: by moonlight they take on a fine shimmering quality and their perfume is delightful. The plants begin to bloom in early midsummer and continue blooming till hard frost. Flowering Tobacco grows quickly in full sunlight in most sorts of soils. *N. Sanderae* having pink or rose flowers, very effective against dark backgrounds, is a hybrid from this and the common tobacco of commerce (*N. tabacum*)—

a plant from three to five feet, occasionally used where a large-leaved tall-growing plant is desired—but its flowers are not so good. If the blossoms of the Flowering Tobacco are picked and the stalks placed in water, the buds will open and remain open if kept away from direct sunlight.

Love-in-a-Mist

Nigella damascena

This prettily named flower has tiny blossoms an inch across nestling in finely cut, fennel-like foliage. Love-in-a-mist grows a foot or two high and should provide continuous bloom all summer. The flowers are blue or white. The petals and sepals are like colored, a distinguishing trait of the Crowfoot family to which Love-in-a-mist belongs. The fruit is a long capsule. The seed may be planted outdoors about May in any available garden soil. Sow in succession for continuous bloom and in the autumn for spring flowers. Love-in-a-mist seems not to transplant well. The flowers are favorites for cutting and are often to be found tucked away in odd corners of borders and rock gardens.

Basil

Ocimum basilicum, O. minimum

The herb gardens of our grandmothers and great-grandmothers no longer exist, and with them have gone out of favor many of the herbs for which they were famous. The brothers Basil, "Sweet" and "Bush," once much esteemed for flavoring, are now very seldom grown. The Bush Basil is a very "bushy" little shrub, and both might be planted for the sake of their long and honorable associations. Sweet Basil grows a foot or two in height and the white or bluish flowers are borne in long racemes in whorls about the stem. Seed may be planted outdoors in the early spring and the plants will do better if thinned to stand no more than ten inches apart.

Farewell to Spring

Godetia

The showy red-and-white blossoms of the flower known as Farewell to Spring fit in well where a large-flowered annual is wanted for a sunny or half-shady spot. These are cheerful stand-bys, prettiest in rather large groups of one kind. The bloom is from July to October and the blossoms an inch to an inch and a half across and of peculiar satiny luster. This annual grows ten feet high at times and is native on the Pacific Coast. Farewell to Spring should to started indoors early if you want June flowers, otherwise outdoors in May. Whether soil be thin or rich seems immaterial. The plants should finally stand twelve inches apart.

Prickly Pear

Opuntia vulgaris

Prickly Pear is a small Cactus and the only one of that large family suited to the border. This Cactus grows about a foot high with curiously jointed, flat, leaf-like stems covered with spines in groups. Flowers are pale yellow, appearing at intervals during the season. Prickly Pear, sometimes also called Barberry Fig, is hardy as far north as Massachusetts. The plants are ideal for shallow soils, cool and underdrained. They may be put outdoors in the spring and arranged as house plants in winter, but because of their spines and bristles they are rather a nuisance indoors. In some parts of the world other species of Opuntia are raised for their edible fruits. They have also served as hedge plants.

Iceland Poppy

Papaver nudicaule

The Iceland Poppy is a pretty, low-growing perennial with the characteristic crinkled petals of the Poppy. The delicate crêpey blossoms about two and a half inches across, ranging from white through greenish yellow to orange and orange-red, are borne singly on hairy, leafless stems, delicately curving at the top. The grayish-green leaves in a clump at the base of the plant are quite decorative. Technically a perennial, the Iceland variety lasts more than two years except in the North. Plant seeds in late summer and the plants should bloom, if not allowed to seed, continuously from May to frost. Select warm, rather rich soil in bright sunlight.

Oriental Poppy

Papaver orientale

"Gorgeous" is the adjective most frequently used in garden manuals to describe the brilliant red of the Oriental Poppy. Certainly the garden in May and June could never be as gay without them!

Oriental Poppies grow three or four feet high with handsome, lobed leaves. The type flower is brilliant orange-scarlet, with a black spot in the centre, but there are numerous variations, even to white. The leaves are large, rough, grayish-green, irregularly and deeply notched, extremely decorative but dying to the ground after blooming season, but growing again in the fall. These Poppies had best be planted where other plants will conceal their foliage after bloom. They should not be crowded as considerable green growth is made in the fall. Sow outdoors in the spring as early as possible in rich loam, in sunshine. Thin to stand a foot apart as they are hard to transplant. Poppies have long, tapering roots and are difficult to transplant except in the autumn when partially dormant. If transplanted in the spring they will not bloom the same season. There are many shades of color and named varieties, but the type flower can hardly be improved upon.

Corn Poppy

Papaver Rhoeas

This little field Poppy, scarlet with black spot, glorifies the grainfields of northern Europe and is the stock from which our modern varieties of "Shirley Poppies" have been developed. The Shirley Poppies are always single with a white base, yellow or white stamens and no trace of the black spot. The bloom comes in summer and when self-sown will be earlier than the planted groups. As the plants do not bear transplanting well they must be put in the ground quite small where intended to flower, but it is best to sow where wanted and thin. Make the soil fine and scatter the seeds, which need only very light covering. Allow about eight inches of space per plant and do not let the flowers run to seed if continued bloom is wanted.

TIGER LILY
(Lilium tigrinum)

MONKEY FLOWER
(Mimulus luteus)

FOUR O'CLOCK
(Mirabilis Jalapa)

LOVE-IN-A-MIST
(Nigella damascena)

AUTUMN ACONITE
(Aconitum autumnale)

JAPANESE ANEMONE
(Anemone japonica)

BOUQUET STAR FLOWER
(Aster ptarmicoides)

FALSE CHAMOMILE
(Boltonia latisquama)

The Opium Poppy (*P. somniferum*) is a gorgeous annual, three feet high, with bold glaucous foliage and large single or double flowers in a great variety of colors.

Geranium

Pelargonium hortorum, P. domesticum

Geraniums are easily raised; it is necessary only to slip them into the ground and await results. They do not object to poor soil and will grow better than almost any plant of standing in a dry place. They never stop flowering till frost comes, throwing out new blossoms well above the leaves in truly decorative fashion. No wonder experts chide the amateur for his passion for the Geranium!

Garden Geraniums are cultivated forms from species imported originally from South Africa. Rose, Ivy-leaved, Fish, and the old-fashioned Show or Lady Washington, represent different distinct species. Geraniums are very easily grown from cuttings. In culling out it is well to remember that stocky, many-branched plants will produce the best flowers. Discard the tall and spindly. Plant in full sunlight, keep the soil loose, and see that there is plenty of water in blossoming time.

The old-fashioned Lady Washington Geranium (*P. domesticum*) has a short blooming season and cannot stand the heat of midsummer. In September the plants should be pruned, repotted in light compost, and kept in a frame till cold weather. The flowers, not so many in a truss, are larger and more striking than in other varieties. They usually appear on a white ground, marked or blotched with red or purple.

The common or Zonal Geranium (*P. hortorum*) is a

mixed hybrid of indefinite origin. Very variable in flower, etc.

Petunia

Petunia hybrida

The gaudy colors of this soft, frilled flower have perhaps advertised it so much that the Petunia has fallen a little into disrepute; if only the pure purple and white varieties were seen in gardens, the flower would have quite a different reputation. The Petunia is a most profuse, sweet-scented bloomer, growing from one to two feet in height with flowers from July to September; resists drought well but is inclined to be of weedy habit. Sow indoors in April, transplant in May, selecting a warm sunny spot, or sow outdoors for later bloom. Petunias make a handsome display in window boxes and rock gardens. The finest varieties are grown from cuttings, as plants propagated from seed generally show a variation from the parent stock. Cuttings should be made of soft, young growth potted quite firmly and kept shaded a few days.

Scarlet Runner Bean

Phaseolus multiflorus

The Scarlet Runner Bean, grown as a vegetable in economical Europe, is cultivated with us more for the bright, cheerful scarlet flowers that appear in June and July. Normally a perennial, though in actual practice usually an annual, the Scarlet Runner grows about ten feet long, twining and twisting about whatever is near by. This Bean can be used successfully about old tree stumps or wherever vines of its length are desired. The leaves

are compound, the leaflets thin, acute. Plant where you
wish the Bean to grow, sowing not until the ground gets
warm. Place the seeds eye down, about an inch deep
and about a foot apart. They grow anywhere and repay
small effort both in beauty and in food value.

The Butterfly Runner Bean (*P. multiflorus papilio*) is a
variety having pretty rose-and-white flowers.

Wild Sweet William

Phlox divaricata

The pretty little bluish gray blossoms of the Wild Sweet
William are to be seen along the edges of moist woods and
beside the banks of shady streams. The flowers are flat,
somewhat fragrant, profusely borne in small loose clusters
at the end of slender leafy stems sometimes eighteen
inches high. The Wild Phlox is spring blooming, very
adaptable, seemingly accepting with gladness whatever
choice of soil is offered. This Phlox looks well in masses.
The country cousin is perhaps best suited to rock gardens
and to carpet dampish spots by the waterside. *P.
Laphami* is an improved form with bluer, larger flowers,
raised in Europe.

Perennial and Annual Phlox

Phlox paniculata; P. Drummondi

The Perennial or Hardy Phlox is a native plant that has
forged its way from obscurity into considerable promin-
ence in the floral scheme. Coming nowadays, in all
shades of pink, scarlet, cerise, lavender, purple, white with
or without a pink eye, the Phlox is easy to manage, solid

and orderly in habit, quickly increased, fragrant, beautiful.
The bloom runs from late June through September, and
the flat flowers one inch or so across are profusely borne in
close elongated heads on erect, leafy stems from two to
four feet high.   The modern hybrids must have good rich
food, and plenty of water in dry weather.   All varieties
will thrive without any attention for many years, but better results will be obtained if the clumps are divided every
three or four years in late autumn; otherwise the plants
show a tendency to become rootbound and by the growth
of surrounding seedlings seem to revert to type color.   If
late and early blooming varieties are planted together, one
should obtain bloom from July to November, but bloom
may be delayed by pinching back the tips of the shoots.
There are two strains, *viz.:* paniculata, the taller and
with colors usually in the reds; suffruticosa, any early
flowering hardy Phlox with white, flesh-pink, or purple
blossoms.

Annual Phlox (*P. Drummondi*) may be planted in the
open or preferably started indoors earlier.   It is a low-
growing plant with flat round flowers and comes in a great
range of colors, and there are strains of star-like blooms.
The parent of the annuals was introduced into England
from Texas in 1835 and was immediately seized upon by
English gardeners as a subject of experimentation.   It is
one of the most popular garden annuals now.

Cape Fuchsia

Phygelius capensis

Cape Fuchsia is an attractive native of South Africa,
rather partial to warmer climates than ours.   With us,

except in California, the Cape Fuchsia has been seen more
as a curiosity in greenhouses than outdoors in beds. Yet
the plant lives under the same conditions as do Geraniums
except that it is more susceptible to early frosts. The Cape
Fuchsia grows from two to three feet high; the flowers are
about two inches long, tubular and drooping, borne in
groups of one to four on long pedicles straight out from the
stalk. It can be raised from seeds and cuttings and will
make an excellent novelty for the home garden or window
box. Seeds should be started in midsummer and the
plants transplanted in May. They are not at all hardy
and must be moved back indoors in good season, but
south of Philadelphia will live outdoors with protection in
winter.

False Dragon Head

Physostegia virginiana

False Dragon Head, also known as Obedient Plant and
Lion's Heart, is a good reliable perennial of easy culture in
a strong, rather moist and rich soil. The flowers are small
and curiously shaped, often a half-inch long, ranging in col-
or from purplish red through rosy pink and lilac to flesh-
pink, closely borne in graceful terminal spikes on erect
stems. The foliage is fine, persistent—an excellent foil
against plants of coarser texture. The period of bloom is
July and August, but if the flowers are kept from going to
seed, the bloom will be prolonged well into autumn. To
keep the plant at its best old clumps should be divided and
replanted frequently. Set out about two feet apart in
good moist soil. There is an excellent white variety and
an allied species, *P. denticulata*, smaller and more delicate
with very neat pinkish flowers.

Chinese Bellflower

Platycodon grandiflorum

The Chinese Bellflower, or the Balloon Flower, with blossoms three inches across, is the largest Bellflower that can be easily grown. The blossoms are large, wide-open, purplish blue, with curiously inflated buds, borne very freely at the tips of leafy stems which sprawl if not supported. They must be tied to light supports as soon as they are a foot high; if once allowed to flop over to the ground, they will not straighten up without breaking. A fine specimen may have ten or twelve spikes of flowers during July and August. The name Balloon Flower comes from the inflation of the bud just before it opens. Good drainage is essential and a sandy soil preferable. To secure bloom well into autumn make sure that seeds do not form. In the autumn the dying stems should be left to protect the crown. Divide early in spring when the growth starts, or grow by seed. The method by seed is rather uncertain as the seedling frequently does not come true to parent either in form or color. The lovely white variety *album* is faintly tinged with blue, reminding one garden commentator of the fresh blue-and-white aprons of little girls.

Tuberose

Polianthes tuberosa

The Tuberose, once quite fashionable, is now rather infrequently planted, probably owing to its heavy, almost sickening odor. Also it is very stiff-growing and does not seem to form happy combinations with other plants.

Tuberose is of the Amaryllis family and is not related to the Rose, the name being merely a corruption of the adjective tuberosa. The flowers are white on a foot-long spike carried on the end of an erect three-foot stalk, and the time of bloom is August and September. The foliage is grass-like and arching. If bulbs are planted outdoors about the first of June there will be late summer and early autumn blossoms. The soil should be fine and light. The "bulb" need be covered with no more than an inch of earth. Allow about eight inches between bulbs. Before the time of frost the bulbs (in reality they are tubers) should be taken out and kept dry for next season's use. In the spring examine stock with care. If bulbs are green at the top, they are sound and may be replanted.

Portulaca

Portulaca grandiflora

Portulaca, most gaudy of coverings for very dry spots and first cousin to the weed "Pusley" of unenviable reputation, will grow in hot, dry, shallow soil where no other flower will; for seaside gardens it is indispensable. Portulaca, or Rose Moss, grows six or eight inches high, but owing to its trailing habit seldom appears to attain even its own meager real height. The blossoms are red, magenta, orange, and white, appearing from July to October. The leaves are succulent, well-rounded. Culture is simple: the seeds need merely be scattered over the surface of raked ground when the weather is warm. Plants may be thinned to stand three inches apart. Portulaca often self-sows and persists for years.

Shrubby Cinquefoil

Potentilla fruticosa

Cinquefoil has bright yellow flowers like small single
Roses that bloom all summer. Though the plant may
grow four feet high, it is generally met with much smaller.
The bark is shreddy, the leaves compound with three to
seven leaflets. The Shrubby Cinquefoil is favored for the
garden on account of its long season of bloom. On a rich
and moist soil it is inclined to grow rank and weedy. On
drier soil the vigorous little plant will keep itself in better
shape. Potentilla is quickly propagated by division of
rootstock in the spring or they seed quite freely. The
plant often shows up very effectively along a border or in
a rock garden.

Mignonette

Reseda odorata

Sweet Mignonette is undoubtedly the most popular
flower cultivated solely for fragrance. The little plant
grows from ten to eighteen inches high, with red, white,
and yellow finely cut flowers borne in a dense spike but
not at all conspicuous. Shorn of fragrance the Mignonette would indeed be a very minor plant. Sow outdoors in
the sun rather early, for the bloom is late. You had best
thin the plants to stand ten to twelve inches apart.
Mignonette is a favorite for bouquets and in the garden
is often put to use to break up undesirable color combinations. By a second sowing one may have bloom and fragrance till November. There is a fine dwarf form, var.
suffruticosa, which is also inclined to be somewhat woody.
Florists own a number of named strains.

Flowering Raspberry

Rubus odoratus

The Flowering Raspberry, often miscalled the Mulberry, will make a pretty semi-wild effect in a domestic garden. This sub-shrub is vigorous, three to five feet high, with shreddy bark and leaves somewhat like a Maple. The flowers are in clusters, rosy purple, fragrant like single Roses; the fruit edible but not desirable. It had best be isolated on a lawn both because of its color and because it seems to sap the strength of plants growing near it, and is useful for planting in waste places. This Raspberry grows rapidly from the root in rich soil, as its natural habitat is along rich woods and shady banks. Buy small plants and set out in the early spring.

Roses

General Introduction

No flower name brings to mind more beautiful or more varied pictures—pictures of the wild flower of the roadside as well as of its more delicately reared cousins, the Rose of the garden and the greenhouse! The Rose has played its part in history in the famous English Wars of the Roses. In literature the references from Chaucer and Shakespeare down the long line of poets are constant. The books on Rose culture are legion, the possibilities of selection bewildering, the pitfalls all too many.

Yet any one with a little space, a little attention, and a little patience may have Roses as beautiful as any planted by high-priced landscape artists for indifferent million-

aires.   If one wishes to start at first with only a small Rose
garden, where shall it be made?   How tended?   What
standard varieties had best be tried?

In selecting space for a Rose garden, find if possible a
site protected from cold winds and open to the sunlight
several hours a day.   Deep, rich loam is wanted for all except the Hybrid Teas, which can be grown in sandy,
gravelly soil. All Roses require good drainage. Artificial drainage can often be arranged with small stones or
gravel placed well under the top soil to carry off the excess
water.   Mix the soil to the depth of a couple of feet a few
weeks before planting, using about one third well-rotted
manure.   The general rule is to plant in the spring, though
some Roses may be planted safely in autumn. When
Rose stems are received from the greenhouse, see that the
roots are protected with burlap from the drying action of
the wind.   Holes should be dug deep enough to permit
the roots to point downward and to slant outward.   For
watering and weeding, beds should not be over five feet
wide and plants eighteen inches to two feet apart, according to their spreading habit.   A point in successful Rose
culture is to remember that the surface soil should be kept
raked loose during the growing season. When buying
Roses it is economy in the end to get only the best quality
of stock from thoroughly reliable dealers.   A light mulch
had best be left on the raked surface of the Rose bed all
summer and in the winter a heavy three-inch covering of
rough manure.   Keep the covering undisturbed as long as
possible, but avoid waiting until the sap is running freely.

The matter of pruning is quite important.   All pruning,
is best postponed until after February. The Hardy Roses,
both climbing and non-climbing, should be pruned first

and Tea varieties a little later. In pruning, first cut out all dead wood and weak shoots; then you must decide whether you prefer a few Roses of superlative size or if you prefer a greater quantity of smaller blossoms. Drastic pruning will produce the former, and more lenient wielding of the shears the latter.

Unfortunately, of all the ornamental garden plants the Rose suffers most from insect pests, bane of the Rosarian, important among which are the rose beetle and the rose slug, the aphis, or green fly, the leaf hopper, and many others. Rose manuals devote pages to the enumeration of insecticides and fungicides, but the timid amateur may be cheered with the thought that all these diseases seldom come to any one garden and that many well-tended vigorous Rose bushes run along for years with very few "bug troubles."

Hybrid Perpetual Rose
Rosa gallica, etc.

The large group of Hybrid Perpetuals includes the old-fashioned, large-flowered varieties that have made June the Rose month of the year. They are all fairly hardy, though they appreciate winter protection; but very few are "perpetual" bloomers in America. Mostly, though there are notable exceptions, they flower with us only in the early summer. Hybrid Perpetuals generally have dull green, wrinkled but not shiny foliage, and prickles generally strong and fairly abundant. These Roses had best have good garden soil, rich and deep inclined to heavy, and plenty of sunshine. To get larger and of course fewer flowers prune down heavily after flowering season.

Frau Karl Druschki is snow-white of remarkable vigor, attaining a height of over five feet the first year. Louis Van Houtte, rather capricious but if once well established a fine deep velvety red and very fragrant. Paul Neyron is strong growing, almost equaling a Peony in size and color. Very effective in masses, and profits by hard pruning. Ulrich Brunner is cherry-red, Victor Hugo a brilliant crimson.

The York and Lancaster Rose, petals striped red and white, is a variety of the gallica Rose.

Tea Rose

Rosa odorata

Tea Roses, unsurpassed for delicate colorings, are the tenderest of the Rose family. Pink, yellow, coppery bronze are the most frequent colors; there are really no dark reds; all are delicately tea scented. Foliage is smooth and shiny. Prickles are moderately abundant, in some varieties almost absent. Tea Roses require a very rich soil thoroughly drained and winter protection except in California and the Far South. Though somewhat capricious growers, their almost continuous bloom makes them well worth the time and pains taken in cultivation. If heavily mulched they can be grown in the latitude of New York.

Madame Jean Dupuy is a very fine reddish-yellow, an abundant autumn bloomer. The buds are long and carried on single stems. *Maman Cochet* is a pink Tea Rose, full flowering and very desirable for cutting. This is considered perhaps the hardiest of all Teas. The bloom is profuse, the growth spreading and rather low.

Hybrid Tea Rose

Rosa odorata hybrida

The Hybrid Tea, mainstay and joy of amateur Rosarians, combines the merits of the Hybrid Perpetuals and the true Teas, the brilliant colors and hardy character of the one and the more delicate colors and continuous bloom of the other. Foliage is slightly rougher than in the Teas and wrinkled; prickles are generally large and strong, though not very abundant. Flowers are well formed with a large number of petals and an elongated bud. They bloom constantly. As a class they require less protection than the Teas. New varieties are constantly being pushed into notice but can hardly supersede the best known favorites.

Etoile de France is velvety crimson, continuous and free-flowering, the brightest colored of all the very dark Roses. The famous Killarney is pure pink with a white counterpart in every way the same except the color. La France is silvery pink with a tendency toward a bluish tinge and very fragrant. Madame Ravary is deep apricot-yellow, a decorative Rose of great merit. Prince de Bulgarie is rosy flesh, shaded salmon, and orange.

Crimson Rambler Rose

Rosa multiflora

The Crimson Rambler, introduced into this country as late as 1893, leaped immediately into popular favor, and it is safe to say that more Ramblers have been sold for outdoor cultivation than any other variety of Rose. Crimson Ramblers are most commonly trained as climbers for porches, trellises, archways, or over rustic posts. The profuse trusses of bright crimson flowers make a brilliant June picture and this Rose seems reasonably free from the attack of insects except red spider. They grow with great vigor in any well-manured soils. After flowering the old canes should be cut out and the plant fed freely to encourage the young shoots which will produce next year's flowers. The foliage should be frequently sprayed to avoid mildew. From the Crimson Rambler as a parent there are continually being produced new varieties, often of the highest merit.

Ramanas Rose

Rosa rugosa

Shrubby Roses have always been favorites for massing and for landscape effects in mixed borders and shrubbery, and in the less-cared-for parts of the garden. For this purpose foliage is fully as important as bloom. *R. rugosa* makes a bush five or six feet high, a favorite for ornamental hedges and for seaside planting. The thick, dark green leaves are very attractive and the large, conspicuous fruits, like small apples, are held well into winter. The flower is purplish rose, or you may have, if you prefer, the white variety, *alba*. This Rose makes a brave showing on very light, very poor soil. Many charming hybrids of this Rose will be found listed in catalogues.

Harison's Yellow Brier, a fine golden yellow, and W. C. Egan, a *R. Wichuraiana* hybrid, light pink and nearly always in bloom, are often used as shrubbery Roses. *R. lucida*, the native New England dwarf wild Rose, is largely planted in Boston parks, making very attractive displays both in the white and in the pink varieties.

Prairie Rose

Rosa setigera

The original Prairie Rose, of which there are several improved garden varieties, grows wild in the Middle Western States where it is often known as the Illinois Rose. Of the hybrids, the Baltimore Belle, a fine double Rose with light green foliage and creamy white blossoms, is perhaps the best known. The Prairie Roses thrive over a greater extent of territory than any other group. They are rapid growing, flowering but once late in the season. The foliage is five to seven leaflets, dark green, rough, and large. The prickles are stout and generally numerous. It is pleasant to be able to write that Prairie Roses are absolutely hardy and not particular as to soil. Plant in spring or autumn.

Memorial Rose

Rosa Wichuraiana

The Wichura Rose, also introduced in 1893, the same year as the Crimson Rambler, hardy with pure white single flowers and resplendent green foliage, is the type Rose from which many charming hybrid Ramblers have been, and are still being, produced. All the Wichuraiana daughters may be quickly recognized by the glossy character of the foliage. Dorothy Perkins, best known of pink climbers, may be likened to a pink Crimson Rambler, but is more elegant, with glossy foliage. All these trailing Roses answer the requirements of the average American garden better than many of the other types, and though they will not be grown as flowers for cutting like older varieties, they are already—both literally and figuratively—filling a large place in our gardens. It is not too much to say that two Roses—the Crimson Rambler and the Wichuraiana—have taught millions to learn that a Rose garden is a possibility wherever there are a foot or two of soil and a few rays of sunshine.

Salpiglossis

Salpiglossis sinuata

Salpiglossis is a rather unusual little annual on the order of the Petunia, with most delicate aesthetic color schemes, smoked pearl, amaranth, rose, burnished purple, delicate buff among others, all with pencilings and flashes of deeper color. The flowers are funnel-shaped with very open-spreading throat. Tender annuals such as this had best be started indoors early and transplanted outdoors in late May. The plants are customarily placed no more than six inches apart as the lower part of the stems has a bare look. Salpiglossis will grow in any usual garden soil and will bloom constantly from July on, unless the season be too dry. This annual, though quite old, will still be a novelty to many amateur gardeners and is well worth trying.

Saxifrage

Saxifraga ligulata, etc.

The Saxifrages, some early but more midsummer blooming, are a large family of small, hardy, modest plants that have their habitat in stony ground, clefts in rocks, or anywhere in thin soil; found mostly in the cold and temperate regions of the Northern Hemisphere. The stalks rise usually no more than two feet high. The foliage varies, sometimes mossy, sometimes leathery-leaved, sometimes silvery. The blossoms are all colors and the many tiny seeds are usually enclosed in capsules. The leaves of some of the European species are eaten as salad and the root is used in medicine.

S. ligulata, a sturdy rock-garden plant not hardy as far north as Boston, is commonly catalogued as *Megasea ligulata*. Mother-of-Thousands, or Strawberry Geranium (*S. sarmentosa*), is a great favorite as a window-box and pot plant. The flowers are small, whitish pink, on a long stalk. The Pyramidal Saxifrage (*S. Cotyledon*), the largest and showiest of the family, grows to the height of twenty inches with leaves in silvery rosettes and pyramidal inflorescence of small white flowers.

London Pride

Saxifraga umbrosa

London Pride, Nancy Pretty, None-so-pretty, St. Patrick's Cabbage—all these names sound at least like a flower with a history. This Saxifrage is a little evergreen edging plant, four inches high, with small summer white flowers often dotted red, borne loosely on foot-long stalks. London Pride thrives, even increases itself, in the cold shade next to walls where few other plants will live. This modest little Saxifrage has always been a prime favorite in English cottage gardens, but has never been used in America to any great extent. Try a few plants, if you have a rock garden, selecting preferably a spot with half-shade and well-drained soil. Set out young shoots allowing

between a space of ten inches.   When the growth gets too
mat-like, they may be taken up and divided without harm.

Butterfly Flower

Schizanthus pinnatus

The Butterfly Flower, a native of Chile, seems to have
the fate of being grown mostly in pots indoors whereas it
is quite hardy for outdoor planting and one of the most
charming of variegated flowers.   Colors range from white
through violet, lilac, and yellow, frequently with markings
which immediately suggest butterfly wings.   Schizanthus
grows about two feet high and the general effect is one of
daintiness.   Poor Man's Orchid is another name but not
so appropriate as the Butterfly Flower.   A further reason
why this plant should be tried outdoors is that it will require no special care or richness of soil.   Plant seed outdoors in May and thin to stand six inches apart.

Steeplebush

Spiraea tomentosa

Steeplebush, or Hardhack, is a late-blooming Spiraea
with flowering season from July to September.   The pretty
little rosy-pink flowers are densely arranged in rather stiff
terminal spikes.   They blossom from the apex downward
and before the lower blossoms begin to open the upper
have already faded to a light brown.   The plant reaches
four feet in height with upright brown branches and leaves
woolly on the under surface.   This late bloomer should be
planted in low moist ground and looks best in fair-sized
groups and masses.   Unlike most of the members of the

family it does not sucker. Steeplebush is somewhat similar to Meadow Sweet and is often found growing near it in low moist ground and along the sides of hillside pastures. If you have a wild tangle in one corner of your garden, there will be the place for this Spiraea. May be propagated by seeds or cuttings but much more easily by a small shrub from a nurseryman.

Great Sea Lavender

Statice latifolia

The Great Sea Lavender grows about two feet high, sending up flower spikes from a tuft of rather coarse leaves. The large heads of mauve-colored, mist-like bloom form a fine combination with August-flowering Phloxes. The bloom is in June and July and the dried flowers may be kept indefinitely. Statice likes a deep, loose, sandy soil in full sun and is one of those plants that do best if not disturbed. The effect of the mist-like flower clusters may be brought out in fine shape in a rockery. The plant is not so frequently used in borders. Start indoors in February and transplant outside in May, allowing at least a foot between plants.

Marigold

Tagetes erecta, T. patula

The old-fashioned yellow African Marigold brings the glitter of sunshine into the garden and into the house, too, where few flowers are its equal in lighting up dull rooms. The colors range from rich orange to pale lemon and the pungent bloom from August till frost. The flowers are compact solid masses of bloom up to two and a half inches in diameter, on a freely branching shrub-like bush two feet high. The old-fashioned *T. erecta* never was difficult to raise and produces the best blossoms with plenty of sun and good rich soil. Sow about four inches apart and thin to twelve or eighteen inches, as they need space.

The French dwarf Marigold *T. patula,* growing round twelve inches in height, makes an excellent border plant and a very fine combination with Sweet Alyssum. In color yellowish to red brown, this dwarf has darker foliage and a velvety look uncommon in a Marigold. The seed may be planted outdoors in May or started in pots indoors to induce earlier bloom. *T. signata* is still another good dwarf form, but has single yellow flowers.

Trumpet Vine

Tecoma radicans

The Trumpet Creeper is a great boisterous vine best planted where bold striking effects are desired. It climbs by aërial rootlets and will cling to wood and stone. The Trumpet Vine is generally considered the best orange-red-flowered vine for arbors and rough places. This vine flowers only in spots turned toward the sun. The blossoms are trumpet-shaped, four to six inches long, in loose clusters, lasting usually from June till September. As might be anticipated, it may be planted in all sorts of soils and will triumph over all sorts of conditions.

Wishbone Flower

Torenia Fournieri

The Wishbone Flower is an annual edging plant with yellow, blue, and purple flowers on the order of the Pansy.

TUNICA
(Tunica Saxifraga)

HOARY SPEEDWELL
(Veronica incana)

The foliage is dark green, becoming bushy and compact. The plant grows ten to twelve inches high, and the flowers are funnel-shaped and two-lipped in terminal racemes. They have nearly all the Pansy shades and bloom from July to October. The plants had best be started indoors in March with a covering of very light soil. Transplant to the open as soon as the ground is warm, spacing to stand a couple of inches apart. Torenia has no special soil requirements to worry over and will grow in sun or shade. There is a fine, large-flowered, free-blooming variety, *grandiflora*.

White Clover

Trifolium repens

The ubiquitous White or Dutch Clover of the roadsides is often brought into the garden where with a little attention the plant will grow so large and luxurious as to astonish the casual visitor "who is not in on the secret." Clover is also valuable for enriching poor pieces of soil for future use. The stems, it hardly seems necessary to say, are creeping and the leaves three-parted. The Red Clover makes a good combination with the White. The Crimson Clover (*T. incarnatum*) is very handsome, the stem rising one to three feet high and the flowers varying from crimson to scarlet.

Blazing Star

Tritonia crocosmaeflora

Blazing Star, also known as Montbretia, has gay color and decorative habit, qualities much sought for in the late summer garden. The flowers are orange-scarlet and starlike on long graceful spikes from slender, much-branching stems three to four feet high. The leaves are tall, narrow, and stiff, springing from the ground. The bulb is half-hardy south of New York and will survive the winter even in the North with a proper amount of protection. But it is best in the North to winter indoors in dampish earth and replant in the spring. Plant outdoors fairly early in rich, well-drained soil in full sunlight. There are a number of modern named varieties offering a charming selection of color.

Tall Nasturtium

Tropaeolum majus

The Nasturtium is another cottage flower considered too commonplace for city parks and great gentlemen's estates, but affectionately abbreviated to "sturshun" by many generations of small garden lovers. *T. majus* is a trailing species, reaching a length under favorable circumstances of twenty feet or more. Plant outdoors in April an inch deep and six inches apart; bloom should be forthcoming in June. Keep the flowers well picked and give plenty of climbing support. It will not endure frost.

The possibilities of the Nasturtium as a cover for stone walls or corners of a backyard should not be overlooked. Indoors, arranged just as they are with stems, disk-like glaucous leaves and seed vessels attached, they are wonderful brighteners of dark houses and dull north rooms.

The Dwarf Nasturtium (*T. minus*) with familiar scarlet, yellow, maroon blossoms, making dense masses of leaf and bloom, hardly needs mention.

These plants are popularly called Nasturtium because of

the peppery flavor of the leaf. The Watercress is the true Nasturtium.

Canary Bird Flower

Tropaeolum peregrinum

The Canary Bird Flower is a vine that loves to ramble, peering here and there over a rustic fence, climbing a trellis, or creeping up an old tree stump. The vine may be drooped over window boxes, but it never seems as vigorous as when given opportunity to climb. This is reputed our best yellow-flowered annual of its sort, attaining twenty feet in a hot sunny location on dry ground and often in bloom from July until frost. The leaves are five-lobed and the odd-shaped flowers canary-yellow. This is not a showy vine but very advantageous for spots where quick growth is desired. Sow indoors in February and transplant after danger of frost is over.

Tunica

Tunica Saxifraga

T. Saxifraga is the only one of the Tunicas grown in this country. The flowers are small, pink or purplish pink, not striking but very dainty. When in bloom Tunica presents something of the appearance of the Gypsophila. The leaves are also small, dark green, and persistent, forming a tufted, spreading mat. Tunica grows six to ten inches high, blossoming from late June through August, and is customarily used for edging and in rock gardens. Propagate by seed or by division indoors or outdoors. Growth will be excellent in all soils except perhaps one that is poorly drained.   There are a half-dozen Tunicas native of Europe.

Valerian

Valeriana officinalis

Common Valerian, or Garden Heliotrope, has minute, pinkish-gray clusters of flowers with a spicy odor that will scent the whole garden in June.   The stems are two to five feet high, downy and branching; the leaves compound, showy, fragrant, and persistent.   Valerian spreads rapidly, tending to form large clumps, and looks well naturalized along the edge of shrubbery.   This is not a capricious plant and will obtain satisfactory growth in most sorts of poor, unimproved soils.   Plenty of sunlight is advisable. Plant outdoors in May, allowing generous space between plants.   Large old clumps may be divided without injury in the early spring.

Speedwell

Veronica longifolia, etc.

The Speedwells are a family, small in size though not in numbers, widely distributed over the temperate zones. *V. longifolia*, one of the most charming of border plants, has small, intense lavender-blue flowers in numerous, showy, slender spikes rising above vigorous, leafy stems. The leaves are saw-edged, narrow-pointed, green, persistent.   This Speedwell does best in deep, rich loam.   Start indoors in February and set out young plants in May, at least a foot apart.   Summer blooming.

V. incana, or Hoary Speedwell, another striking though smallish flower, has rich blue blossoms in many graceful, slender spikes three to six inches long, borne on branching leafy stems often eighteen inches high.   The leaves, two or three inches in length, are rather narrow and pointed, downy, grayish green.   This species has a fresh, trim appearance both in and out of bloom.   Likes a sandy soil and plenty of sun.   Summer blooming.

V. repens, a little creeper, develops a dense mass of shining green moss-like foliage.   It will grow where grass will not, and in May is covered with tiny blue flowers.

V. rupestris, the Rock Speedwell, also spring blooming, is very well liked for edging on account of its dense foliage habits and profusion of bloom, growing only four inches high.

There is also a variety of *V. longifolia* known as *subsessilis* which produces fine, high sapphire spikes of flowers from August to October.   So with one variety or another the Speedwells manage to spread over most of the outdoor season.

Wayfaring Tree

Viburnum Lantana

The frequently seen Wayfaring Tree has white blossoms in dense cymes with showy white rays along the margin. This Viburnum blooms in May and June, often growing twenty feet high and more.   The fruit is a striking red berry that slowly fades to black, remaining on the tree till well into winter.   The Wayfaring Tree is a favorite for dry and limestone soils and is no exception to the general statement that all the Viburnums are hardy, satisfactory growers.   This species may be started from seed sown in the autumn, a process hardly to be recommended on account of its slowness, or from greenwood cuttings, but it is best to buy plants from a nursery.

Japanese Snowball

Viburnum tomentosum plenum

The Japanese Snowball blooms later and is more effective generally for specimen purposes than the old-fashioned common Snowball. The flower heads are rounder and cleaner, the leaves crinkled and a deeper green. Altogether, the Japanese Snowball may well be esteemed the best white, large-flowered summer shrub. This Snowball grows from eight to ten feet high under favorable circumstances and may be trained quite effectively over walls. Cuttings may be taken and the young shrubs set out in the early spring in any good garden soil. The Snowball will be effective with shrubbery or by itself as a specimen on a lawn. There is an excellent variation, *rotundifolium,* which is particularly attractive, flowering two weeks earlier.

Pansy

Viola tricolor

The Pansy is one of those flowers that come to our gardens laden with many names and a weight of much tradition. Shakespeare was familiar with "Love-in-idleness," another good Pansy name, and we may infer from a reference in "A Midsummer Night's Dream" that the Pansy was a "western" flower and a component of love potions. The English wild mountain Pansy is purple and pale yellow. Heart's Ease, Love-in-idleness, Johnny Jump-up, and Ladies' Delight are all well-accredited names for this best known of flowers.

Quantity of bloom, wonderful range of color, the velvety

texture of the darker shades, are among the fine points of
the Pansy. Standard colors are purple, yellow, blue; the
variations are countless. The Pansy bed had best be
arranged in cool, deep loam and in partial shade. Start
seeds indoors in a seed pan in March and transplant in the
garden in May. Another plan is to sow in August and
cover over the thinned plants with a light protection of
leaves. The next season you should have luxuriant bloom.
Pansies run out quickly unless care be taken to renew old
stock.

V. cornuta, known as the Horned Violet and also as the
Bedding or Tufted Pansy, has smaller flowers with longer
range of bloom. After July, cut back, manure heavily,
water often. Plants should be in fine shape for September
bloom.

Monk's Pepper Tree

Vitex agnus-castus

Monk's Pepper Tree, Chaste Tree, or Hemp Tree, is an
aromatic shrub belonging more strictly to tropical and
subtropical regions than to the temperate zones. The
flowers are bluish lilac, quite effective, and the leaves
grayish in color and generally star-shaped. The shrub
blooms late for its type. The height varies considerably
according to locality, but is most likely to be around six to
eight feet. Any soil will do, but a rather dry sunny situation is much to be preferred. If possible, buy a small
shrub and set out in the spring. This will bring much
quicker results than the slow process of raising from seeds
or cuttings. The Chaste Tree may be planted in a sheltered spot as far north as New York with the reasonable
anticipation that it will be found hardy.

Immortelles

Xeranthemum annuum

The double-flowered Immortelle has a rather somber, old-fashioned look. This annual grows about two feet tall and the flower heads are violet and purple, rather Aster-like in appearance. The showy parts are the stiff bracts, which as cut flowers will last all winter. This Immortelle is easily raised and is very attractive grown with perennial Grasses. Seeds may be sown in early May in the open, or to get a better start, indoors in February. The plant, a native of the Mediterranean regions, is grown quite commonly in European gardens but less frequently in this country.

BUTTERFLY FLOWER
(Schizanthus pinnatus)

SALPIGLOSSIS
(Salpiglossis sinuata)

AUTUMN

AUTUMN

Japanese Maple

Acer palmatum

The Japanese Maple, with fine deeply lobed leaves, growing into low specimens no higher than twenty feet, is a very handsome, distinctive shrub for foregrounds, for planting near houses, and in the rock garden. The color of the leaf is various yellow, purple, scarlet, giving excellent choice of varieties. The Japanese Maple needs well-drained, rich soil and partial shade. The varietal names are descriptive of the plant. Thus: *palmatum* has a divided leaf; *atropurpurea* is deep purple red, etc.

Autumn Aconite

Aconitum autumnale

Autumn Aconite, with vigorous but not so open bloom, is a very timely successor to the summer Aconites or Monkshoods. The growth is from three to five feet, the flowers blue, lilac, whitish, holding on from September to November; the foliage finely divided, dark and handsome. This perennial is sometimes exasperatingly slow in establishing itself, but when it once has a good footing you need give yourself no further concern over your Autumn Aconite for a number of years. Aconite will thrive in sun or shade, but the flowers seem to last longer in shady spots. Rich,

moist soil is preferable. Plants require a foot of space in
the garden. Growth for seed is very slow and it is better
to set out young plants if procurable. A new species from
China, *A. Wilsoni*, grows five to six feet with violet-blue
flowers. This is considered the hardiest of all Aconites.

Silver Sweet Vine

Actinidia arguta, A. polygama

This best of arbor vines has attractive dark green leaves,
quite tough, with reddish petioles. The vine twines but
does not cling. The flowers are greenish white in June
followed by yellow fruit with fig-like flavor. The Silver
Sweet is remarkably free from insects and fungi and is
easily increased by seeds, cuttings, and layers. *A. poly-
gama*, flowering in July, is a lighter green, quite silvery
above the middle of the leaf; grows more slenderly and is
not so vigorous a climber. It possesses a great fascination
for cats who will very quickly play havoc with young
plants if opportunity be given them. Both species may
be grown without difficulty in all sorts of soils and are
very satisfactory as vines for arbors and trellises.

Hollyhock

Althaea rosea

The Hollyhocks stood like sentinels before the doors of
the first houses of the Plymouth Bay Colony. Nowadays
we see them mostly in bold masses amongst shrubbery
where, while they last, they are most effective. Hollyhocks grow from six to eight feet high and are among our
tallest flower-garden plants. The flowers are rose, pink,

FEATHERED COCKSCOMB
(Celosia plumosa)

SHRUBBY CLEMATIS
(Clematis heracleaefolia)

PLUMBAGO
OR BLUE LEADWORT
(Ceratostigma plumbaginoides)

TICKSEED, CALLIOPSIS
(Coreopsis tinctoria)

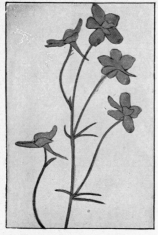

CHINESE LARKSPUR
(Delphinium chinense)

BURNING BUSH
(Evonymus alatus)

BLANKET FLOWER
(Gaillardia aristata)

SUNFLOWER
(Helianthus annuus)

white, pale yellow, madder-purple, in single and double
varieties.   These biennials or perennials are unfortunately
subject to disease which has caused them to be less frequently planted than formerly.   To get bloom the first
year start indoors in February, transferring the seedlings
promptly in early May.   The plants like deep, fertile
soil, but rank manure is not safe and the ground had best
be prepared quite a little while before planting.   Allow
about two feet of space per plant, and always cover the
Hollyhock bed over winter with leaves held in place by
branches.   The yellow and white fig-leaved Hollyhocks
(*A. ficifolia*) have a widening circle of admirers and look
well beside the older varieties.

Pearly Everlasting

Gnaphalium margaritaceum

This prettiest of Everlastings is no doubt still used for
decorating mantelpieces in the parlors of houses in remote
and backwoods districts.   Pearly Everlasting grows two
or three feet high.   The leaves are alternate, green and
downy on the upper surface, woolly below.   The little
flower heads are formed of many dry, pearly white, overlapping scales enclosing a tuft of numerous fuzzy yellow
tubular florets.   This is the common Everlasting found
growing wild on dry hillsides and recent clearings.   In the
garden this white effect of late summer will appear surprisingly well against a background of border plants.   It
is entirely hardy and no garden soil is likely to be too poor
for it.   Sometimes it runs into the lawn and becomes a
weed.

Japanese Anemone

Anemone japonica

Anemones in the autumn may seem a mere freak of nature to the uninitiated, but the Japanese Anemone, or Windflower, which is to be found more frequently every year in our gardens, blooms gloriously from August till hard frost. The flowers are usually rose or white, two or three inches across, and the bloom is prolific in September. The leaves, generally in clumps at the bottom of the plant, are much lobed and quite decorative. This visitor from over seas likes partial shade and cool, loose, moist, rich soil. The plants had best be covered over winter and they do not like to be transplanted in the autumn. Drought in early midsummer will affect the bloom. The Japanese Anemone is chiefly to be seen in clumps amid shrubbery or under trees. There is much choice of named varieties, both single and double.

The Snowdrop Anemone (*A. sylvestris*), a white flower, will give similar bloom in summer if planted in the spring. Like most of its kin it also prefers half shade. The Windflower (*A. nemorosa*) is a late spring and early summer bloomer with solitary white or white-tinged purple flowers like small single Roses. These natives of woods and meadows are easily coaxed into wild home gardens and will make a brave showing in any good garden soil in partial shade.

Hercules' Club

Aralia spinosa

Hercules' Club, also called the Devil's Walking Stick, is a shrub oddity with twisted, club-like branches that stand out grotesquely in winter. It grows some forty feet high with fine white-clustered flowers in August, and later black berries much relished by the birds. The leaves are large, pinnate; the stems armed with vigorous spines. Hercules' Club is quite tropical looking and is just the choice for those who want "something a little different."

True Goat's Beard

Aruncus astilboides

True Goat's Beard is often mistaken for the False (*Astilbe decandra*) and both True and False are often mistaken for Spiraeas. They are not greatly different one from another and either is well worth growing for bold, massive, half-wild effects and especially for connecting the flower garden with shrubbery. True Goat's Beard is a perennial growing about two feet high with graceful panicles of minute whitish flowers rising on long, slender, forking spikes. There is a companion form, *A. Sylvester*, growing wild in woods but not so trim and graceful. The plants need about eighteen inches of space each. They should be grown without difficulty and increased by division of the roots.

Butterfly Weed

Asclepias tuberosa

The Butterfly Weed in full bloom is the handsomest of the Milkweeds and one of the most gorgeous bits of color of the garden. The flowers are large, fragrant clusters of brilliant orange, more rarely yellow, carried on erect stems two to three feet high, but after blooming the plant had

best be cut down or hidden by shrubbery.   Pleurisy Weed
and Orange Mullein Weed are perhaps the best known of
the other numerous popular names this plant has gathered
to itself.   The stalks are stout and hairy, only thinly
provided with the milk that is characteristic of the Milkweeds.   The seed pods are also more slender than those
of the common Milkweed and no more than one or two
are produced at a time.   As might be anticipated from the
name, Asclepias in full bloom is surrounded by such hordes
of butterflies and flying insects as to be called the Butterflies' Mecca.   Transplant from the wild either early in
spring or after flowering is over in September.   This is
one of the plants that do well in dry banks and fields in
full sunlight.   If you bring along a little of the soil with
which the plant was surrounded, success will be doubly
sure.

Aster

Various species

The Windflower and the Violet, they perished long ago,
And the Brier-rose and the Orchis died amid the summer glow;
But on the hills the Golden Rod and the Aster in the wood,
And the yellow Sunflower by the brook, in autumn beauty stood.
                                                —Bryant.

The Hardy Aster, or Michaelmas Daisy, as it is called
in England, is par excellence the September flower.   The
hardy Asters adapt themselves with supreme grace to
domestic gardens; a beautiful autumn garden would indeed be difficult to draw up without their aid.   It seems
extraordinary to think that great, showy, delicately tinted
varieties have all sprung from the little country Aster that
mingles happily enough with the Golden Rod and the

Ferns by dusty roadsides. The Hardy Asters—there are several hundred species—show considerable ranges of color from white to dark purple and including bright rosy lilac, pink, rose, crimson, pale blue, and violet. The colors are not vivid and dazzling, but commonly rich, warm, and harmonious with a tawny subdued glow both arresting and appealing. On large estates borders are sometimes made up almost entirely of Asters, and every carefully planned home garden should have a corner at least of these indispensable, daisy-like flowers.

They will grow under practically all soil conditions and will come through the severest winters unharmed. Old clumps should be broken up and separated, as the increase is rapid, the plants becoming untidy and unmanageable. While they do well on all soils, they will naturally grow taller and flower over a longer period if planted in deep, rich, moist ground.

A. amellus is a small, free-blooming Aster good for neat, restricted areas; grows from two to three feet tall, is thoroughly reliable, offers the maximum of bloom to the square inch. The leaves are oblong, lanceolate, the flowers purple in fine large heads. The dwarf Aster (*A. alpinus*) is spring-blooming.

The New England Aster and the New York Aster (*A. novae-angliae* and *A. novi-belgi*) are conspicuous tall, loose-growing species. The New England Aster in particular grows as high as eight feet on good moist soil with plenty of sunlight. The flowers are in heads, the ray flowers purple, white, blue, pink, lavender, the disk flowers yellow, often changing to purple. The New York Aster is a more slender-growing plant with violet-colored flowers. These may be started from seed indoors in February or planted outdoors in August for the following season's bloom. In this case thin in September so that the little plants stand six inches apart and have the bed carefully covered over winter. The New York Aster in particular has some very attractive named varieties: *roseus*, clear rose color with yellow center; F. W. Burbidge, light pinkish lavender with yellow or brownish centers; and Top Sawyer, clear Parma-violet blue with yellow or brownish-yellow center.

The Smooth Asters (*A. laevis*) with sky-blue flowers are among the best of the family for dry soils and dry wood-lands, and may be easily naturalized by merely scattering seeds. There is also a white variety excellent for late bloom.

A. cordifolius and *A. patens* are among the finest of the wild species. *A. cordifolius*, the common blue Wood Aster, has been greatly improved under cultivation. In the wild this Aster is very spreading, bushy, small-flowered, grow-ing from one to five feet high in partly shaded roadsides and thickets from early August often until the first snow-fall. *A. patens* has fine blooming qualities; twenty or thirty showy rays of a deep rich violet surround the yellow purple-stained center of disk flowers which are set in pleasing green cups of overlapping parts. The rays close inward with recurved tips at night.

The Bouquet Star-Flower (*A. ptarmicoides*) is a dwarf variety of neat, upright habit with small, pure white, star-shaped flowers in great profusion. The foliage is finely cut and dainty. The individual flowers are not so full or well formed as in some Asters, but the thickness with which they cover the plant makes up for their thinness in detail. This prime favorite prefers dry, loamy soil and, transplanted into the garden, should be given a dry or at least a well-drained soil. If native Asters are to be found in near-by woods or fields, it is much better to transplant than to grow from seed.

A. grandiflorus is the latest of the hardy Asters to come into bloom. The flowers do not appear till late in September. They will continue to bloom till really severe winter sets in. The flowers are large, dark bluish violet and starlike, with yellow centers borne freely on bushy plants two or three feet tall.

The White Heath Aster (*A. ericoides*), the last Aster the limits of our space will allow us to mention, has masses of small white, bluish, lavender-gray, or pinkish mauve blossoms in September. White Heath also "owns up to" a long list of popular names, including Frost-weed, Farewell Summer, Dog Fennel, Mare's Tail, Scrub Brush, and White Rosemary. This is an Aster for a dry soil. The little white flowers scattered over the bushy plant look like frost particles.

False Chamomile

Boltonia latisquama

False Chamomile with lilac flowers in late July through September is a flower for bold, wild effects, very attractive in rough places or at the back of borders. The flowers are large, Aster-like, with yellow centers, carried in profusion on tall, much-branching stems. The foliage is bright green, oval, pointed. False Chamomile differs from the Asters only in technical characteristics. The plant in the woods grows no more than four feet tall, but often six and eight in cultivation. False Chamomile blooms profusely and will not require staking. For a plant whose natural habitat is moist ground, it will do astonishingly well on light dry soil; but of course the richest growth will only be obtained under more favorable circumstances. Division of the roots is the best method of propagation. Another Boltonia (*B. asteroides*), also called False Chamomile, has white, pink, or purplish flowers that come earlier.

Shrubby Calceolaria

Calceolaria integrifolia

Calceolaria, or Slipperwort, is a low, shrubby, evergreen plant whose blossoms are somewhat the shape of a pouch or slipper. The leaves are large and close-growing; the flowers, abundant and showy, yellow. It grows about two to six feet high and, as our summers are not suited to the outdoor growing of this South American importation, is more of a greenhouse and indoor plant with us. The Calceolarias of the florists are hybrids of allied herbaceous species and are variously colored yellow, brown, maroon, mottled and spotted. Sow the seeds in rich soil, in pots or pans, during early June in a greenhouse; they need not be covered, merely sprinkled over the top of the soil. Shift to small pots and then larger as occasion requires.

French Mulberry

Callicarpa purpurea, C. japonica

The French Mulberry has pretty pink flowers in July, but is grown rather for its lilac-violet fruits which persist in dense clusters well into winter. *C. purpurea* grows three to four feet high, not quite so high as the American species (*C. americana*).   Choose a spot with good sunlight but if possible sheltered from heavy winds.   Sandy loam is desirable but not at all essential.   Callicarpa must have some winter covering, but will spring up from roots apparently dead and flower the same season.

The Japanese species (*C. japonica*) is extremely ornamental and hardy.   The flowers in pinkish or whitish cymes are succeeded by the shrub's great attraction, large, purple, drupe-like fruits.

China Aster

Callistephus hortensis

The China Aster is one of the most satisfactory of the none too many survivors of the old-fashioned garden flowers.   More modern improvements of forms and colors have been made on this charming annual than perhaps on any other of the Daisy family.   There are many desirable types: some tall and branching; some pyramidal in shape; some with overlapping, recurved petals; others with narrow, twisted petals.   The prettiest tints are shell-pink, pale lavender, white, and strong purple. China Asters had best be started indoors, or in a frame, and transplanted to the open only after all danger of frost is past. Although seed may be sown in the open for late bloom they prefer a light loam, deeply dug and well manured, and must always be watered in times of drought.   If early, midsummer, and late-blooming strains are planted, one may have a succession of bloom till frost.   The plants show a tendency to rust; for this rapid growth and well-cultivated soil are the best of antidotes.

Canna

Canna indica

Everybody knows the Canna, most frequently seen in circular beds in parks and in the centers of lawns. You may have Cannas without difficulty if you wish to grow them and if you do not think this tropical-looking flower has not been somewhat overplanted. The modern large-flowered varieties are wonderful improvements on the old-time Indian Shot, as it was called. The truth is that the Cannas give bold, brilliant color effects, but it is excessively difficult to reconcile them with most of our northern flowers. Perhaps the best that can be done—a variation at least from the eternal circular bed—is to make one isolated corner devoted to tropical effects, with Bamboo, Eulalia, and tall decorative Grasses.

The Cannas grow from two to six feet high, with red, pinkish, pale yellow, and nearly white flowers from August till frost. The flowers are in branching spikes above large sheathing leaves. Cannas like a rich moist soil with plenty of water. They are sensitive to chill and must not be planted till the ground is well warmed; and the roots must be wintered indoors.

Blue Spiraea

Caryopteris incana

Blue Spiraea you will certainly wish to bear in mind, if for no other reason than that it is the only blue-flowered shrub of late summer and autumn. The flowers are lavender-blue conical spikes somewhat suggesting the Larkspur, blossoming in August and September. The shrub grows from three to four feet high, dying to the ground at the close of each season. Blue Spiraea does well along the sea coast and in sandy soil generally. The shrub may be bought and set out early in the spring; or seed sown in the autumn and protected over winter should produce good growth with the advent of mild, balmy weather. It grows easily, too, from cuttings of "half-opened wood" in summer or fall. This fine blue is most effective at the back of the flower border or massed with other shrubs.

Cupid's Dart

Catananche caerulea

Cupid's Dart, which seems by name at least a flower with a history and a long and honorable past, is a pretty, well-behaved perennial with a blossom like a blue Daisy. The plant grows about two feet high; the flowers are blue-rayed, measuring two inches across, borne on long slender stems. Cupid's Dart is easily grown anywhere and will do astonishingly well on light, thin soil. Plants may be started from seed or old roots. The *bicolor* variety has flowers of blue center with white margin, and *alba* is all white. The flowers in olden time were much used dried, as Everlastings.

New Jersey Tea

Ceanothus americanus

New Jersey Tea, Red-root, or Wild Snowball, is said to have been used by American soldiers in the Revolutionary War when other supplies failed, for brewing tea. It is a shrub, late-blooming and very free-flowering, a member of the Buckthorn family. The numerous tiny white or cream-white flowers are densely crowded into oblong, terminal clusters. The astringent, reddish roots possess some medicinal qualities and also yield a brown dye. New Jersey Tea ranges wild from Ontario and Manitoba to Florida and Texas in dry open woods. Somewhat the same type of situation should be picked out in the home garden or grounds. The plant will grow three feet in height with profuse bloom from July to September. There are many attractive hybrids under the general name *Ceanothus hybridus*, having flowers in various shades of blue.

Bittersweet

Celastrus scandens

Bittersweet is a native vine of rapid growth with bright orange-red berries that hold their own even amid the brightest of the bright hues of autumn. By contrary, the blossoms in June are altogether inconspicuous. Bittersweet attains a height, or rather length, of some twenty feet, advancing vigorously along whatever solid is within reach of its tendrils. The leaves drop off early leaving the fruit exposed. The berries are in an orange-colored pod which, when ripe, bursts open in three divisions. The vine seems to grow indifferently in either sun or shade and may be started from seed, layer, or root cuttings. A Japanese species, *C. orbiculatus*, grows more vigorously but the fruits are hidden till very late by the foliage.

Cockscomb

Celosia cristata, C. plumosa

The Cockscomb makes fine masses of color in red, scarlet, salmon and old gold, but is not a very attractive plant otherwise. The flower heads grow into a monstrosity somewhat of the appearance of a rooster's crest, eight to twelve inches across in various shades of color from crimson to orange and creamy white. Cockscomb, of which you probably will not wish any great amount, is mostly seen in borders and occasionally in beds by itself. Sow indoors and transplant into any available garden soil, one that is moist being preferred. Moisture either natural or artificial must be provided. The crested and the plumed or feathery are the two main types. The feathered (grown as *C. pyramidalis*) grows from two to three feet in height, much higher than the crested, and is on the whole more satisfactory for general garden use.

Plumbago

Ceratostigma plumbaginoides

Plumbago, perhaps more commonly known as Blue Leadwort, is the finest low-growing blue perennial for autumn mass effects. The flowers are a fine cobalt blue and the bloom will run through September and October. They somewhat resemble Phlox in form and are great favorites for bedding plants. The flowers are small, profusely borne in dense heads on shrubby, branching red stems. The plants will produce their finest, deepest blue in a warm light soil with full sun.

The shrubby Plumbago (*Plumbago capensis*) is a climbing shrub in South Africa and California, a greenhouse plant in the eastern United States. This Plumbago may be put outdoors in early summer and will produce fine, deep blue flowers up to frost. There is also a white variety of this but hardly of the attractiveness of the type flower.

Pyrethrum

Chrysanthemum coccineum

The Pyrethrum, also called the Colored Daisy, is a favorite of old-fashioned gardens that in recent years has been more grown in England and on the Continent than with us. The plants are single or double with color range from white to pink, to scarlet and to lilac. The leaves are finely cut, the blossoms terminal and solitary on stalks eighteen inches high, the ray flowers are usually red. Pyrethrums had best be started indoors in midwinter. The plants should be set near the front of borders as they are close, neat dwarf growers. In fairly dry soil set out eighteen inches apart; in rich, deep moist soil as much as thirty inches. Ground should be dug deeply and manured well. If the foliage rots in midsummer cut it away unsparingly. The roots lie close to the surface and the plants cannot stand too much sun.

Chrysanthemum

Chrysanthemum hortorum

Volumes have been written on the Chrysanthemum; the number of named varieties is legion; the flower is generally conceded to be the most important of the late-blooming plants of the garden.

The hardy garden Chrysanthemums are single, semi-double, or double flowers varying in size from over two inches to no more than a quarter of that, and in color from pure white, pale yellow, and pink, through orange and red to bronze and dark, deep crimson. The stems are two and three feet high, the leaves deeply cut and lobed.

The Chrysanthemum bloom is the most resistant to frost of any garden flower and is often in bloom even after the first fall of snow. Unfortunately the large-flowered, show Chrysanthemums seen in florists' windows are unattainable without skilled personal attention, but there are plenty of varieties well suited to gardens, most of which may be wintered outdoors if provided with light covering. The plants should grow easily and increase in size from year to year without any great attention. Cuttings taken in the spring and early summer root easily. By pinching back the growth till the end of May, plants can be made quite bushy, developing often an extraordinary number of flowers. The hardiest garden varieties are known as Pompon Chrysanthemums, and all are crosses and strains of *C. indicum* and *C. morifolium* (*sinense*). Chrysanthemums show great diversity of form but are mostly separated into well-defined types among which are the single, resembling a Daisy; the double quilled; the double with expanded rays; and the reflexed. The greenhouse and florists' Chrysanthemums are commonly of the types designated as Incurved, Japanese (the most popular decorative sort), Reflexed, and Large Anemone.

Clematis

Clematis recta, C. heracleaefolia, etc.

When the wild Clematis comes, with
her wealth of tangled blooms reaching up and drooping low.

In September, when most of the summer flowers have come and gone, the sprays of white or purple Clematis trail over rocks and fences or swing lightly from the tops of

shrubs. In the cities and in suburban towns the culti-
vated varieties riot over veranda, trellis, and arbor.
Wherever it grows, exquisite, airy grace belongs to the
Clematis.

White Bush Clematis (*C. recta*) is the Common Bush
Clematis of southern Europe, with fragrant flowers an
inch across in dense corymbs borne two to three feet high
or erect leafy stems. This charming perennial is unfortunately very susceptible to drought and must be kept
well sprayed in dry weather. The best soil for it as for
most sorts of Clematis is deep, rich, well-drained loam improved by a very slight addition of lime.

C. heracleaefolia Davidiana is a stout, fairly erect form
with small china-blue, hyacinth-shaped flowers possessing
a fragrance like orange blossoms. The leaves are bright
green and very large—larger than the leaves of any other
cultivated species. This Clematis used with the white
recta will be a success as a border plant, but is seldom
strong enough to stand without support.

The Japanese Virgin's Bower (*C. paniculata*), of Japanese origin, throws out masses of creamy bloom in August
and September. This is a rapid grower reaching out in a
single season a distance of as much as twenty feet. Virgin's Bower prefers good sunlight, but it is thought that
some shade for the lower stems and roots is necessary to
ensure best results.

Jackman's Clematis (*C. Jackmani*) is one of the large-
flowered showy hybrids enormously free-flowering in July
and occasionally thereafter through the summer. The
deep violet flowers are produced on the new wood and
even if the plants should become frozen in the winter, they
will blossom from the new season's growth.

EVERLASTING
(Helichrysum bracteatum)

SWAMP MARSHMALLOW
(Hibiscus Moscheutos)

RED-HOT POKER
(Kniphofia Pfitzeri)

MOCK CYPRESS
(Kochia scoparia)

HENRY'S HARDY LILY
(Lilium Henryi)

JAPANESE CLOVER
(Lespedeza japonica)

BLUE LUPINE
(Lupinus hirsutus)

BAYBERRY
(Myrica carolinensis)

Another exquisite, exotic-looking, large-flowered Clematis with white blooms is Virgin's Bower (*C. Henryi*).

The hybrids all favor shades of white, blue, or purple. There is also the red-cupped *C. coccinea* which looks well anywhere and is particularly fine when artfully mingled with the white-flowered sorts. Lastly, in one's zeal for the large-flowered and the over-cultivated, one should not forget the many small-flowered forms which are all generous and charming climbers and practically never fail to respond to reasonable anticipations.

Sweet Pepperbush

Clethra alnifolia

Sweet Pepperbush grows three to ten feet high and has, for garden points, lateness of bloom, attractive blossoms, and a willingness to grow vigorously in moist, sandy soils. The flowers are white in fleecy spires with spicy fragrance very alluring to the bees. The shrub is native and its sweetly fragrant odor should make its presence manifest quite a little way off in the open woods and along the country lanes. This is an adaptable shrub that will do well under most conditions and is particularly effective naturalized along streams and ponds.

Autumn Crocus

Colchicum autumnale

After the flowers have withered to nothing and the Grasses and Sedges have been gathered for indoor use, the astonishing Autumn Crocus makes the garden observer wonder whether the old year has really taken on a second childhood! These Crocuses are all the more surprising

because after a fine growth in May and June the foliage
dies away to nothing before midsummer. The flowers
that appear quite late are larger than the spring Crocuses,
generally measuring as much as four inches across. The
standard colors are purple, pink, and white; there are also
purple-veined varieties and a white, striped lilac. Bulbs
should be planted in the early autumn for the next season's
blossoming or in midsummer. Place the tips three inches
below ground and cover the top of the bed with old manure
or leaves. Mass the bulbs in beds in the rock garden or
in light grass that is not expected to be frequently cut.

Meadow Saffron

Colchicum speciosum

This is indeed the Queen of autumn Crocuses! The
large blue-purple bowl is carried on a fine long stem and
within burns the flame-capped stigmata, "like a candle or
perhaps the torch of its hardy little spirit." (*Wilder.*)
They bloom late, generally well into October, with colors
varying from a violet to a pure pink. All the late-
blooming Crocuses should be planted in the autumn with
their spring brethren, and they all need a good warm covering against the winter's cold. These Crocuses, placed
on damp pebbles or on a window-sill, without earth or
moisture other than that to be obtained from the air, will
bloom in cheerful, quite astonishing fashion.

Tickseed

Coreopsis lanceolata

Tickseed has large daisy-like flowers that, if kept well
picked, will give the garden a brilliant note of yellow

throughout the entire summer season. The foliage is small, rather sparse, and had best be concealed or sheltered by near-by shrubbery. The Tickseed blooms from August till frost and is easily grown in all soils. Rich, damp soil in open spots is preferred, but lacking natural dampness the Tickseed responds vigorously to midsummer watering. The plants had best be staked, and in setting out where they are finally to stand, allow twelve inches of space between plants.

C. tinctoria, generally listed in seed catalogues as Calliopsis, is a showy, easily grown annual very attractive for cutting. The flowers have reds, maroons, and browns, as well as yellow.

Red Twigged Dogwood

Cornus stolonifera

The Cornels and Dogwoods have many-colored fruits and brightly colored barks that put them among the most effective of late season and winter shrubs. They are slender-twigged trees of small size, with simple entire-leaves, strongly ribbed and of exceptional beauty. For winter color bark is often as effective as fruit and more lasting. *C. stolonifera* is considered by more than one garden commentator to be the best red-barked shrub for winter effects. The berries are an attractive white, but after all, it is the brightly colored branches that give the shrub its undeniable charm. Dogwoods have soft willow-like wood and are easy to raise from cuttings. Take cuttings in summer and start in sand. For finest effect the shrubs should be cut back every two or three years to induce new growth. The shrub is quite hardy and you should enjoy your Dogwoods for years and years.

Another fine Dogwood for autumn effects is *C. san-guinea*, growing about twelve feet tall with purple or dull blood-red branches and blackish fruit. *C. sibirica* has very bright coral-colored branches, grows about ten feet high, and is known as the Red Osier. The Cornelian Cherry (*Cornus mas*) often grows twenty feet high with bright, shiny scarlet berries about the size of an olive. This Dogwood will light up to fine effect a mass of dull, uninteresting shrubbery. The Flowering Dogwood (*C. florida*) has bright scarlet berries, but is generally better known for its exuberant spring bloom.

Cosmos

Cosmos bipinnatus

The familiar Cosmos is a fine, tall, late annual with white, pink, or crimson daisy-like blossoms. Our seasons are really too short for Cosmos, which is generally coming into its own about the time of the first frosts. The plant grows seven to ten feet high; the disk flowers are invariably yellow. Sow the seed as soon as frost has left the ground in a dry, sandy soil. Cosmos does not care to have the ground too rich, but appreciates full sunlight. If started indoors in February, you are naturally more likely to get the full benefit of the bloom. The Yellow Cosmos (*C. sulphureus*) grows not so tall and the flowers are smaller and come into bloom even later.

Gourds

Cucurbita, various species

Gourds are grown for their bright-colored and often fantastically formed fruits. Old walls used to have gourd

dippers, and housewives darned stockings over a gourd.
Some of the fruit, in the South particularly, grows to
enormous size. Negro cabins in the Southern States often
have large hollowed gourds hanging from poles in the door-
yard for bird houses. Gourds belong to the same family
as the Squash and the Pumpkin. Plant three seeds in a
hill no more than an inch deep. The vine grows very
rapidly and had best be trained over supports from which
the fruit will hang effectively. The Gourd vine is good for
quick screens over unsightly places, but is rather a rank
and undesirable annual otherwise.

Dahlia

Dahlia variabilis

The famous Dahlia responds to cultivation in a way that
flatters and encourages the timid amateur. In spite of
the obvious shortcomings of the flower, once a Dahlia
grower, always a Dahlia grower! Dahlias have thick
stems, large leaves, huge bulk. The trouble with the
modern Dahlia is chiefly the result of too much breeding
for bloom and too little breeding for strong, sturdy stalks.
Far too many of the otherwise fine modern varieties have
flowers too heavy for the stalks so that they hang over
and are half or entirely hidden by the leaves.

The Dahlia grows two to six feet high and comes in all
colors except blue and pure scarlet. They are easily
grown from seed, flowering the same season. In brilliance
of form and color they are the most effective of tall-growing,
late-flowering plants. Dahlias are heavy feeders with
moisture as a first essential. Special soil is not a matter of
importance, but it is highly desirable to avoid a wind-

swept site. Dahlias are best planted by themselves in beds; they are rather too gross feeders to do well in association with other plants. The original Dahlia was somewhat star-shaped, with slender pointed ray flowers; in process of cultivation the rays have become broader and wider so that the small original flower is hardly recognizable. The cultivated forms are all variations within the species.

The numerous forms have been classified as follows: Show, regularly quilled rays, self-colored, or lighter at the base; Fancy, regularly quilled rays darker at the base; Cactus, petals variously twisted and revolute, all colors; Decorative, an intermediate group with broad and flat petals; Peony-flowered, very large, irregularly formed, of semi-double decorative type; New Century, single, very large, with rich colorings; and Collarette, single or semi-double with a row of enlarged florets in white or yellow. The Pompon group includes miniatures of the Show, Fancy, and Single types.

Dahlias may be raised from seed planted indoors in February; the little plants should stand six inches high by May. After the first frosts cut to the ground and dig up the tubers, storing in a cool but not freezing cellar. In replanting it is best to divide the old roots.

Larkspur

Delphinium belladonna

With its early and very late blossoms and its rare turquoise blue tints the Belladonna Larkspur is one of the finest of the Delphinium hybrids and invaluable for the border or for massing against shrubbery. The plants are low-growing and very sturdy; the flowers, curiously shaped, sky-blue with white centers, borne on graceful, stalky spikes about twelve inches long. Seed should be started indoors, and plants will thrive in any good garden soil in sun or partial shade. If you have a choice of soils, plant in deep, rich, sandy loam, exposed to the sun. The first-year plants should be spaced about eighteen inches apart and the second year double this. Every three or four years Belladonna Delphiniums should be taken up and the ground respaded and refertilized; reset the plants somewhat farther apart than they were before.

Chinese Larkspur (*D. chinense*) has Larkspur leaves and blue or white flowers. The stem grows from two to three feet tall, very slender and not much branched. This native of China is a general garden favorite.

Cinnamon Vine

Dioscorea Batatas

The Cinnamon Vine grows thirty feet in a season with profuse white, cinnamon-scented flowers borne in loose clusters in July and August. Other names are Chinese Yam and Chinese Potato. The roots are huge tubers, potato-like in flavor and considered edible in the tropics. The leaves are shiny and opposite, quite attractive. The flowers are borne on the axils where appear also little tubers about the size of a pea. These tubers sown like seeds will produce the second year a full-sized vine. Cinnamon Vine likes the sun and is not at all capricious as to soil. The small tubers had best be started indoors in pots for quick growth.

Hyacinth Bean

Dolichos lablab

Hyacinth Bean is a rapid-growing annual vine with good ornamental qualities. Flower spikes are borne well out from the foliage and the fruits—flat pods three inches long—follow similarly colored, purple or magenta and white. The leaves are three-parted, broad at the base and pointed at the tip. The autumn effect is so attractive that it is too bad the Hyacinth Bean succumbs so easily to the first frosts. It is a good climber and an excellent drought resister. Sow the small black seeds outdoors in any garden soil about an inch deep and eight or so inches apart. Hyacinth Bean comes from the tropics and is commonly supposed to be the ancient Bean of India.

Purple Coneflower

Echinacea purpurea

The Purple Coneflower is rather somber looking but has good habit and its numerous dull pink flowers persist through a long period of bloom. The flowers are large and daisy-like, sometimes five inches across with high-pointed, purple central cone. The plant is coarse, rather bushy, growing from two to three feet and a half and, in exceptional cases, four feet high. This perennial likes rich soil and sunshine; is tolerant of drought. The very black roots may be divided infrequently or the Coneflower may be started from seed. The variety *serotina*, considered by some gardeners to be a better variety than type, is later-flowering with brighter colored, broader, flatter petals.

Willow Herb

Epilobium angustifolium

The Great Willow Herb, or Fire Weed, attracts attention by its tall, showy, magenta spikes of midsummer flowers. Low moist land is the preferred habitat, particularly recent clearings and land newly burnt over. Willow Herb is a fine plant for bold effects, grows vigorously and spreads freely. The plant often reaches seven feet high; the leaves are willow-like, the flowers purplish pink in long racemes, blooming during midsummer and well into autumn. Willow Herb grows wild from Labrador south to North Carolina and westward to California. In the garden the flower makes rank growth in moist spots and pretty effects along the edges of small ponds. Propagate by division of the root or by seed. Start preferably indoors, remembering to keep the soil moist. There is also a white variety, *alba*, that will make a delightful contrast.

Sea Holly

Eryngium amethystinum

The Sea Holly is a thistle-like plant with blue-flowered heads that show up well in a border but look quite out of place with other plants in the restricted areas of small garden beds. As the season advances the whole plant, especially in sandy soils, where it does admirably, takes on a metallic blue sheen. Blue Thistle and Star Thistle are also popular names incorrectly applied, for Sea Holly is not of the Thistle family. Growth is about three feet, the stems very stiff, steel-blue in color. Sea Hollies thrive vigorously in poor soil. Seeds germinate slowly; if sown in a pot, keep in a cold frame over winter; the seeds will germinate in the spring. The roots do not stand division successfully. There is a desirable dwarf form, *Bougati*.

White Snakeroot

Eupatorium urticaefolium

White Snakeroot is native and may be found wild in rich and moist woods in many parts of the country. The flower grows three or four feet high with opposite dark green leaves sharply toothed. The blossoms are tiny white florets loosely grouped into small fringy heads gathered in a terminal and somewhat flat-topped cluster. These appear in August and September, making a very attractive border plant. White Snakeroot must have good moist ground and preferably part shade. Sow indoors in fine soil and transplant the early part of May, allowing a space of eighteen inches between plants.

There are several other species occasionally found in gardens: *E. aromaticum melioscoides* grows four feet high with a mass of all-white flowers in August and September.

Mist Flower

Eupatorium coelestinum

Mist Flower, in general appearance somewhat like Ageratum, has for its claim to distinction among the host of competing flowers dainty heliotrope-color blossoms very charming in the late autumn. These flowers come in compact, flat-topped clusters on somewhat downy, leafy stems one to two feet high. The Mist Flower is just the right selection for the front of a small border. Good blooming season will be obtained even if the plants are started outdoors in May. A sunny corner is desirable. The young plants should be thinned to stand twelve inches apart. Mist Flower is a hardy perennial requiring only a light litter of leaves over winter.

Burning Bush

Euonymus europaeus, E. alatus

The Burning Bush, a well-named shrub, has fine scarlet fruits that wax brighter till midwinter finally robs them of their glory or until the birds spy them out. In October there is a purple husk that gradually parts and curls back revealing the red berries. Burning Bush has yellowish flowers in May, but there are more flowers in May than there are colorful shrubs in late autumn and winter, so it is rather for its autumnal radiant foliage that Euonymus gets its popular name. There is close family relationship between this small tree and the woody vine Bittersweet, both flowers and fruits being alike in many features. *E. europaeus* has pinkish pods and orange-colored seeds. There are varieties with deep purple, scarlet, and whitish berries.

E. alatus is rather spreading with its eight feet in height, and has corky wings running down its branches. The fall husk is a pinkish purple that opens and displays orange fruit. A blending of these in a group of autumn shrubbery will make an exhibition that all will stop to admire.

Blanket Flower

Gaillardia aristata

The very gay, daisy-like flowers of the Gaillardia will last from early summer till frost if no seed forms. The colors range from brilliant yellow at the tips to red or maroon toward the center. The foliage is rather deficient and, to compensate for its own lack of leaves, the Blanket Flower should always be planted with a setting of good foliage plants. The bloom is exceedingly profuse and continues even after light frost. The only double-flowered variety is *splendidissima plena*. In the variety *Kelway's King* even the disk is yellow. The Blanket Flower will provide blossoms for cutting from July to October and their fine long stems will make them especially attractive. The Blanket Flower likes the sun and will do well in any good garden soil. Sow early in the season and allow ten or twelve inches space between plants. They are likely to winterkill in too heavy soils.

Horned Poppy

Glaucium flavum

The Horned Poppy is very delicate and short-lived, but as it blooms almost continuously one really has no serious cause for complaint. This Poppywort branches and grows low, no more than one or two feet in height. The leaves in form of a rosette lie close to the ground and from them rise the flower stalks, sparingly leaved. The flowers are orange and yellow, two or three inches across and very poppy-like, blooming from July to September. They will

bloom till frost if the seed pods be kept constantly removed. The plant is short-lived as a perennial and had
best be treated as an annual. Start seed indoors in April
and transplant to the garden as soon as the soil is warm,
in an open sunny situation, allowing about eighteen inches
between plants. The Horned Poppy makes an attractive
display in a flower border. If you wish a change from the
familiar yellow, *G. corniculatum* will provide red or purplish
flowers.

Witch Hazel

Hamamelis virginiana

This is the American Witch Hazel, a shrub or small tree,
inconspicuous through the summer but offering autumn
flowers and fruits at the time when other shrubs are wind-
ing up their season's activities. The American Witch
Hazel grows as high as twenty-five feet with yellow and
brown flowers in September and October. The pods that
contain the seeds eventually pop open, throwing the tiny
black pellets far and wide for a considerable distance.
The lining of the pod is believed to shorten, producing a
spring that drives the seed forth with surprising force.
Frost and sun decide when to spring the trap. The gathered pods will burst indoors, but not so promptly. The
Witch Hazel likes moist earth, either peaty or sandy, and
makes a handsome, interesting autumn shrub; it grows
extensively in native woods, and a little investigation
ought to bring to light fine young material for transplanting. Select straight stock no more than four feet
high. The Japanese Witch Hazel is similar but is spring
blooming.

French Honeysuckle

Hedysarum coronarium

The French Honeysuckle is an old-time garden plant, quite inadequately named; it does not climb at all nor does it in flower resemble in any way the more familiar Honeysuckles. The French Honeysuckle grows two to four feet high with reddish, pea-like, fragrant blossoms in crowded axillary clusters. The leaves are compound with from three to seven pairs of roundish leaflets. The blossoms come in August and September, and are usually prolonged till the first frosts. Plants are rather straggly in growth, preferring light, open, well-drained soil with plentiful sunlight. Seeds may be started outdoors in May, but preferably indoors in February. There is a white variety that goes well in combination with the red. The variety *multijugum* grows taller than type with purplish blossoms and very attractive gray-green foliage.

Sneezeweed

Helenium autumnale

The bright yellow Sneezeweed is our best large, yellow, daisy-like flower for late summer and autumn. Sneezeweed grows up to six feet high with smooth, toothed leaves. The showy and quite effective flowers are one to one and a half inches across with drooping rays and hemispherical yellow center. There is also a variety, *rubrum*, less commonly planted, with drooping rays of red terra-cotta color and maroon and gold center. Sneezeweed has its habitat in swamps and moist meadows; as a garden plant it is

most commonly seen massed against shrubbery. Sow
outdoors in May and thin to stand twelve inches apart.
Old large plants should be dug up in early spring, divided,
and replanted in freshly prepared ground.

Sunflower

Helianthus annuus, etc.

Eagle of flowers! I see thee stand,
And on the sun's noon-glory gaze;
With eye like his, thy lids expand,
And fringe their disk with golden rays.

—MONTGOMERY.

The Sunflower, certainly to be included in any list,
however short, of the better-known garden flowers, is
obviously so named from its great flower head with en-
circling rays of gorgeous yellow petals. The modern
varieties grow from three to twelve feet with individual
flowers six to fourteen inches across. This annual plant
makes a valuable quick-growing screen available for almost
all soils or even lack of soil. The large seeds should be
planted an inch deep and six inches apart. Even plants
two feet high may be successfully shifted provided plenty
of water is put into the newly dug holes. The Sunflower
family is a very large one. *H. Maximiliani*, a perennial,
is one of the latest to bloom and is also one of the tallest,
especially suitable for the back of a flower border. It is a
Western species and does well in dry soils.

Of other perennials, *H. multiflorus* grows about five feet
high, is compact and controlled as to growth, with dark
green foliage and many globes of bloom. *H. mollis* is a
fine Sunflower of moderate height with large yellow flowers

that contrast pleasantly with the grayish foliage. *Helianthus rigidus* var. Miss Mellish, or var. Rev. Wolley Dod, are fine September Sunflowers with semi-double, deep yellow bloom.

Jersusalem Artichoke

Helianthus tuberosus

This Sunflower was brought to England from Italy in 1617 and was called the Sunflower Artichoke from the tubers which are edible and have somewhat the flavor of Artichokes. It varies from five to twelve feet in height. The leaves, rough on the upper surface, are four to eight inches long. The ray flowers vary from twelve to twice that number; the disk flowers are yellow. This Helianthus when in good condition will bloom from September to November. Propagation by tubers is easy. Plant outdoors in early May and thin the small plants to stand two to three feet apart. If tubers are to be planted in the spring, they need be no more than barely covered with soil. Sunlight and good rich but not too heavy soil are desirable.

Everlasting

Helichrysum bracteatum

Everlastings are brilliant yellow to dull crimson and white flowers that bloom in August and endure indefinitely if cut and dried when only partly unfolded. *H. bracteatum* grows two and three feet high and is the largest flowered Everlasting. These are African and Australian forms accustomed to dry, sandy ground and indifferent to lack of moisture. Scatter the seed in drills half an inch in depth and eight inches apart, and thin to stand eight inches apart. Sandy soil and full sunlight will exactly suit this Ever-

ZANZIBAR BLUE WATER LILY
(Nymphaea zanzibariensis)

WINTER CHERRY
(Physalis Alkekengi)

NINEBARK
(Physocarpus opulifolius)

SACALINE
(Polygonum sachalinense)

ALLAMANDA
(Allamanda Hendersoni)

LILY OF THE PALACE
(Amaryllis aulica)

VARIEGATED PINEAPPLE
(Ananas sativus var.
variegatus)

ARDISIA
(Ardisia crenulata)

lasting. If desired to be preserved indefinitely the flowers should be cut when only partly unfolded and hung up to dry with their heads down.

Swamp Marshmallow
Hibiscus Moscheutos

The various forms of Hibiscus deserve more general cultivation. To many flower lovers this perennial is quite unknown; yet Hibiscus is easily raised, quite hardy, and of attractive bloom. The Swamp Rose Mallow is a good-sized expanded flower, rose or white, often four inches across, sometimes with crimson eye, blossoming in August and September. This is the best rose-colored flower for swamps and brackish marshes by the sea. The leaves are large and roundish, grayish green, handsome, persistent. Young plants should be easily bought or they may be raised from seed. They should be planted one or two feet apart in good garden soil and will need no especial care. A fine new race of hybrids is springing up from the native Mallows of the North combined with some of the tropical species. These hybrids have slender arching stems and flowers in various colors, chiefly shades of pink and madder, often as much as six or eight inches across, and are known as *Mallow Marvels;* striking and effective for planting in groups at the back of a border.

Sea Buckthorn
Hippophae rhamnoides

Orange-red berries in clusters set off by grayish and silvery green foliage make the Swallow Thorn, or Sea Buck-

thorn, a splendid shrub for vivid late autumn color effects.
This Buckthorn is very capricious as to growth in different
soils and temperatures, causing such extreme varieties as
a height of twenty feet and then again in a poor location of
no more than two. Its liking for sandy soil makes it
preëminently a seaside plant, but fair growth is obtained
under average garden conditions. There are yellow blossoms in May, pretty but in no way remarkable. Staminate plants are more upright than the pistillate, which are
quite twiggy. In order to make a fine showing of autumn
berries be sure that you have both staminate and pistillate
plants among those you set out.

Hypericum

Hypericum Moserianum

The largest of the St. John's Worts, and a graceful,
showy plant for borders and shrubberies. The single
flowers, golden yellow with bright orange stamens, are
wild rose shaped, about two inches across, borne one to
three on a stalk on a low-growing, erect shrub with drooping branches. The flowers bloom a few at a time throughout the season, and this Hypericum should always be
planted in clumps as it will not look well singly. The
plant (it is technically a shrub) grows about two feet
high, is not hardy in New England, and except in the Far
South should be protected by leaves or litter over winter. The flowers will bloom longer in partial shade than
in sun, and the plant will make good growth in any
light, sandy soil. Propagated easily by seed, suckers,
and cuttings.

Hyssop

Hyssopus officinalis

Hyssop is a very charming little herb with small, dark foliage and bright blue flowers which last a long time. The little plant grows about eighteen inches high with linear leaves and flowers in whorled spikes, blue and occasionally white or pink. The blossoming season is from June to September and the plants are quite suitable for a low, hardy border. Hyssop is one of the old-time plants that have dropped out of notice but which are still quite well worth cultivating. Plant the seeds outdoors as soon as the ground is warm in light, sandy soil and thin so that the plants stand twelve inches apart.

Ilex

Ilex laevigata, I. verticillata, etc.

A number of the Ilexes offer fine red or black effects desirable in selecting shrubs for autumn color. Winterberry makes an excellent choice for border and hedge purposes, being low-growing, erect, and of good habit. The Winterberry (*I. lævigata*) and Black Alder (*I. verticillata*), both natives, have bright red berries. The leaves blacken after heavy frost but the abundant berries remain, untouched by birds, late into winter. The fruit-laden branches of the black Alder gathered in the wild are sold for Christmas decorations. The Ilexes like moist ground, grow slowly, and object to being moved about. The Ilexes bear the two sexes on different plants; so make sure that you have both staminate and pistillate plants in your group.

I. aquifolium is the European Holly, chiefly known to us through the importation of the cut branches offered in the markets for Christmas decoration.   Its sharp leaf, more spiny, more deeply cleft, more lustrous than that of our native American Holly *I. opaca*, makes, it must be confessed, a handsomer, more attractive shrub.   The European Holly must be protected for the winter in the latitude of New York or Boston; yet the little trees, if successful, will amply repay the extra labor they entail.

Our native American Holly (*I. opaca*) ranges from southern Maine to Florida, throughout the Gulf States and north into Indiana and Missouri.   Carloads of this Holly are shipped northward before Christmas and even in the remotest hamlets it is generally possible to buy a sprig for a buttonhole or a wreath for Christmas morning, but this collection of wild material has almost destroyed the plant in many sections.

Red-Hot Poker

Kniphofia Pfitzeri

Red-Hot Poker, also known as Tritoma and the Torch Lily, bears foot-long cones of bright, orange-scarlet, tubular flowers, picturesque and sometimes startlingly effective along a garden border.   The plant grows three or four feet high and is in bloom from early August till October.   The leaves are often three feet long, narrow and grass-like. Named varieties give a color range from yellow to brick-red.   The root is a rhizome from which the plant is commonly started.   Red-Hot Poker will do best in warm, well-drained soil and the color will be most vivid if the flowers rise against a dark background.   The rhizome should be planted outdoors in May with a space of fifteen inches between plants. They are hardy south of Philadelphia but farther north may have to be lifted and stored over winter; otherwise they are quite easy to raise.

Mock Cypress

Kochia scoparia

Mock Cypress is a foliage plant, a dense, neat, little bush with linear branches that turn a fine scarlet in the early autumn. The plant needs only to be sown in the open in May to grow in amazing fashion into a vigorous bush in a couple of months. Mock Cypress has a straight, soldierly look that is effective in a formal border or as a temporary hedge. Allow two feet space between plants. Clayish soil and a sunny situation are advantageous, but there should be good growth in any average garden soil. There are flowers of a sort in July, but quite inconspicuous. Mock Cypress dies completely to the ground after the first frosts.

Lavatera

Lavatera trimestris

Pink and white Mallows (*Lavatera trimestris*) are conspicuous in the late summer and autumn garden. They are easily raised from seed, and in deep rich soil will grow with large spreading clumps. They grow from three to six feet high with heart-shaped leaves and large characteristic flowers four inches across. The flowering season is quite extended, running from June through September. Lavatera likes rich, deeply dug soil and sunny exposure. Plant the seeds indoors in February and allow a space of two feet between plants when the seedlings are transferred outdoors in May. In dry weather the plants need careful watering.

Japanese Honeysuckle

Lonicera japonica

This vine, with small, dark-green foliage and neat, black berries, is ideal for a situation that demands winter foliage as a screen and where flowers are wanted to lend attractiveness in summer. This Japanese plant grows to the height of about fifteen feet and the lower portions of the vine do not become leafless and unsightly. The flowers are white changing to yellow, blooming in June, July, and August.

The Belgian Honeysuckle (*L. Periclymenum Belgica*) is a dwarf becoming somewhat bushy and particularly esteemed for its reddish, very fragrant blossoms which persist all summer. There is also a fine variety, *serotina*, blooming later in the autumn.

Honeysuckles flower on new wood and should be cut back severely to produce long shoots of vigorous scented flowers. If desired for effect as a vine, prune only lightly for form. Honeysuckles may be transplanted in either spring or autumn and young plants can be raised in any quantity by layering. Honeysuckles like the sun and thrive in any average garden soil.

Column Flower

Lepachys columnaris

The Column Flower is suitable for massing and makes an attractive cut flower. This yellow perennial, sometimes also treated as an annual, will grow from three to five feet tall. The leaves are divided with three to seven segments. The flowers, two inches long and somewhat drooping, are borne on thin wiry stalks. The ray flowers are yellow; the disk flowers are an elongated thimble-like, reddish-brown cone. Column Flower is easily grown from seed which is best started indoors in March for early growth and blossoms. Outdoors, plants should stand eighteen inches apart in a light garden soil exposed to full sunlight. Column Flower is a native composite; the garden varieties, however, have been greatly improved through cultivation largely in Europe where Lepachys is much used as a bedding plant.

Bush Clover

Lespedeza Sieboldi, L. japonica

Bush Clover has graceful, slender growth and small, pealike flowers in rosy, pink or white clusters in September. Bush Clover, so infrequently planted that the sight of it is quite a rarity in some sections, is hardy in central New England. Growth should be four to six feet, but winterkill generally keeps the plants a good distance from the maximum of eight feet. Bush Clover has all the Clover earmarks and is well to remember because of its late bloom which can be depended on for September and October. The two species are somewhat alike, *L. japonica* being slightly later in bloom and its white flowers very numerous. These Bush Clovers should be used in the backgrounds of borders. Plants may be bought and set out a foot apart, or the seed may be scattered broadcast or in drills. *L. bicolor*, shrubby, has charming purple flowers in July and more or less steadily through the summer and autumn.

Hardy Flowering Privet

Ligustrum ibota

Japanese Privet is an excellent evergreen Privet with dense foliage. These shrubs, though somewhat over-planted, are really indispensable as hedges. Left to them-selves they become quickly long and leggy, but deprived of new growth and sickish blossoms, their really extraordinary vitality is immediately turned to the upbuilding of dense undergrowth. The flowers which we seldom allow to come to maturity appear in small white clusters in the early summer and the fruit is a berry which often persists on the branches all the autumn and winter. Privets may be planted in any soil or sort of exposure. Though mostly clipped short for hedges, they are occasionally to be seen growing at full length in half-shade with other shrubs. Cuttings start easily. *L. japonicum* and *L. lucidum* are well-known species in the South. The so-called California Privet is a Chinese plant, *L. ovalifolium.*

Henry's Hardy Lily

Lilium Henryi

Henry's Hardy Lily, a sturdy, free-growing species, is one of the finest of late-blooming Lilies. This native of China grows in favorable circumstances as high as eight feet and the flowers may be produced to the number of twenty on a single plant. The flowers, dark salmon-orange spotted with red-brown, make a superb showing in August and September massed against shrubbery or in borders. The leaves are slender, rather inconspicuous. Bulbs may be planted in the spring or autumn as are other Lilies. A well-drained soil is essential; manure must not come in direct contact with the bulb; shade or a top dressing to keep the ground cool and moist are very advantageous. This Lily is hardy, vigorous, free from disease and, though still somewhat expensive, as are most novelties, will better repay anticipations than many novelties do.

Great Blue Lobelia
Lobelia syphilitica

The Great Blue Lobelia has perhaps suffered too much by the comparison with its gorgeous sister, the Cardinal flower. The flowers, about an inch long, light blue marked with white, are borne on dense, leafy, wandlike spikes. In the wild they are commonly to be found from July to October, in low, moist soil frequently along the banks of streams. The formation is similar to that of the red Lobelia, but the lobes are much shorter and the stamen tube does not stand out beyond the corolla. The Great Lobelia is a swamp plant and to make a success of it in domestic surroundings you must have a corner that is more or less permanently moist. The plant may be raised from seed started indoors in February, but it is far better if possible to select your own stock in the woods, transferring very early in the spring. There is also a white-flowered variety that grows on dry soils but far more vigorously on wet ones.

Blue Lupine
Lupinus hirsutus

Lupines are especially effective when massed apart in large groups in a setting of rich, dark green foliage. The

Hairy Blue Lupine grows two and three feet high and is
the largest flowered of its kind with purple, rose, and white
blossoms in July and August. The hairy leaves, quite
finger-like in appearance, are compound with seven to nine
leaflets. Lupine seeds may be started outdoors as soon as
the ground is warm. Sow lightly no more than half an
inch deep and allow a space of six inches between plants.
Bloom extends over a period of four weeks, but may be
much prolonged by frequent sowings. Lupines cannot be
successfully transplanted, so their corner or plot must
be selected with care.

Matrimony Vine

Lycium halimifolium

The Matrimony Vine, or Box Thorn, is a shrub with
trailing branches and orange-red, very attractive berries.
The foliage is gray-green and makes a fine contrast amidst
the berries. The flowers are light purple fading to yellow,
appearing solitary or, in clusters, in early summer. The
shrub will frequently grow twelve feet high and is very
effective trained over light support. Arranged on a wire
trellis it may occasionally be seen doing duty as a hedge.
Box Thorns may be grown in any soil that is not too moist;
a sunny situation is desirable, as the plant is much given
to mildew. Shrubs may be started from cuttings or
seeds. The plants throw out suckers rapidly and had best
not be set out too near flower beds. There are two closely
related species. *L. halimifolium* is smaller and less vigorous with grayish green leaves and orange berries; *L.
chinense*, more vigorous, has bright green foliage and large
scarlet berries. The name "Matrimony" is given the vine

because the flowers often grow side by side in the axils of
the leaves.

Osage Orange

Maclura pomifera

Osage Orange is a small, thorny, North American tree
now planted chiefly for ornament but at one period widely
used in the Middle West in the pioneer's task of bringing
the prairies into cultivation. Osage Orange should be
hardy as far north as Massachusetts and if kept continually cut back will make an attractive, dense, defensive,
high hedge. As an ornamental shrub on a lawn the Osage
Orange displays brilliant leathery leaves that turn to a
mass of gold in the autumn, and conspicuous orange-like
fruits. There are also minute blossoms in May and June,
attractive but quite likely to be overlooked at the exuberant height of the vernal season. This native of the
middle Mississippi Valley is by nature of sturdy, vigorous
growth doing well in all sorts of soils. Young shrubs may
be set out in the early spring or seeds may be planted in
spring or autumn. The roots are unusually long and in
transplanting may be chopped back without harm.

Tar Weed

Madia elegans

Tar Weed has a very attractive yellow, daisy-like flower.
The blossoms close in full sunlight so that Tar Weed is
generally chosen for shady places. The plants grow a
foot or two high, of graceful, open habit; the leaves are
linear or lanceolate; the flowers, daisy-like, with three-
lobed yellow ray flowers having a brown spot at the base of

each. If frequent sowings are made, there should be bloom from July to October. Sow outdoors in May, half an inch deep, and space the young plants to stand eight inches apart. Except that the Tar Weed should be planted in shade, there are no special soil requirements. The name comes from the heavily scented foliage.

Musk Mallow
Malva moschata

The old-time favorite Musk Mallow, two feet high, is but little cultivated in domestic gardens nowadays. Perhaps it is most frequently seen outside deserted farm grounds, from which it has escaped and about which it runs wild in riotous fashion. The Mallows are showy and are among the most easily grown of all plants in any soil or situation. All Mallows contain a sticky substance resembling mucilage. The Hollyhock and the Hibiscus as well as the common Mallow or Cheese Flower, which has become a widely scattered weed, are all members of this family. The Musk Mallow grows from one to two feet high with single, well-expanded, rose or white flowers that bloom from July to September. The name "Musk" comes from the faint, musk-like scent of the foliage. Plant outdoors in May and thin to stand twelve inches apart; or more safely for early bloom, sow indoors in February. *M. Alcea* has deep rose flowers in clusters and is lower in stature.

Stock
Matthiola incana

The Stocks are lovely in form and foliage, color and fragrance. The Ten Weeks' Stock is summer blooming;

the autumn Stock comes later. The plant grows quite
straight, about two feet high, and the flowers are in terminal racemes, white, pink, or purple in color, with strong
clove fragrance. There are single and double forms, the
double being particularly desirable. The Stocks like sun
and have no objection to water. They are generally
ordered by color in many varieties and seeds should be
started indoors very early. The plants will flower in
autumn and, carefully removed indoors, will also send
forth blossoms a large part of the winter. The older name
of the Stock was the Gilliflower—a name, however, shared
with the Carnation and Wallflower, as well. In England
to-day the Wallflowers in spring and the Stocks in summer
and autumn represent in somewhat improved and advanced forms the Gilliflowers of the Elizabethan period.

Bayberry

Myrica Gale, M. carolinensis

Bayberry, or Wax Myrtle, has as its autumn attraction
bluish white, wax-coated, and quite aromatic berries
prized for winter indoor decoration and much sought for
by the birds. The shrub grows compactly four to eight
feet high with dark green foliage that shows up the berries
to full advantage. The Bayberry is just the shrub for
semi-wild effects and will cover dry, exposed slopes where
grass can with difficulty get a foothold. Bayberry may
be found growing wild the entire length of the Atlantic
Coast, in the Far South often forming a tree thirty feet
high. No soil is too poor, apparently, but of course better
rounded more luxuriant specimens will be found in richer
soils. Seed may be planted in the spring in drills, or

suckers may be removed from the base of old plants of *M.
Gale.*

Zanzibar Blue Water Lily

Nymphaea zanzibariensis

The royal blue Zanzibar Water Lily is on all counts the
best of the large family of Water Lilies, adapting itself
readily to varied sorts of conditions, even producing its
large, sky-blue flowers in small pots indoors.   The superb
starlike, solitary flower, ten inches or more in diameter, is
carried about a foot above the water. This is a day-
blooming Lily lasting four or five days and remaining open
from eleven in the morning to perhaps five in the afternoon.
The underside of the leaf is colored similarly to the flowers.
The type flower is sky-blue and there is a rose-pink variety
equally attractive. Tropical Water Lilies require rich,
deep soil and are commonly planted in tubs or boxes.
They must be moved into warm quarters during the cold
months.

Sour Wood Tree

Oxydendrum arboreum

Sour Wood or Sorrel Tree, with terminal clusters of white
flowers in June and highly colored foliage in autumn, is an
attractive addition to a home garden all the year round.
The Sorrel Tree is slow-growing and quite variable as to
size; in cultivation small, slender-stemmed, dainty, the
tree is known to reach a height of sixty feet along the slopes
of the Big Smoky Mountains in Tennessee. The young
wood has crimson bark and the conspicuous seed pods
that follow the flowers remain white a long time. The
Sorrel Tree will grow in shade and does well in any moder-

ately good garden soil. The leaves have a sour taste somewhat like that of the herbaceous Sorrel.

Boston or Japanese Ivy

Parthenocissus tricuspidata

Boston or Japanese Ivy differs from its chief rival, the Virginia Creeper, in its leaf and in its method of climbing; clinging closely to its support by suckers, and forms a solid, compact tapestry of green. This vine is rampant, pervasive—too much so for many situations. "A single plant has covered a stone retaining wall over one hundred and fifty feet long and twenty feet high in twelve years." (*Blanchan.*) Unpainted and rough surfaces suit it best. The Boston Ivy clings by little adhesive disks at the tips of its pink fingers and in time the large, overlapping leaves of older growths conceal any surface, rough or smooth, they may grow against. When the fall frosts turn the leaves to as brilliant a crimson as any Maple, even the most careless of passers-by will stop and survey this Ivy with interest. With all its faults the Boston Ivy is the best all-round "Ivy" yet developed for this country; it is perhaps better known under its older name of *Ampelopsis Veitchi.*

Winter Cherry

Physalis Alkekengi

The older Winter Cherry, or Strawberry Tomato, with red or yellow fruits, used formerly to be planted for its cherry-like, edible fruit which was much relished in preserves. Nowadays the bright, decorative red husk of the other species is the attraction, the practical use of the fruit having gone out of fashion. The plant is a perennial, commonly treated as an annual. Winter Cherry grows twelve to eighteen inches high with whitish flowers, not at all showy. A bladdery dry inflated calyx an inch or more across encloses the round fruit which grows a brighter red as it matures. Many birds for whom the Winter Cherry is a superlative attraction help disperse the numerous kidney-shaped seeds. The Winter Cherry likes the sun. Sow indoors in light fine soil and transplant as soon as the condition of the ground warrants in May. The plant creeps under ground and in rich soil is likely to become troublesome. Newer species, *P. Franchetti*, is twice as big and even brighter than the older one, and the cut stalks furnish a charming red for Christmas decorations.

Ninebark

Physocarpus opulifolius

Eight and ten feet high grows the Ninebark, and its greenish white flowers are followed by bright red fruit; very showy and effective in the late summer and early autumn. With its spreading arching branches and its good garden habit, this is one of the prettiest of native hardy shrubs. The leaves are three-lobed and the whitish clusters of bloom remind one a little of Spiraea, and it was formerly classed under that name. Ninebark goes well massed with other shrubbery, but is perhaps more frequently seen by itself as a specimen shrub on lawns. All the usual methods of propagation are available, and good growth is assured on practically all garden soils. There is a dwarf variety (*nana*) which should be planted in front of

INDIAN AZALEA
(Azalea indica)

FANCY-LEAVED CALADIUM
(Caladium bicolor)

COMMON CAMELLIA
(Camellia japonica)

FLORISTS' CINERARIA
(Cineraria hybrida)

GENISTA
(Cytisus canariensis)

GREENHOUSE CARNATION
(Dianthus Caryophyllus)

THREE-FORKED
CLERODENDRON
(Clerodendron trichotomum)

CROWN OF THORNS
(Euphorbia splendens)

tall shrubs; *lutea* has bright yellow leaves that change to golden bronze, and so offers a variation of color.

Mountain Fleece

Polygonum amplexicaule

Mountain Fleece with feathery, white, fragrant plumes in September and October, is a splendid perennial for late borders. The plant grows two to three feet high with glossy leaves and flowers in great rose-red or white masses. The Mountain Fleece may be easily started from seed planted indoors in February and transplanted outdoors in May to stand fifteen inches apart. The var. *speciosum* has flowers of deeper red, almost purplish. There are other species grown, including Sacaline (*P. sachalinense*), a Japanese plant, growing very rapidly to a height of from eight to ten feet. The soft, dull green leaves are unusually large, sometimes eighteen inches long and half as broad; the small greenish flowers are borne in axillary clusters late in August and September. This Polygonum grows so rapidly and spreads with such vigor as sometimes to become a pest. A vine, *P. Auberti*, is white-flowered and is sometimes seen clambering over the trellis.

Kudzu Vine

Pueraria hirsuta or *Thunbergiana*

If you do not believe it possible for a vine to grow fifty feet in a season, try the Kudzu in a sunny soil with plenty of water. It will make a dense screen and where speed of growth is a main consideration this Japanese importation should certainly be selected and it gets along well after once being established. The foliage is a good green, but succumbs to the first touch of frost, and there are no autumn colorings. The flowers are pea-shaped, in color dull purple, appearing in August and September. The fruit is a pod. In the North the Kudzu dies to the ground in the autumn and should be taken up, or be very heavily mulched over winter except on dry soils. Old plants are difficult to remove, as their thong-like roots penetrate deeply into the earth, this helps the vine to get additional moisture of which, indeed, it hardly ever gets too much. Plants may be started from the tuberous roots. Either plant indoors in pots (the better way) or else outdoors in the spot where the vine is to remain permanently. Kudzu will grow in any likely soil, but best growth will only be obtained in full sunlight with plenty of moisture added.

Buckthorn

Rhamnus cathartica

The Buckthorn, a clean-leaved, handsome, thorny shrub, makes the best strong hedge, as dense and tight as Honey Locust but not so high. The flowers are greenish, four-petalled, rather inconspicuous. The glory of the shrub is the display of attractive black autumn berries clustering close to the twigs. These berries yield a valuable medicinal principle oftenest sold in the form of a syrup and the bark furnishes a yellow dye. The leaves are opposite, a shiny pretty green. This prefers a dryish soil and is to be propagated from seed sown in the autumn or from layers. Old hedges that get out of condition are easily recovered by cutting back. Waythorn, Harts'thorn and Rhineberry are popular names for this English shrub.

Jet Bead

Rhodotypos kerrioides

The Japanese White Kerria or Jet Bead growing with us generally no more than six feet high is often planted for autumn and winter effects. The white May blossoms are very fine too; but in May the entire garden is alive with competitive color, whereas the black, shiny, berry-like fruits have few competitors in the late autumn and early winter. The White Kerria grows in the country of its origin to a height of fifteen feet with slender pendulous branches and profuse flowers and fruits; in this country the shrub appears more dwarf, but very ornamental and successful in most sorts of soils. The White Kerria is hardy as far north as Massachusetts.

Staghorn Sumach

Rhus typhina

No tree carries its autumn foliage longer or blazes with greater splendor in the softened light of October than the Sumach. After the leaves have fallen the full red, fuzzy fruit persists, slowly fading to brown as winter advances. Staghorn Sumach reaches to a height normally of ten to twelve feet, but sometimes as high as thirty, with velvety, hairy foliage and, in July and August, flowers in dense panicles. The Sumach is particularly successful in dry soil in wild or semi-wild situations. The var. *laciniata* has deeply cut foliage.

The Poison Sumach (*R. vernix*) is unfortunately the prettiest of the species, with shiny leaves and clear white berries in drooping clusters.   Poison Ivy, the familiar bugbear of children, is a member of the Rhus family (*R. toxicodendron*).

The Smoke Bush, or Venice Sumach, an old favorite not so frequently seen nowadays, and very effective in autumn and early winter, is a close relative.

Japanese Currant

Ribes japonicum

The Japan Currant, after the custom of its country, produces its bright scarlet berries in September and October rather than in May and June, and holds its foliage quite late.   The shrub grows about four feet high, and the berries are valuable only for color and ornament, being quite insipid as to taste.   The flowers in May and June are small, inconspicuous, generally unnoticed in the height of the floral season.   The Japan Currant would hardly be planted were it not that the autumn season is so little overcrowded.   The shrub does well singly or with contrasting shrubs in groups.   Too much shade is not desirable and this member of the Ribes family will do well in practically all soils where it is likely to be planted.   Propagation is easily arranged through the side shoots; cut off shoots about six inches long, insert two thirds their length in sandy soil outdoors in a shady position.

Castor Oil Bean

Ricinus communis

The Castor Oil Bean has large palmate leaves that produce a remarkable subtropical effect along the back of a border.   Rising three to eight feet high according to the

CONE FLOWER
(Rudbeckia speciosa)

SALVIA
(Salvia azurea)

variety planted and the richness of the soil, the Castor Oil
Bean is the boldest of annuals and very satisfactory as a
screen for unsightly spots. The leaves are large, with
seven or more lobes, the flowers small and borne in racemes.
Plant the seeds two in a hill no more than two inches deep
and allow the same distance between hills. The plant is
one of those that will put forth extraordinary efforts in
rich heavy soils; is of easy culture, requiring practically no
attention after planting, and will continue looking well till
nipped by heavy frosts.

Golden Glow

Rudbeckia laciniata (*.flore-pleno.*)

Golden Glow, a double form of the wild Rudbeckia or
Corneflower, has both good and bad points. The blossoms
are pretty and excellent for cutting; but the plant itself
is quite long-legged and gawky, spreading rapidly without
encouragement and frequently quite swallowing up its
next-door neighbors. This Rudbeckia grows six or eight
feet high with masses of aster-like, bright yellow, double
flowers. If cut back after flowering, there is quite likely
to be a second crop of blossoms. Golden Glow is most
frequently planted in straight rows at the back of flower
borders or else massed against walls that it is desired to
hide. The plants increase with great rapidity and may be
said never to die out. Roots may be divided at any time
and, as may be easily surmised, the plant is adaptable to all
common soils. To kill the red plant lice with which
Golden Glow is commonly troubled in midsummer, any
common soap may be dissolved in water and sprayed over
the insects.

Cone Flower

Rudbeckia subtomentosa, R. speciosa

There are other Rudbeckias besides the best known Golden Glow that will well reward planting. Black-eyed Susan, the yellow or Ox-eye Daisy, or the Niggerhead (*R. hirta*), has lively familiar orange and black heads that are found glowing in dry, open, sunny fields from Canada to Florida, Colorado, and Texas. *R. subtomentosa* is a long and vigorous bloomer, a native perennial to be found on the prairies from Illinois to Texas. The leaves are thick, the flowers in excellent heads with yellow rays. *R. speciosa* grows about two feet tall and bears throughout the summer and autumn large Daisy-like flowers with a dark center cone. This is very successful massed in borders and for naturalizing in dry places. Also a favorite for cutting. *R. triloba* is a Western biennial having medium-sized flowers gracefully borne on stiff black stalks.

Salvia

Salvia azurea, S. splendens

The Scarlet Sage (*S. splendens*) is probably the most popular of red-flowered plants rivalled only by the Canna as a display plant for suburban lawns. It is a tender perennial, more commonly planted as a half-hardy annual. The plants grow about three feet tall and the flowers appear as long tubular-shaped spikes, the entire plant glowing like a flame during July and August. Seeds had best be started indoors in February for May transplanting. Any soil will do and plenty of sun is essential.

The tall, hardy Blue Salvia (*S. azurea*) is planted far less frequently than its more showy sister. The flowers are small, tubular, sky-blue varying to white, on long terminal spikes borne on erect leafy stems two to five feet high. The lower leaves are oval and toothed along the margin; the upper narrower with smooth edges. This hardy Salvia requires a sunny situation and in a cold climate should be given a light covering of leaves over winter. Wet seasons and soils play havoc with the growth and bloom of Salvias sometimes giving them a reputation for capriciousness which they hardly deserve.

S. patens, not often seen, has quite large deep blue flowers.

Sage
Salvia officinalis

The Sage of stews and stuffings is the one herb sure to be found in every kitchen garden. *S. officinalis* is a fine spreading bush with beautiful velvet gray-green leaves and spikes of blue-purple flowers much frequented by bees. The sub-shrub is perennial, a native of southern Europe, but will become acclimatized without difficulty in this country. The leaves are grayish green, thick, oblong, the flowers two-lipped, in terminal spikes, blue, white or purple. The seeds germinate but slowly and had best be started indoors in early spring. The leaves should be cut before the flower stems develop and carefully dried indoors. Sage is used chiefly to flavor sausages and cheeses and for meat stuffings.

Red-Berried Elder
Sambucus pubens

The Elders are quick growing, stout-branched trees and shrubs with pithy branchlets and ill-smelling sap. Many

of the family are of fine appearance in the late months of
the year, turning a soft yellow and bearing rich ornamental
fruits. These berries begin to ripen as early as June in
large clusters, a bright attractive red. The leaves are
compound, made up from five to seven leaflets. The
bark is warty and if a small twig be cut, the pith in the
center will be found to be brown. Seeds dropped on the
ground will spring up of themselves and the Elders will
grow in any soil no matter how thin. If there is a poor
strip of land to be hidden, plant the red-berried and the
common black-berried Elders together.

Bouncing Bet

Saponaria officinalis

Those who like to speculate on the origin of flower
names may perhaps discover the reason why this naturalized European adventurer, long ago escaped from colonial
gardens, should be called Bouncing Bet. The beautiful,
clustered, pale pink flowers of this wandering Soapwort
are to be found from July to September along dusty roadsides and railroad banks. Wherever it grows, it grows
luxuriantly in great patches constantly increased by under-
ground runners or stolens. The root when agitated in
water forms a soap-like lather that has given the plants
the common names of Soaproot and Latherwort. Bouncing Bet grows two feet or more in height with blossoming
time in July and August. Double flowers are not uncommon and are even more attractive than the singles.
The calyx often splits apart after maturity, causing the
faded petals to present a dilapidated appearance in strange
contrast to that of their days of mid-summer glory.

Bouncing Bet may be most quickly procured by dividing old plants in the early spring; or seed may be planted indoors in March.

Scabiosa

Scabiosa atropurpurea

The garden flower known as Scabiosa, Mourning Bride, Pincushion, or Blue Bonnet, is like a large double Daisy with dark blue, rose, or white flowers from July to October. Scabiosas are fine for cutting, having excellent stems and lasting well in water. The leaves are small, narrow, and divided, grayish green and insignificant. The hardy Scabiosas are not so well known or as much raised as the annual varieties. They are, however, of easy culture in any good garden soil, needing only to be protected with a cover of leaves over winter.

S. atropurpurea, Sweet Scabious, much used as an annual, grows three to ten feet high with flower heads on long stalks. The outer row of the florets is much larger than the inner; the styles are club-shape and protrude on the inner flowers so that they give the impression of pins on a pincushion. The seeds need only to be sown outdoors in May and the young plants thinned to stand six inches apart. Sweet Scabious grows in all sorts of soils and is avid of sunlight. *S. caucasica*, white or lavender, is a perennial.

Autumn Squill

Scilla autumnalis

None of the autumn-blooming bulbs ever seem as satisfactory as those of the spring, nor are there as many of them. The Autumn Squill, or Starry Hyacinth, usually but not invariably, sends up its flowering stems before the leaves appear. The blossoms that last from July well into September are in racemes, hyacinth-like. The leaves which are never numerous, die down in the spring and come up in the autumn again after the blossom stems appear. Any well-drained garden soil will do and the bulbs should be planted in good season, three inches deep and three inches apart. Every three or four years Autumn Squills should be gone over with care and the poorest discarded.

Showy Sedum

Sedum spectabile

Showy Sedum is a sturdy plant with small flowers in broad heads borne on stout, erect, leafy stems one to two feet high. The leaves are wavy in form, opposite or in threes, smooth, grayish, evergreen. The colours are rose-pink, varying to purplish and whitish, and the time of bloom from mid-August well into October. This Sedum is a favorite for the fronts of borders, for rock gardens and for massing in barren spots. Showy Sedum grows on all garden soils in full sunlight and is propagated quickly by offsets or more slowly through seeds. Many other Sedums are in gardens.

S. maximum is bushy, the largest and stoutest of the Family. The leaves are opposite, fleshy, purplish in color; the salmon-colored flowers are in clusters; the flowering season runs from August into late autumn. Live-forever (*Sedum Telephium*), a well-named flower, flourishes in all sorts of thin soils, in sunshine and in shadow; it will not live up to its name in wet lands or spots where water will stand and settle about the roots. Live-forever is not abundant in bloom or conspicuous in height, but will be found useful in odd corners and spots where few other plants will do more than wither and die.

Mountain Ash

Sorbus americana

There are about thirty species of Sorbus widely distributed over the Northern hemisphere and chiefly inhabitants of mountain slopes. In the wooded uplands of New England and lower Canada, along the borders of swamps, or climbing the rocky bluffs, the frail scarlet-berried Mountain Ash leaps up in the crisp autumn air like a yellow flame. Dainty and slim on its red stem, there is no handsomer leaf at any season. On a lawn a Mountain Ash is a very neat and decorative addition the year round.

The American Mountain Ash or Dogberry is in general appearance shrubby, attaining an extreme height of around thirty feet. There are clusters of greenish white flowers in large corymbs in May and June, and early in the autumn come the red fruits. The tree or shrub will grow vigorously even in sandy or rocky soils. The Dwarf Mountain Ash (*S. spuria*) grows about fifteen feet high with branches slender and often drooping. Hybrids of various sorts, many very interesting, have been grouped under the name *S. spuria*. They mostly bloom in May and June and have berries dark purple or black, according to parentage.

Stokes' Aster

Stokesia cyanea

Stokes' Aster, or the Cornflower Aster, with large Thistle-like flowers blue or purplish blue, will furnish brilliance to dwindling summer color from August till well into October. The flowers, sometimes three to four inches across, resemble a China Aster and are borne on erect, leafy stems one to two feet high. The leaves are long and narrow, rather inconspicuous. The flowers are in heads; the darker tubular flowers in the center, the marginal flowers composed of short-tubed corollas. Though found in wet ground in the wild, this Aster in cultivation decidedly prefers well-drained sandy soils and full sunlight. Stokesia is perfectly hardy in the South and with light winter protection may be successfully grown as far North as New England. Stokes' Aster is mostly used in borders but is occasionally seen quite effectively massed in beds. Allow usually twelve inches between plants. Procure young stock if possible, as growth from seed is very slow.

Snowberry

Symphoricarpos racemosus

The Snowberry, or Waxberry, an old-time favorite, not as much planted as formerly, still peeps through many tumbledown fences on the outskirts of New England villages. Snowberry grows about five feet high sometimes, with tiny pink flowers which are quickly followed by large, gleaming, white berries. These berries remain till well into winter, and their weight is sufficient to make the branches bend quite noticeably. Tucked in with Dogwood and other shrubs, the attractive white of the berries shows up splendidly. Snowberry nowadays is chiefly massed in front of shrubbery borders or used as a cover plant for banks and bare slopes. This charming shrub

SCABIOSA
(Scabiosa caucasica)

SHOWY SEDUM
(Sedum spectabile)

seems to thrive almost equally well in all common garden soils. They sucker freely, making propagation a quite simple matter.

The Coral Berry (*S. vulgaris*), another member of this family, is planted for its dark-red berries considerably smaller than those of the Snowberry which form in July and remain on the branches all the autumn and winter. The shrub grows five feet, sometimes ten under favorable circumstances but usually only three feet, and the foliage also turns reddish in autumn, making an attractive combination with the berries. Coral Berry is a native of the Middle States.

Tamarisk

Tamarix gallica

Tamarisk is considered the best hardy shrub for feathery effect in windswept places. The general impression is of a big, feathery plume borne on drooping, red-barked branches. The leaves are small and scale-like; the flowers pinkish or white, almost three inches long. The range of growth is from twelve to fifteen feet and the shrub is particularly to be recommended for alkaline and salty soils. The Tamarisk may be cut back severely with good results. Flowers are commonly produced on the old wood but in one species *T. narbonnensis*, on the new. *T. gallica* blooms in May; *T. chinensis* and *T. hispida* in September. The last with carmine flowers and foliage rather more bluish than green, is particularly to be recommended as an autumn shrub. Young plants should be procured from nurserymen if possible, as growth from seeds and cuttings will be found generally too tedious for amateurs.

Japanese Toad Lily

Tricyrtis hirta

The Japanese autumn-blooming Lily known as the Toad Lily will be a novelty for most gardens. The plants grow one to three feet high and the flowers are Lily-like, many on a stalk, cream-white with purple-black spots. The var. *nigra* earliest to bloom, has black instead of purplish spots and is generally considered the most satisfactory for domestic gardens. The other Toad Lilies are so late blooming that they hardly reach maturity before they are nipped by frosts. Toad Lilies have a short rootstalk and are not bulbous. The plants flourish best in light, well-drained, sandy loam. Set the roots out in spring, covering very lightly with moist rich earth. A mulch of old manure spread an inch or so thick will keep the foliage in fine shape during summer. Roots divide easily and beds may be left as they are for years without deterioration.

High Bush Blueberry

Vaccinium corymbosum

Few country people perhaps would think of transplanting the High Bush Blueberry to garden surroundings, yet the foliage in the autumn is as fine and brilliant as the much prized Sumach. This familiar denizen of swamps and moist woodland will well repay the labor of transplanting provided you can offer a moist corner. The shrub grows from six to fifteen feet high, and the fine, large, juicy berries are the late Blueberry of commerce. It is best to select your own bush in the autumn and transplant then and there. Select a young shrub, of course; moist land is essential; it is only the little Low Bush Blueberry that flourishes on dry soil. If there are no High Bush Blueberries in your vicinity, you may possibly get a small shrub from a nurseryman.

Great Virginia Speedwell

Veronica virginica

The Great Virginia Speedwell, sometimes called Culver's Root, growing five and six feet high with August and September bloom, is the best tall blue flower of late summer. The leaves are in whorls of from four to six, finely toothed, lance-shaped, the flowers are on rather stiff-looking spikes, white or pale blue. Plant this tallest of the Veronicas in rich soil in full exposure to the sun. Set out young plants about four feet tall in the early spring. Veronicas present no garden problems and you should have fine September bloom.

Another Veronica (*V. longifolia subsessilis*) has a much prolonged flowering season. The purple spikes are nearly a foot long, the longest spikes of any autumn flower. This late Veronica responds luxuriantly to the influences of deep, rich soil and sunny position and will be found very successful for distant mass effects.

Viburnums

Viburnum dentatum, etc.

Handsome foliage, showy flowers, and attractive fruits justify the great popularity of the Viburnums in gardens and parks. There are about one hundred species, and many offer charming autumn leaf and fruit effects.

Arrow-wood (*V. dentatum*) is a fairly common native shrub, an upright bush frequently fifteen feet high. Its special attractions are its creamy white June flowers and striking blue-black fruits that appear in September. If not crowded by other shrubs, Arrow-wood will keep its symmetrical appearance year after year with practically no pruning. This Viburnum will grow in all sorts of soils and is often used as a screen for boundary planting.

The Japanese Bush Cranberry (*V. dilatatum*) with large, abundant, bright scarlet autumn berries, is an importation that will certainly obtain a permanent position in our domestic garden scheme. This Bush Cranberry grows ten feet high with bright green, rounded leaves that make excellent foils for both flowers and fruits. The shrub seems to develop best in deep loamy soil, but fair results are obtainable under more difficult conditions. *V. dilatatum* is usually propagated by layering; that is, lower branches are bent down and partially buried, allowing the tips only to protrude; if this is done in spring the layers will be rooted by autumn and may be dug up and planted separately.

The American Wayfaring Tree (*V. lantanoides*) is especially to be recommended for large handsome foliage, broadly ovate, turning in early autumn to a deep rich claret color. The flowers are white in cymes and the berries bright red changing to black. This Viburnum is preferred for limestone soils and dry situations, sometimes becoming tree-like in height and in extent of spreading branches. All in all, the Viburnums offer excellent variety of choice for autumn effects.

White Watsonia
Watsonia Ardneri

The Watsonias, charming plants somewhat on the order of the Gladiolus, are newcomers from South Africa, the culture of which is not as widespread as it ought to be. Watsonias are "bulbous" plants growing three or four feet tall, with September bloom. *W. Ardneri* white, and *W. iridifolia* pinkish, are the species commonly planted either singly or together. The bulbs require a somewhat sheltered position and soil that is light and sandy. Plant in May and June six inches apart, covering with about four inches of soil. When the foliage dies down after the blooming season, dig up and store in dry sand in a cool cellar. The Watsonias lend themselves very successfully to indoor forcing.

Zinnia

Zinnia elegans

Zinnia with red, scarlet, yellow, magenta, and intermediate tints, is considered the best showy annual for very late bloom. This is a native of Mexico and blooms lavishly in all sorts of garden soils from July till nipped by heavy frosts. Individual flowers are often two to three inches across, but flowers of this size will hardly be produced except in deep rich soil. In making selections avoid the magenta and greenish tinges. The plants may be used in borders or massed in beds. Wherever the effect of distant masses is desired Zinnia may happily be called into use. This native of Mexico transplants easily and plants need stand no more than six inches apart. The primitive Zinnia had both ray and tubular flowers, but in process of time the tubular flowers have been slowly eliminated, producing larger, more intense, and generally more satisfactory bloom.

WINTER

WINTER

White Fir

Abies concolor

The garden picture includes both the background and the frame. To give diversity of outline and color, to form windbreaks and boundary belts, to afford shelter and shade to emphasize and to slur over, we must have trees. In gardens of Europe and in our Eastern states, the Silver or Blue Fir is probably the most frequently planted of the highly ornamental family of Firs. All Firs are tall, pyramidal trees with widespreading horizontal limbs and branches that grow in whorls and spread like Fern fronds.

The White Fir (*A. concolor*) is a rapid grower and withstands successfully the extremes of heat and drought. The Colorado form is usually grown by nurserymen and is considered superior both in beauty and in hardiness to more Western forms. The foliage is dense, the leaves large and broad, blue-green above and silvery beneath. The height is rather variable, depending on the nature of the soil where planted. The Fir should have plenty of room to develop, and in well-drained, rich soils may grow to a height of two hundred and fifty feet.

Nordmann's Fir (*A. Nordmanniana*), a native of the Caucasian region, is one of the stateliest of the species with broadly conical outline and glossy dark foliage. This Fir grows thicker and wider than most Conifers and is un-

231

injured by salt spray.   Nordmann's is also a rapid grower and should attain a height of from one hundred to one hundred and fifty feet.   The common method of propagation of most cone-bearing trees is to sow the seeds, as soon as they are ripe, in a bed of sandy soil in the shade.

Maidenhair Fern

Adiantum cuneatum

The Maidenhair Fern, so called from the delicacy of its stalks, may be easily grown in conservatories, but not with any great success in the hot, dry atmosphere of the average dwelling house.   The delicate tracery of the graceful branching fronds makes the Maidenhair perhaps the best known of Ferns and the Fern par excellence for cutting and for decorative purposes generally.   Maidenhair will be best grown in six-inch pots using as soil equal parts of sandy loam, peat, and leaf mold.   When the plants get to be too large divide into parts and repot.   *A. Farleyense*, the culture of which is similar to that of *A. cuneatum*, produces enormous fronds with large pinnæ of a delicate rose color later turning to light green.   The temperature where this Fern—certainly among the most marvelous of Nature's creations— grows must never fall below sixty degrees.

Century Plant

Agave americana

The so-called Century Plant is very useful to the amateur.   Of good symmetrical habit, and with a predilection for dry atmospheric conditions, the plant is attractive for winter indoor growing and in summer for porch decoration.

A large plant will have forty or fifty fleshy leaves, each about three or four feet long and three to four inches across, which gradually taper to a point that is tipped with a very sharp spine. The edges also have a few sharp spines. The leaves are light glaucous green in the type; some of the varieties have a broad or narrow yellowish stripe running through the center, while in others the leaves are edged with yellow. The Century Plant will grow in any sort of soil, but the soil must be well drained. The plant seldom blooms in cultivation but under most favorable conditions has been known to flower in twenty years. The flowers are borne in clusters at the top of a tall, stout stem and have a weird candelabrum-like sort of effect. Should you have a Century Plant flower do not be alarmed that the plant dies as soon as the seeds mature. Perpetuation is commonly accomplished by means of the numerous suckers which are to be found about the base of the old plant.

Allamanda

Allamanda Hendersoni

There are several Allamandas natives of tropical South America, often grown in greenhouses for their large, yellow, sweet-scented blossoms which are produced almost continuously. *A. Hendersoni* is of vigorous nature and should be given plenty of room to spread. This plant may be successfully trained over pillars, rafters, and conservatory walls. *A. Williamsii* is more frequently grown as a pot plant. The potting soil should consist of two thirds loam and one third well-rotted manure. In a greenhouse where a temperature of from fifty-five to sixty degrees is maintained either of these species should be very successful.

During their period of rapid growth Allamandas must be watered copiously.

Coppery Alocasia

Alocasia cuprea

Alocasias are foliage plants, as are Caladiums. The leaves are of great variety, some of almost metallic appearance, others bright green or variegated with white. These leaves are heart-shaped and sometimes on well-grown specimens as much as eighteen inches in length. The plants grow to perfection in humid greenhouses in which the temperature does not fall below sixty-five degrees. If cultivated as a house plant, Alocasia will need copious supplies of water. Alocasias may be treated as Caladiums, allowing them to lie dormant for six months and then forcing them forward, or they may be treated as all-the-year-round plants. Another desirable kind is *A. macrorhiza variegata.*

Lily-of-the-Palace

Amaryllis aulica

No window garden would be complete without some bulbous plants like Amaryllis or the Calla. There are some sixty or seventy species of Amaryllis or Hippeastrum, which is the more approved name, many of great beauty and quite able to withstand the special disadvantages of indoor culture. The Lily-of-the-Palace is a late winter bloomer with enormous flowers which are red in color with a green base to the petals. The flowers are produced before the leaves and until the latter appear water must be given sparingly. The large bulbs should be potted in early

winter in soil composed of two parts loam, one part decayed manure, and one part sand. The bulbs should succeed in the temperature of an ordinary living room. As
soon as the flower bud is seen emerging from the bulb, put
the plant in a window where it may obtain plenty of sunlight.

Variegated Pineapple

Ananas sativus variegatus

Variegated Pineapple has leathery leaves of hard smooth
texture with fine color—striped green and pale yellow with
a suggestion of red along the margin—and on both counts
is well adapted for house decoration. This plant is a variety of the Pineapple of commerce and in habit of growth
somewhat resembles a Screw Pine. Variegated Pineapple
grows most luxuriantly in a humid greenhouse with a
minimum temperature of sixty-five degrees; but in default
of these ideal conditions the plant will thrive in fair shape
in a dry atmosphere and much lower temperature. Preferred soil should consist of two parts fibrous loam, two
parts fibrous peat, and one part sand. Keep always well
watered. Propagation is by suckers or, if the plants fruit,
the leafy part at the top may be treated in the same way.

Lily-of-the-Valley Tree

Andromeda floribunda

The Lily-of-the-Valley Tree forms a neat bush usually a
foot or two high but occasionally seen much taller. In
late autumn the blossom buds appear. These buds remain on the plants all winter, not opening up till early
spring. The flowers are produced on upright stalks, but

the individual flowers are drooping. Seeds should be sown in a cool greenhouse as soon as they are ripe. The plant may be propagated by layers and cuttings. The various species of Andromeda are closely related to the familiar Stagger Bush and also to Leucothoë.

Japanese Andromeda (*A. japonica* often listed as *Pieris japonica*) has the fine combination of dark green foliage and drooping white flowers that open in early March. This Andromeda has masses of fibrous roots which may be dug up and potted in the autumn. In the cool greenhouse its charming blossoms will be certainly appreciated. Soil should be light, containing humus and free from lime.

Anemone

Anemone coronaria, A. blanda

The Poppy-flowered Anemone (*A. coronaria*) or the blue Winter Windflower (*A. blanda*) may be grown in the window of a cool room, and these charming, delicate harbingers of spring will be a constant joy. The Poppy-flowered Anemone has a pretty, finely divided leaf and a flower often two and a half inches across, red, white, or blue in color. The Winter Windflower has deeply cut leaves and sky-blue flowers superficially like those of a Marguerite; there are also charming color variations ranging from pure white to dark blue. For house use tubers should be potted in September, placing ten or a dozen in an eight-inch pan. Plunge in ashes outdoors till December, when they may be brought indoors for forcing. If more people knew how easily these little bulbs are to be grown, we should have far more colorful January and February window boxes.

Flamingo Flower

Anthurium Andreanum

The Flamingo Flower with scarlet, waxy blossoms and white, tail-like appendage, is one flower to which the sometimes abused epithet of "striking" may well be applied. The blossoms have good staying quality, often lasting eight or ten weeks, and the foliage, too, is attractive. Flamingo Flower in full bloom will never fail to excite comment. Plants are propagated from seeds sown in fine peaty soil and kept in a temperature of seventy-five degrees. Young plants should be potted in fibrous peat and sphagnum moss with a few lumps of charcoal. The plants, of course, are at their best in the even temperature of warm greenhouses but, unless they experience too violent changes of heat and cold, should do well as house plants. There are also several varieties grown especially for foliage.

Norfolk Island Pine

Araucaria excelsa

The branches of the Norfolk Island Pine are produced in regular tiers of diminishing size as the top of the plant is approached, and are studded with tiny, well-proportioned, bright green leaves giving altogether an attractiveness that easily explains the popularity of this evergreen for house culture. Select a well-lighted cool room and success should be sure. Soil should consist of one part leaf mold and two parts loam. The plant is usually grown from seeds, as those made from cuttings from the side shoots do not produce shapely plants. Cut off the terminal shoot of an old plant and a new growth of young shoots should appear just below the cut. These are to be snipped off and inserted in sandy soil, covered with a bell glass and placed in shade in a cool house. There is also a variety, *glauca*, with silvery leaves, and another variety, *robusta compacta*, stronger and more compact of growth.

Ardisia

Ardisia crenulata

Ardisia with bright red berries and shining green foliage in successive tiers is much seen in florists' windows round Christmas time and at first glance reminds one of Holly. Ardisia is usually grown as a small tree, the crown of leaves occupying the upper part with leaves and berries projecting on long stalks below. Growth of young plants from seed is not difficult, but rather inclined to be exasperatingly slow. Seeds sown in March or April will bloom the following spring and the desired berries should appear the next winter. Cuttings taken from vigorous plants in June and inserted in sand in a warm greenhouse should produce much quicker results. The plants lose beauty as they get older, so they are seldom more than three years of age. The best temperature is one ranging round sixty degrees. Unfortunately, the plants are subject to attack by scale insects which must be met promptly by a careful bath in lukewarm soapy water.

Asparagus Fern

Asparagus plumosus

The light green, feathery sprays are like fairy lace and, when cut, the Asparagus Fern holds both color and freshness for a remarkably long time. For pot plants the dwarf forms, *nanus* and *compactus*, should be selected. Rich soil, loam two parts and decayed manure two parts, is essential; when new growths get to be a foot or so in length the ends may be pinched out to keep the plant shapely. For indoor vines use the more vigorously growing type and prepare support along which to twine as for Smilax. Your Asparagus Fern, if you have good luck with it, should make a very attractive table decoration.

Smilax

Asparagus medeoloides

The florists' greenhouse "Smilax," with its light green, heart-shaped leaves, an almost indispensable decorative accompaniment of formal social occasions, is not a Smilax at all, but a twining species of Asparagus; it is also one of the best vines for the amateur's window garden, particularly as it will grow in a shaded corner where other plants often make but little progress. Seeds are started in January or February. When the young plants are a few inches high, transplant singly to two-inch pots and later to three-inch pots. For a window garden a long narrow box capable of holding a half-dozen plants is more satisfactory than pots. The soil should be fibrous loam to which may be added half-rotted cow manure and sand, one part each to three parts of loam. Strings on which the Smilax is to climb should be provided as soon as the seedlings are arranged in their permanent position. New sowings of seed should be made each year rather than to attempt to hold the plants over. The night temperature ought not to fall below fifty degrees.

Aspidistra

Aspidistra lurida

Aspidistra, with broad green or variegated leaves springing from a creeping rootstock is an interesting foliage
plant for indoor growing. Even the most careless and
forgetful of indoor gardeners will have success with this
sturdy plant, which however, will not stand frost.
Aspidistra seems not to mind dust and dry air, or spas-
modic watering or insufficient light. Aspidistra never
gets very tall, but it broadens out luxuriantly on rich soil
and plenty of moisture. The plant has no ascending stem,
the leaves coming directly from the rootstock or rhizome.
These leaves are from fifteen inches to two feet long, green
or variegated with white stripes; but the white stripes are
almost lost if the plant makes rapid growth, and on no
two leaves of the plant are they alike.

Indian Azalea

Azalea indica

The Indian Azalea, long considered the best Easter-
flowering plant for indoor growing, has white to deep red
flowers, either single or double, and small, shiny dark
green leaves. Azaleas are showy little shrubs of bushy
habit, easily grown and surveyed year after year with in-
creasing satisfaction. For early flowering they should be
brought indoors on the approach of cold weather and
placed in a light, airy corner, where the temperature may
be allowed to vary from thirty-five to forty-five degrees.
When you are ready to force them, bring the plants into a,

living room where you can watch the rapidity with which the flowers develop. If started early, they may even be in full bloom by Christmas. Azaleas are injured by too much or too little water: the soil must be kept just moist making sure that it becomes neither over dry nor waterlogged, and it must not contain any lime. After flowering pick off the dead flowers and water freely to induce good growth. Pinch back faster-growing shoots in order to form a symmetrical plant.

Quite recently a number of varieties of a new race of Azalea, called "Kurume" is becoming popular. The plants are more delicate in appearance and smaller in leaf and flower, and of almost the same general nature as to soil, water, heat, etc.

Begonias

Begonia coccinea, B. sanguinea, etc.

Begonias are an enormous family divided into a few well-marked groups. Next to the Geranium, among flowering plants the "fibrous" Begonia is probably best adapted for indoor gardens, and is offered to the ambitious amateur in standard forms and in numerous and sometimes rather capricious hybrids. These Begonias are easily grown and will remain in bloom for long periods, new clusters of flowers being produced as the old begin to fade. The colors range from red through pink to white, the reds being particularly attractive in dull winter surroundings. They are easy to grow and easy to take care of. Soil should be light and fibrous, of equal parts loam and leaf mold, and with a liberal sprinkling of sand. Pots must be well drained. Repotting is done preferably in the spring. During the summer the plants should remain outdoors in a sheltered spot protected from heavy winds and strong sunlight.

Another group has rhizomes which are cut into pieces an inch or so long which are planted much as large seeds for propagation purposes. And a third group is the "tuberous," which is described by that term. They are usually raised from seed and the tubers dried off for keeping over winter, although they may be kept growing.

The showiest house Begonia is undoubtedly the Coral Begonia, *B. coccinea*. The stems are bright green, stiff, and upright, the leaves three to six inches long and half as wide with wavy red margins. The flowers, which in a sunny situation should be produced pretty steadily through the winter months, are about half an inch across, deep coral red, in good-sized clusters. Out in the greenhouse the Coral Begonia will grow eight to ten feet high, but in pot culture three feet is commonly as much as may be anticipated. This is the old-fashioned *B. rubra*.

The Beefsteak Begonia (*B. sanguinea*) is grown chiefly for the beauty of its foliage. The leaves often measure six to eight inches in diameter and are roundish, leathery in texture, dark green above and red below. This Begonia will do better in darkish corners than others of the family. *B. metallica* is probably the best with variegated foliage.

The upper surface of the leaf is dark green and has a lustrous bronze shaded effect. The under sides, flowers bluish white. *B. Thurstoni*, a hybrid of *B. sanguinea* and *B. metallica*, has the unusual combination of leaves that are red above and purple beneath. *B. albo-picta* and *B. argentea-guttata*, the spotted-leaved Begonias, have numerous admirers.

The hybrid Begonia, Gloire de Lorraine (*B. socotrana*,

B. Dregei), is very popular but somewhat capricious, even professional gardeners being reported to have had troubles with it. Yet if you ever see the plant in full bloom—a mass of soft, rosy pink flowers from October till April— certainly you will be tempted to give it a trial. There are several other named varieties of this type; Turnford Hall and Glory of Cincinnati, among others, are "sports" of the Lorraine type that vary only in the color of the flower. These are very popular in the florists' shops about holiday time.

Air Plant

Bryophyllum calycinum

The old-fashioned Air Plant is still occasionally to be seen as a curiosity in window boxes. This Bryophyllum is tall-growing, of easy culture, with long, pinnately divided, fleshy leaves. The plant has little decorative value and is cultivated largely because of the curious fact that if a leaf is laid on a damp surface it will produce a new plant at each indentation. Leaves pinned to a wall or window casing will produce new plants which, of course, die as soon as the nourishment contained in the old leaf is exhausted. If mature leaves be laid on the surface of moist, sandy soil, young plantlets will appear on the notches along the margin of the leaf, and these may be placed in small pots as soon as they are large enough to handle. There are several species, all very similar in appearance.

Fancy-Leaved Caladium

Caladium bicolor

No other foliage plants exhibit the bright varied colors of this Caladium. Plants are often grown outdoors in shady sheltered spots, but to attain the finest development of their fragile beauty they really demand the protection of a greenhouse. The brightness of the colors is greatly enhanced by the semi-transparency of the leaves. Caladiums lie dormant for long periods during which they should be left in dry pots in a cool spot. Through the growing period they need plenty of water. For soil, fibrous loam and peat in equal parts, a little sand and a few small lumps of charcoal are recommended. Young plants should be started in quite small pots, transferring to larger receptacles as needed. Plenty of light is necessary to develop fine shades of color, but strong direct sunlight is undesirable. When the colors begin to fade and the leaves to lose their lustre it is time to put the plants back into retirement. Withdraw water slowly and store in a dry cool cellar.

Florists' Calceolaria

Calceolaria hybrida

The reports of the difficulties of growing Calceolaria are rather discouraging to the timid amateur, but if difficulties are overcome, the mottled, often brilliantly colored flowers will be all the more a triumph. Seeds had best be sown in June or July and the young plants kept in a shady cold-frame till the approach of frosts, when they should be brought into a cool greenhouse. In January pot in six or eight inch pots in two thirds fibrous loam and one third well-decayed manure. Till they begin to bloom in May they must be kept watered, and aphids, if discovered, smoked out with nicotine.

The shrubby Calceolarias grow taller and more bushy

but are less varied in color.   They are mostly used for out-door bedding, but are rather pretty in pots.

Camellia

Camellia japonica

The popular Camellia, hardy in the South, well deserves to be grown in smaller compass as a window plant in the North.   The wild Camellia is a single red flower, but hundreds of variations are in cultivation, single and double and of various colors and shades of white, pink, and red and even mixtures of these in one flower.   The leaves are dark green, shiny, laurel-like, setting off the large blossoms most effectively.   The plants are best grown in a greenhouse where the winter temperature does not exceed fifty degrees.   Soil for potting should be rotted peat three parts, sand one part.   If the plants are placed in a temperature of from sixty to sixty-five degrees, bloom will be much hastened.   They should have plenty of water, especially while flower buds are forming.

Dumas's famous play translated into English as "Camille," was called in the original "The Lady of the Camellias."

Japanese Cypress

Chamaecyparis [Retinispora] pisifera, etc.

The somber but very decorative Cypress is often arranged in groups or allowed to stand alone as a specimen tree on lawns.   The Japanese Cypress is of slow growth and only the young trees are seen in garden cultivation.   The tree has nearly horizontal branches with tiny dark green leaves forming a beautiful, feathery, frond-like arrangement. Varieties with yellow and sulphur-colored foliage offer opportunities for unusual color schemes. The little trees (in cultivation they are seldom to be seen over six feet high) may be set out in spring or early autumn. In moving them at any time avoid disturbing the dirt about the roots any more than is necessary. There are many varieties: *filifera* has long-drooping branches and thread-like, light green foliage. *R. plumosa* and *R. plumosa aurea* have short branches; *aurea* with golden. *R. squarrosa* is silvery blue.

R. obtusa differs from most varieties in having dark green, arborvitae-like branches. Growth is dense and compact. All the Retinisporas do best in heavy, rich, but well-drained soil sheltered from cutting winds. These types of Cypresses are all increased by means of seeds or cuttings; the finer sorts by grafting upon seedlings of one of the common varieties in winter in a greenhouse.

Marguerite or Paris Daisy

Chrysanthemum frutescens

If you buy plants of white Marguerite in flower from a florist in early winter, you should have bloom all the season. The Marguerite makes an excellent plant for the window garden if care be taken to keep the temperature as uniform as possible; in greenhouses where a temperature of about fifty degrees is maintained, the plants almost never disappoint the growers. Young stock for another season is to be procured by making cuttings of the ends of the branches in the early part of May and, as soon as rooted, plant outdoors and pot early in September.

BEGONIA GLOIRE DE LORRAINE

THE SWAMP LEUCOTHOË
(Leucothoë racemosa)

Old plants are best not kept over a second season. There is also a double-flowered Marguerite and a fine yellow, variety, Étoile d'Or, or Gold Star.

Florists' Cineraria

Cineraria hybrida

Cinerarias are pretty annuals with a varied range of vivid coloring that makes the dwarf varieties valuable as house plants and the taller sorts useful in more spacious conservatories. Sow in April or May in light sandy soil, cover lightly and keep the young plants moist, cool, and partially shaded through the hot months. On the approach of autumn pot in rich fibrous soil and bring indoors. The dwarf varieties will hardly exceed a foot in height and at the other extreme are enormous thick plants four or five feet tall. The varieties range in color from purple to blue and white and often in combinations such as blue and white. Troubles more or less serious with aphids will be best warded off by vigorous sprayings with nicotine solution.

Clerodendron

Clerodendron Thomsonae

C. Thomsonae or *Balfourii*, perhaps the most frequently cultivated species and a very attractive plant, flowers quite young, and is among the best climbers for window culture, producing immense clusters of crimson flowers with large white calyx. The flowers are unusual in their balloon-like, inflated calyx, which is very conspicuous and in sharp color contrast with the rest of the flower.

The Three-Forked Clerodendron, *C. trichotomum*, is a hardy sub-shrub in the North, but is more commonly to be seen growing in greenhouses. It has white flowers in a reddish-brown calyx. Soil should be rich and fibrous. Propagation is commonly by cuttings. Clerodendrons, though often grown, have somewhat of a reputation of being especially susceptible to attacks by mealy bugs.

Coco Palm

Cocos Weddelliana

Cocos Weddelliana as seen in our greenhouses is a very small Palm with finely pinnated leaves, not too large for table decoration, and often considered the most graceful of this numerous group. It grows slowly and is very slender both in stem and in leaves. It requires heat and moisture and the foliage will be benefited by frequent sprayings. Fibrous peat and loam with a little well-rotted cow manure and a dash of sand will make an ideal soil; the pots should be comparatively small and well drained. Propagation is usually from seed sown in a temperature of seventy-five degrees. The Coco Palm is not of difficult culture and will endure ordinary house conditions fairly well. *C. plumosa*, a larger-growing species with feathery leaves, is also often to be seen in conservatories and is used for avenue planting in California.

Croton

Codiaeum variegatum

The plants known commonly as Crotons have large, leathery, finely colored leaves vying in brilliance of color with the Caladiums and displaying a diversity of form which is always a surprise and a delight. Small plants make attractive table decorations and large plants find a place on summer lawns. The full beauty of the leaves can be maintained by frequent and vigorous spraying. Culture is easy: sun, rich fibrous soil, and plenty of water at the roots are all that is required. Propagation is by half-ripe cuttings in a warm place or by seeds. For winter plants the Crotons offer an unusual choice of varieties, nearly all of which are excellent and fancy can run free in making a choice, for example: Andreanum, leaves large, broadly lanceolate with yellow veins; Disraeli, particularly to be recommended, with leaves hastate with red and golden veins; undulatum, leaves lanceolate with wavy edges, bronze with red and crimson; variegatum, heavily blotched leaves, green and yellow, with pale rose-colored leaf stalks. The names of these garden varieties often, as here, describe the particular plant.

Dracaena

Cordylene terminalis

Dracaenas with straight stems and large tufts of gracefully recurving leaves are often seen decorating large entrance halls. Young plants are used in window boxes and for table decoration. There are many species and varieties and hybrids, some very highly colored, and altogether the Dracaena, or Fountain Plant, as it is more popularly called, is one of the most useful and adaptable of winter plants. In *C. indivisa* the leaves are long, arching, strap-shaped on slender green stems. *D. terminalis* has red leaves and its varieties have bronzy leaves striped white, red, yellow, spotted, mottled, or variegated. Dracaenas are increased by means of stem cuttings laid down in sand

(a method impracticable in dwelling houses) or very slowly
by seeds sown in a temperature maintained at sixty degrees.
Fibrous loam, leaf mold, well-decayed manure, with the
usual sprinkle of sand, make a satisfactory soil. Frequent
spraying or careful washing of the leaves with soapy water
will be necessary to prevent disease and to keep the plant
on its best appearance.

Hawthorn

Many species of *Crataegus* as *C. punctata*, etc.

The Hawthorns are often planted as specimens on lawns
with the anticipation of their wonderful, late seasonal,
ornamental qualities in mind. The Hawthorn family are
generally undersized trees with stiff, zigzag branches set
with thorns. Over a hundred species have been catalogued by botanists. The Hawthorn has fine leaf coloration and striking fruit scarcely equalled by any autumn
shrub. Often the bright red berries will persist through
winter into early spring. Hawthorns should be planted
by themselves rather conspicuously on lawns, or in groups
against a background of shrubbery. The ideal soil will be
rich and moist with underlying clay. They may be started
from seed planted in the autumn and take two or more
years to germinate, but quicker results are obtained from
small trees purchased from nurserymen.

Cyclamen

Cyclamen persicum

Our Cyclamens are beautiful plants of the Primula
order, which have been greatly developed and improved
from the original much smaller Persian parent. The

blossoms, which should last all winter, are white or varying shades of pink to dark rose, often with a purple blotch at the mouth. It will take fifteen months to grow Cyclamens from seed to flowers. Seeds may be sown in September or not until the end of the year, according as one is planning for midwinter or early spring bloom. Sow in pots well-drained and filled with light, sandy soil; keep in temperature of sixty degrees till sprouted and repot once or twice during the winter; store in a cool, shady place over summer. The plants may be rested after flowering and often are thoroughly successful a second year, or they may be kept growing. Indoors a temperature round fifty degrees will suit the Cyclamen best.

Sago Palm

Cycas revoluta

Sago Palms are of many kinds, all highly ornamental, all with leaves of hard texture that are proof against the ordinary accidents of the indoor life of plants. They grow slowly, and, if a small plant is bought, it may be depended upon for some years before it will become too large for house culture.

C. revoluta, perhaps the most frequently grown species, has leaves two to four feet long, six or eight inches wide, very closely pinnate and deep glossy green. One whorl is produced in a year; the new leaves unroll like fern fronds and are upright; as they grow older they gradually bend and when new leaves begin to appear the following year they are horizontal or slightly drooping. The Sago Palm is easily grown in any well-drained soil and makes no objection to the somewhat variable temperature of living rooms. Stems are potted in dormant condition and kept in dry soil till the first crown of leaves comes, after which abundant supplies of water should be furnished.

Umbrella Plant

Cyperus alternifolius

The Umbrella Plants, *C. alternifolius,* with green leaves and the variety *variegatus* with variegated, grow one to three feet high and make excellent house plants. The height and luxuriance will vary greatly with the richness of the soil and the amount of water supplied. The leaves of a rich, deep green are produced in clusters at the top of the slender stems. The Umbrella Plant is one of the easiest to propagate by rooting the leaves. Cut off a bunch of leaves with a bit of stem and place in water. In a few weeks a new plant will be seen pushing up from among the leaflets which may be separated and potted. While the new plant is germinating care must be taken that the water does not become stale, which can be easily effected by adding from time to time a bit of charcoal. If grown as a pot plant, Cyperus had best always stand in a saucer of water.

Genista

Cytisus canariensis

Late winter and early spring see this handsome, evergreen shrub covered with spikes of small, yellow, slightly fragrant, pea-shaped flowers that brighten up greenhouses and rejoice the hearts of fortunate possessors of window boxes. Genistas are of easy culture and make successful window or porch plants. Top growth and side shoots should be checked after flowering to make neat, symmetrical shrubs, at which time cuttings may also be taken for new plants. As soon as rooted pot in two-inch pots, transferring to larger receptacles as necessary. During summer the young plants will be benefited by being plunged in ashes out of doors in a sunny position. Take indoors before the time of frosts and transfer to larger pots; then store in a cool greenhouse until ready for forcing; bring out, and in a temperature of fifty degrees the plant should flower in a few weeks.

Carnations

Dianthus Caryophyllus

Most amateurs think of the florists' Carnation as a florist's flower only; yet they are well fitted for house culture, neat in habit, easily grown, plentiful in bloom. During the late winter or early spring take cuttings from vigorous plants and, as soon as rooted, pot in two-inch pots in light sandy soil. Repot several times, plant out in a border over summer, nip long-growing buds and shoots. By September the plants should be large enough for five-or six-inch pots. A good forcing soil will consist of three parts loam, one part manure, and one part sand. Suitable winter temperature for Carnations will be one of about fifty-five degrees. Well-known varieties are: Enchantress, pink; White Enchantress; Portia, scarlet; and Eldorado, yellow.

Aralia

Dizygotheca elegantissima

In the florists' trade this is known as *Aralia elegantissima* and is a charming foliage plant for conservatory or

dinner-table decoration, having leaflets with undulated
margins, red underneath and dark green above. Any good
garden soil will do: as a preliminary cut the thickest roots
available into pieces about two inches long, which are to
be plunged into sand, keeping uppermost the part of the
root that is nearest the stem. A temperature of seventy
degrees should induce growth, and the cuttings may presently be transferred to small pots. The genus Aralia is
comprehensive, including shrubs, small trees, and even
herbs scattered over temperate, sub-tropical, and tropical
regions, but the many decorative plants grown in greenhouses under that name are not Aralias at all. The very
pretty Aralia having pinnate foliage of pale green edged
and splashed with white is *Polyscias Guilfoylei.*

Oleaster

Elaeagnus pungens

Oleasters may be successfully grown as pot or tub plants
and will form a charming variation from indoor plants most
commonly seen in entrance halls and window boxes. The
Oleaster in a greenhouse or in a well-lighted room from
which frost is excluded should form a spreading shrub
about six feet high. All the Oleasters are handsome with
dark green leaves silvery on the underside, fragrant blossoms in late fall covered with silvery scales. The Oleaster
is most easily propagated by layers and is not fussy as
to soil or situation, except as to good drainage. Excellent choice of foliage effects is offered in several varieties:
leaves with margins yellowish white (*variegata*), and
variegated yellow and pale pink (*Simoni tricolor*), among
others.

CYCLAMEN
(Cyclamen persicum)

PRIMROSE
(Primula obconica)

POLYANTHUS OR ROMAN NARCISSUS
(Narcissus Tazetta var.)

E. multiflora, the Goumi, is a hardy shrub with long-stalked scarlet berries densely covered with scales or spangles in June and July. Another is *E. umbellata*, with small fruits in dense clusters on the older wood and is an easy-growing shrub on any well-drained soil.

Winter-Blooming Heaths

Erica hyemalis, etc.

Winter Heaths, striking bell-shaped flowers, pink with white tops, are more popular abroad than with us because of climatic differences. Heaths are difficult for amateur gardeners to manage successfully, but small plants about to flower may be procured from florists, and you will be at least sure of one year's blossoms. Particular attention must be given to the supply of water given the Winter Heaths, either extreme being fatal to development, and they must be grown in a winter temperature round fifty degrees. They are thought to require very firm potting in a mixture of good peat with plentiful addition of sand. *E. melanthera*, with tiny white flowers, is another Heath often seen in florists' shops during the Christmas season. Other species less commonly grown in this country have yellow, small red or white, or long, tubular flowers in purple umbels. This family is very numerous, especially in South Africa.

Amazon Lily

Eucharis amazonica

Amazon Lilies are tropical plants of great beauty and easy culture producing, sometimes thrice yearly under favorable conditions, attractive umbels of very large white flowers. It was at one time grown quite extensively for cutting purposes, but in recent years has rather gone out of vogue perhaps because the flower is fragile and easily bruised. The Amazon Lily delights in a humid atmosphere and a minimum temperature of sixty-five degrees. Soil should be quite rich and a half-dozen bulbs may be planted in an eight-inch pot, placed so that the tips of the bulbs will show above the surface. The Amazon Lily requires frequent washing of its leaves and plenty of water at the roots during its season of growth. It is preferable that plants remain undisturbed for years. On account of its requirements of heat and moisture, the Amazon Lily is hardly possible as a household plant but will be found very satisfactory in conservatories and greenhouses.

Crown of Thorns

Euphorbia splendens

The Euphorbias are rather grotesque plants grown largely as curiosities. The stems are green, fleshy, often angled, some kinds with a fair crop of leaves, others with none at all and very spiny. The Crown of Thorns has long, sinuous, purplish stems studded with stout spines and much more sparsely with oval leaves. At the tips of the branches are the bright-red flowers produced at all seasons of the year but generally most abundant in winter. Culture is not difficult. Any good soil except a clay will do. In order to keep the plant within bounds it is advisable to train the Crown of Thorns over stout wire or wooden frames.

Poinsettia

Euphorbia pulcherrima

The Poinsettia is grown for the brilliant scarlet bracts, measuring often a foot in length and produced beneath the flowers. In the all too frequent dark days of early winter there is nothing better to lighten a room than a generous display of Poinsettia. For winter flowering the plants should be grown in small pots and kept from too much growth by pinching back and withholding supplies of water. Cuttings taken in late spring or early summer root easily under glass in moist sand. When well rooted, pot in equal parts of fibrous loam, leaf mold, and decayed manure. After flowering the plants had best be given a few months' rest. Fifty to sixty degrees will be an ideal winter temperature and in summer not over eighty degrees. There are white and pink varieties but they can never be as popular as the dashing red. Poinsettia belongs to the Spurge family and is named after Doctor Poinsett of Charleston, S. C., who introduced the flower to American horticulture about 1835.

Spindle Trees

Euonymus japonicus, etc.

The Japanese Spindle Tree is easy to grow and will add a bright dash of color to a garden border or shrubbery in the dead of winter when garden color is at a minimum. This Spindle Bush survives winters in the vicinity of New York without protection. Leaves with gold and with white variegations offer a difficult choice and the tree grows vigorously in a rich, well-manured soil. Altogether the

Japanese Spindle-Bush is one of the most decorative and desirable of broad-leaved evergreen shrubs for winter use.

The Creeping Spindle (*E. japonicus radicans*) is an outdoor evergreen shrub, impregnable to frost and to be had in many desirable varieties. It attaches itself to walls or the side of a house by means of adventitious roots produced along the stems, and in a favorable location will climb fifteen feet high or more. A deep, moist, sandy soil is best for the Creeping Spindle Vine.

Leopard Plant

Farfugium grande

The well-named Leopard Plant makes rapid growth in rich soil but will not survive a winter outdoors farther north than Washington. The leaves are large, orbicular, yellow spotted—in certain varieties white and pale rose—and the leaf stalks tall and vigorous. The Leopard Plant may be grown successfully in the average indoor atmosphere and is easily propagated by dividing old plants in spring and repotting the divisions separately. Soil should consist of two thirds loam and a third leaf soil, and as with so many of the foliage plants, plentiful supplies of water are a necessity. It is thought a good plan to let the Leopard Plant rest outdoors in a shady spot during the summer months and replant in the early autumn.

Rubber Plant

Ficus elastica

The ubiquitous Rubber Plant has an unfailing ability to withstand the disadvantages of house conditions that makes the probability of its being superseded in popularity quite unlikely. More usually grown as a single stem plant, equally decorative specimens may be had by procuring plants with compact, spreading branches. The long oblong to elliptical leaves, glossy and dark green above, dull and light green below, are familiar sights in conservatories and entrance halls. The Rubber Plant is a gross feeder, needing a rich soil and improving on a diet of manure water and other liquid plant food. They grow fast but even a plant grown to a single stem will not become too tall for a living room for two or three years. Propagation is effected by means of cuttings taken from the terminal shoots. Tie together and insert in sand. They need plenty of bottom heat and a constant temperature of seventy-five to eighty degrees. Rubber Plants that have grown well during the winter should not be put outdoors in summer where full sunlight will strike the leaves.

The Fiddle-leaved Rubber Plant (*F. pandurata*) has much broader, fiddle-shaped leaves with creamy white veins and offers a welcome and attractive variation from the standard type.

Freesia

Freesia refracta

No winter-blooming bulbs of easy culture are more charming than the Freesias. Freesias are dwarf, Lily-like plants with fragrant creamy flowers in large clusters on slender stems. The leaves and stalks are quite tender and will require support. Ashes in the soil are useful to counteract this tendency and wire carnation supports will be found neat and satisfactory. The bulbs are small and should be potted as soon as received, placing half-a-dozen or more in a five-inch pot and covering lightly with soil. They are usually kept in a cool spot till growth is well under way. By starting Freesias in August they may be had in flower by Christmas. Hybrids offer carmine-rose, violet-blue, orange-yellow, and other charming color variations, but the most popular form is the white variety *alba*.

Cape Jessamine

Gardenia florida

Gardenias, or Cape Jessamines, hardy outdoor plants of exquisite beauty in the South, have fragrant white double blossoms rising amid shiny, deep evergreen foliage. In the North they can hardly be grown with any degree of success except in a warm humid greenhouse atmosphere. Culture is not difficult provided the proper atmosphere can be supplied. Cuttings should be inserted in sand where there is plenty of bottom heat and the seedlings transferred to three-inch pots, using as soil a mixture of three parts loam and one part manure with a sprinkling of sand and a few bits of charcoal. As the plants mature, frequent spraying of the leaves will be found advisable. Few plants are more attractive than the Gardenia grown under conditions that give it a chance to do its best.

Wintergreen

Gaultheria procumbens

Shining evergreen foliage and pretty red berries that remain on the plant all winter make Wintergreen attractive both indoors and out. The plant is low-growing and the leaves yield a pleasant-tasting, fragrant oil which is used extensively in flavoring. Tea used to be steeped from the leaves, and children eagerly devour the tender new shoots tinged with red that are put forth in June. Small, white, bell-like flowers, usually solitary, hang nodding among the leaves from June to September and later come the bright-red berries. Wintergreen is to be found under great trees and in semi-shaded woods and succeeds best in sandy soil which contains a good proportion of decayed vegetable matter. Wintergreen is well adapted for planting along the edges of woodland paths and indoors for hanging baskets and window boxes.

Gladiolus

Gladiolus Colvillei

The Gladiolus is among the flowers distinctive of the summer season outdoors and may be turned to advantage for late winter and early spring bloom, especially if the Colvillei varieties are grown, as they are excellent for winter forcing. For Easter bloom bulbs need not be started before December and their rapid growth will prove a constant surprise and delight. The secret of success is to grow them cool, a night temperature of forty-five to fifty degrees being recommended. Plant in boxes or pots, placing the bulbs so that their tops are level with the surface of the soil. Water only sparingly till growth commences. Support is generally necessary to keep the shoots in an upright position. These varieties have red and white colorings.

Heliconia

Heliconia aureo-striata

Besides the Palms there are other tropical plants of noble appearance that serve much the same decorative purposes in cultivation.   Heliconia is a plant of this sort, a dwarf with large, deep green leaves obliquely striped with golden yellow, invaluable in a greenhouse but too much a lover of warmth and humidity to remain long a resident of dwelling houses.   Heliconia must have a half-shady position, the richest of soils, and plenty of water.   The plant is quickly increased by division of the rootstock, an operation for early spring during which care should be taken to disturb the roots no more than is necessary.   Heliconias are related to the Banana, and the various species are located mostly in tropical America.

Heliotrope

Heliotropium peruvianum

The beautiful purple of the flowers, the sweet, spicy perfume, the long period of bloom, all combine to make the familiar Heliotrope an ideal window plant.   For winter flowers take stout, soft cuttings in early July, root them in a sandy soil and pot after a couple of weeks, when well-rooted.   Heliotrope for winter use will need moderate sunlight and warmth, rich light soil, and a constant supply of moisture about the roots and in the air.   To make bushy sturdy plants, pinch back the new shoots regularly.   Grown in pots or boxes a plant will ultimately cover a space about eighteen inches square and reach a height of twelve to fifteen inches.   Originally the flowers were violet, but we now have several shades of purple and a white, and the individual trusses have increased from a meager two inches across to a full six inches. If you wish to grow from seed, sow from February to May and plan to keep the plants in pots all summer. Winter Heliotropes are best plunged in a border over summer but without removing from the pots. They should be turned occasionally to prevent rooting through the bottom of the pot.

Christmas Rose

Helleborus niger

The Christmas Rose has pure, snow-white flowers produced out of doors in late autumn and in early winter, too, if the weather be at all mild. To obtain the best-developed bloom cover the plants (as soon as the flower buds push through) with a large bell jar or small coldframe. Give the Christmas Rose a partially shaded position and soil enriched by the addition of leaf mold. These beautiful plants are spoiled by too frequent shiftings. If they must be moved it should be done when they are making new roots in September. Of the varieties available, *altifolius* has perhaps the largest flowers and *praecox* is valuable for early bloom, which may even begin in September.

Kentia Palm

Howea Belmoreana

Tolerant of bad light and sharp variations of temperature, of erect, spreading, dark green foliage, the Kentia Palms are among the best of the big Palm family for indoor purposes and are much used for the embellishment of hallways, ballrooms, and for wedding decorations. The Thatch Palm (*H. Forsteriana*), a variant of the same type, is stronger growing, with broader leaves but more drooping.

Palms require plenty of water and rich soil; three parts loam and one part decayed manure will be none too heavy for them. The leaves should be washed frequently (underside as well as top) with a sponge and lukewarm soapy water, both on account of dust and of insects which frequently get a foothold on neglected plants. Palms do best when their roots are slightly confined, so be sure that pots are not too large. Plenty of drainage must be given at the bottom of the pot and a few bits of charcoal added. During the summer all Palms benefit by being plunged outdoors in a partially sheltered position where they must be regularly provided with water.

Wax Plant

Hoya carnosa

The fragrant, pink clustered blossoms produced during the summer months will make themselves delightfully manifest in any dwelling house that has a Wax Plant. The leaves are thick, leathery, ornamental at all seasons. The Wax Plant likes fibrous peat and sand for soil and plenty of moisture, particularly during the growing season. The plant will climb up a back wall if desired, clinging by adventitious roots as do the Ivies. Bits of stem with a leaf or two attached inserted in sand in a warm temperature will quickly take root, disposing of the matter of propagation. The scale insect known as the mealy bug seems unfortunately to have a particular liking for the Wax Plant, and as it increases rapidly, a careful watch must be kept at all times and the pests exterminated on appearance.

Hyacinths

Hyacinthus orientalis

The Hyacinth is truly a domestic flower, a source of fragrance and a joy to look upon. Hyacinths make thoroughly successful pot plants. The trusses are handsome, the colors brilliant, the habit neat, and the perfume delicious. They may be grown in pots or in glass. If grown in pots place one bulb in a five-inch pot, about an inch of the bulb remaining above the soil, which should be rich with a very liberal sprinkling of sand. After potting place out of doors covered with soil or ashes to a depth of about six inches for a period of five or six weeks. This will check top growth but not root action. At the end of this period bulbs may be brought into a heated room and given free exposure to light and plenty of water.

Glass culture is often more expensive than pot culture, but has all the charm of novelty. The base of the bulb should just touch the water, which should contain a bit of charcoal. As long as the water remains clear it need not be changed. The bulbs are to be kept away from light until roots two or three inches long are formed. Then they may be brought into light and heat as are pot Hyacinths. If the trusses become heavy, some sort of support may be found necessary.

The two well-known groups of Hyacinths are Dutch and Roman. Flowers are smaller in the Roman type, and several spikes are produced from each bulb; they are not so stiff and formal as the Dutch Hyacinths and are more useful for cut flowers. The Roman Hyacinths are often potted in batches from August to November in order to obtain quick succession of bloom.

Hyacinths are single or double and may be obtained in a bewildering variety of whites, reds, blues, and even yellows.

Hydrangea

Hydrangea hortensis

The tender Hydrangea is the most showy early-flowering plant for indoor forcing. Plants brought out of seclusion in January should be in flower for Easter. For forcing purposes Hydrangeas should be grown in pots or tubs, plunging the receptacles up to the rims out of doors during the summer months. In early autumn bring inside and store in a light cool spot. During the summer water should be supplied abundantly, but while stored in autumn and early winter only enough to keep the wood from shriveling. Cuttings rooted in February and March should make plants mature enough to bloom the following season. A rich heavy soil of loam and manure is essential for good growth and well-rounded bloom. Flowers vary from white in some varieties to pink, ranging to light blue in others. Blue flowers are produced by acidity in the soil and that is sometimes obtained by regular watering during the summer with a weak solution of alum. Limestone in the soil assures pink flowers.

Ixia

Ixia hybrida

Ixia, boasting the greatest range of color of any bulb, is also cool-loving, which makes it very desirable for indoor cultivation. A night temperature of thirty-five to forty de-

LEOPARD PLANT
(Farfugium grande)

CAPE JESSAMINE
(Ga denia florida)

GLADIOLUS
(Gladiolus Colvillei)

HELIOTROPE
(Heliotropium peruvianum)

DUTCH HYACINTH
(Hyacinthus orientalis)

HYDRANGEA
(Hydrangea hortensis)

IXIA
(Ixia hybrida)

BERMUDA EASTER LILY
(Lilium Harrisi)

grees with a rise of ten or fifteen degrees during the day is considered ideal. The stems are slender and graceful, the flowers offer white, yellow, purple, ruby, blue, green in many shades and variations, usually with black eye. The flower spikes contain six to twelve flowers, each of which may be an inch or two in diameter. Bulbs should be potted in autumn as late as possible in a mixture of loam, leaf soil, and sand, placing eight or nine in a six-inch pot. Keep cool and dark till growth commences. Then bring into light and heat. If Ixia flowers successfully, you will be many times repaid for any troubles or vexations you may have had at the start.

Juniper

Juniperus communis

The slow-growing dwarf Junipers fit in well with most garden schemes, are unaffected by average winters, and will grow vigorously on thin soil. The common Juniper is to be found covering vast stretches of waste land throughout the temperate zones, even into the Arctic regions, ranging according to locality and soil from a mere low bush to a tree thirty or forty feet high. Junipers are easily distinguishable from other Evergreens by their red, blue, or blue-black berries which they bear instead of cones. The dwarf Juniper forms a loose, open head above a short, stout trunk; other forms are pyramidal. Three years is required to mature the berries, and they hang on the shrub two or three years longer; each berry has several seeds which may require three years to germinate. All forms of the Juniper are useful in the garden; the pyramidal for formal effects, the low shrubby for group planting and for screens.

The Red Cedar (*J. virginiana*) becomes in cultivation a neat symmetrical tree well adapted to the formal garden. The dark blue berries have a pale bloom and resinous sweet flesh. In the autumn the foliage becomes rusty brown to match the stringy red bark. This is the cedar of lead pencils and cedar chests and the cedar used by the railroad companies for railroad ties.

Lantana
Lantana Camara, etc.

Lantanas belong to the Verbena family and produce well-formed umbels of showy flowers more often seen in summer garden beds, but available for conservatories and for window boxes. Lantanas may be propagated at any time of the year when there is suitable young wood for cuttings. Pinch out the shoots to encourage bushy habit and the flower buds until you are ready for them to come to bloom. If it is desired to utilize old plants, they may be dug up from the garden at the end of summer and placed in pots large enough to accommodate the roots without crowding. Cut tops back to leave no more than six inches and keep in warm, moist air till new growth is well under way. Lantanas must have rich soil and plentiful supplies of water at all times. There is a choice of white and yellow varieties with many charming intervening shades.

European Larch
Larix decidua

The delicate curving twigs strung with little cones are pretty enough all winter to compensate for the loss of the needle-like leaves which the Larch, unlike most conifers,

does not retain after they turn yellow in the autumn.
Attractive in winter, the feathery light green of the new
growth in spring makes this Conifer unique among trees
commonly planted. This less vigorous relative of the
Pines and Firs succeeds best in deep, well-drained soil and
is valuable as isolated specimens and for group planting. Of
available varieties *pendula* has drooping branches effective
at all seasons but particularly so in winter, and *glauca* has
needles of a glaucous blue. Larchwood is very durable,
heavy, and hard.

Sweet Bay

Laurus nobilis

The most "architectural" decorative evergreen tree
having lanceolate, leathery leaves, and formerly imported
in great quantities from Europe. Sweet Bay appears in
several different ways, sometimes with a stem and globular crowns, sometimes as a bushy plant with leaves close to
the ground, and occasionally clipped in the form of pyra-
mids or cylinders. Rich fibrous loam is needed and the
plants must never be without a suitable supply of water.
They may endure a temperature below freezing and escape
without damage, but it is better not to take the risk.
Plants may be kept in a cool, light cellar over winter for
summer use on lawns, or in heat and light for indoor decorative effects. May be propagated from cuttings in the
greenhouse in late summer.

Leucothoë or Andromeda

Leucothoë Catesbaei

Leucothoë, the graceful sprays of which are much fancied
by florists in making up decorations, is a relative of the

Rhododendrons. The shining evergreen leaves produced on recurving stems two feet long turn a beautiful bronzy purple in winter. The flowers in May are lily-of-the-valley-like, creamy white, and fragrant. Deep soil with plenty of humus and shade to prevent the burning of the leaves by the sun are required. An ideal place for Leucothoë or Andromeda is along the edge of a woodland path or amongst Rhododendrons. The plant is commonly propagated by division in spring or autumn. Leucothoë grows wild in the South and much of the florists' supplies comes from this source. The related Swamp Leucothoë (*L. racemosa*) is a deciduous shrub attaining a height sometimes of ten feet, also having white tubular flowers.

Chinese Fan Palm

Livistona chinensis

The Chinese Fan Palm vies with the Kentia for the title of the most popular of house Palms. Comparing the two, the Chinese Fan is much broader but not as tall; the leaf stem is as long as the leaf and for half its length is armed with short, stout, sharp spines. The foliage is a deep rich green with gracefully drooping tips and presents a more massive appearance than other Palms commonly grown indoors. The Chinese Fan will succeed in any room where the temperature does not go below forty-five degrees at night. Care must be taken to see that the roots are well supplied with water and the leaves kept free from dust by occasional sponging. Heavy soil is essential and too large pots are to be avoided. Plants with eight or more leaves and a spread of four or five feet may frequently be grown in pots as small as six inches. The purchase of a small

Chinese Fan Palm is an investment that will bring results and be a constant delight for a number of years.

Bermuda Easter Lily

Lilium Harrisi

The most appropriate flower for Easter is unquestionably the Lily, but the Easter Lily of to-day is not the Lily of history and religious painting. The Bermuda Lily which, as recently as the early eighties, displaced the Madonna or Annunciation Lily, is a longer, larger, more trumpet-like flower; and it in fact is only a selected form of the Japanese *L. longiflorum*. Bulbs should be potted when received in August and September; bury outside until late in November when they should be started for growth in a temperature that does not sink below fifty-five degrees at night. If Easter Day comes early in the year, it may be necessary to keep the temperature much higher. Water should be provided as needed and a careful watch maintained for aphids. The Lilies are grown one to a six-inch pot or several to an eight-inch pot; approved soil will be loam, leaf soil, and decayed manure in equal parts. Easter Lilies are not difficult to force and make fine bulbs on which the amateur may try a 'prentice hand.

Manettia

Manettia cordifolia

Bright scarlet tubular flowers with yellow segments amid small, broadly lanceolate leaves make Manettia very beautiful and attractive in December. The plant is a neat and graceful climber and may be trained over pillars or

along rafters. There are some thirty species, many of
which, though little used, would be readily adaptable to in
door conditions. The soil should be quite heavy with a
good sprinkling of sand. A temperature that does not
fall below sixty degrees is advisable, but not absolutely
essential. Manettia increases quickly by means of cuttings inserted in sand and kept till well rooted in a warm,
moist atmosphere.

Japanese Allspice

Meratia fragrans

Japanese Allspice forms a shrub six to eight feet high
with whitish or yellowish blossoms, deliciously fragrant,
produced in late winter. One or two sprays will easily
perfume a whole room Outdoors this Allspice should be
planted in a sheltered position as it is probably not hardy
in regions that experience winter temperatures lower than
fifteen degrees. Propagation is arranged without difficulty by layering in the spring and the shrub will put forth
best efforts in a soil well drained and fairly rich. Meratia,
formerly called Chimonanthus, is related botanically to
Calycanthus floridus, our native Carolina Allspice.

Fig Marigold

Mesembryanthemum cordifolium

Not every flower can be destined to occupy the center of
the floral stage. Fig Marigold is something for poor soil,
sandy banks, rocky spots. It reaches a height of no more
than six to twelve inches, but often has a spread of as much
as eighteen inches. The flowers are pink or white, the

pink fading noticeably as the season advances. The leaves are light green, in whorls about the stems, growing brown and woody in autumn. Start from cuttings taken in September or October. Break off the lowest whorl and plant above the break in sand. As soon as rooted, transfer to a small pot containing a mixture of half sand and half good garden soil. The variety *cordifolium variegatum* has charming foliage and should be remembered for hanging baskets and window boxes.

Ice Plant

Mesembryanthemum crystallinum

The Ice Plant is a little trailer and creeper grown for its succulent thick foliage and tiny white blossoms. It blooms from August to September and is often of service in rockeries and, of course, indoors for hanging baskets and window boxes. The fat, fleshy leaves are covered with glistening dots that have somewhat the appearance of ice; hence the popular name. This unassuming annual thrives famously in the driest and thinnest of soils. The plants may be raised from cuttings or from seed started preferably indoors in February. If to be started from cuttings, make the cuttings about four inches long, dry in the sun two or three days and then keep in a sand bed till rooted.

Musk Plant

Mimulus moschatus

The Musk Plant is an evergreen trailer with small yellow flowers that are produced almost continuously. Out-

doors they are half-hardy perennials needing winter cover
in the North and indoors they are great favorites for house
plants.   Easy to grow, with plentiful, slightly fragrant
bloom, they are admirable by themselves or in combination with other window plants.   Musk is easily propagated
through seeds sown early in coldframes or by means of
cuttings.   The method of cuttings is perhaps preferable.
Some plants seem to possess greater fragrance than others,
which for indoor use is naturally of greatest importance.
Select these for your cuttings, avoiding those that have
but faint perfume.   Musk is a great favorite in English
cottage gardens and is hardy in this country as far north
as the vicinity of New York.   Strangely enough, the very
fragrant form is seemingly becoming obsolete.   Why,
nobody knows.

Partridge Berry

Mitchella repens

No woodland creeper rewards care with greater luxuriance of growth than does the Partridge Vine.   Transplanted from its home beneath forest trees with plenty of
leaf mold or chopped sphagnum, the Partridge Berry
quickly makes thick mats at the foot of Rhododendrons
and other tall-growing shrubs.   Indoors, the bright red
berries displayed to perfection amid the evergreen foliage
are often to be found in glass bowls covered to conserve
moisture.   Certainly everybody ought to have a few
Partridge Berry plants.   The vine is of easy culture in
shady positions.   Propagation is simple: cut old plants
into small pieces four or six inches long with roots attached
and plant separately.

Abyssinian Banana

Musa Ensete

The Abyssinian Banana in a large greenhouse will reach a height of twenty or more feet, the crown of enormous leaves with crimson midribs making a truly impressive sight when the plant is moved outdoors in tubs for mid-summer tropical effects. The young plant should be set out in June in a position sheltered from heavy winds. If rapid growth is desired, a hole three feet wide and the same depth may be dug, filling in with rich loam and decayed manure. Soil should be kept quite moist, particularly during the earlier months. The plant may be wintered in a cool cellar or in growth in a greenhouse; if in a cool cellar, the leaves should be cut down and the water supply kept quite scanty. This and other members of the Banana family are attractive plants but hardly available except for those possessing large greenhouses.

Wax Myrtle

Myrica cerifera

Wax Myrtle with dark-green leaves and wax-coated, bluish-white, aromatic berries, grows wild from Delaware to Florida, sometimes a fairly large shrub, sometimes of thoroughly tree-like proportions. Unfortunately, it is not reliably hardy in Northern states. The leaves are practically evergreen and the shrub, which has no objection to dryness or sand, is a great favorite for seashore planting. The seeds are similar to those of the more common Bayberry and like them are much sought for by birds. The wax obtained by boiling and skimming was in early days used for the making of candles. Wax Myrtle should be propagated without difficulty from the suckers that spring up around the bases of old plants or, if necessary, seeds may be sown out of doors in spring.

Myrtle

Myrtus communis

The Myrtles are attractive in foliage and flower and may be propagated with ease in any dwelling house. This native of Mediterranean countries makes a neat evergreen shrub fairly hardy, with shining, blue-green, long oval leaves and white flowers. The leaves, bark, flowers, and berries are all aromatic and are used commercially in the manufacture of perfumery. Myrtle needs fairly heavy potting soil and is easily increased by cuttings taken from young shoots. The plants will be unharmed by light frosts and may be kept in greenhouses at temperatures lower than advisable for most plants. Among the ancient Greeks the Myrtle, as a symbol of youth and beauty, was sacred to Venus and found a place in all their festivals.

Chinese Sacred Lily

Narcissus Tazetta orientalis

Marvelously rapid growth and abundant silvery-white, fragrant flowers have given the Chinese Narcissus a popularity that is really world-wide. From forty to sixty days after planting will be sufficient to produce bloom in a light sunny window and a temperature that had best never get over sixty or under fifty degrees. These bulbs are most frequently grown in glass bowls filled with pebbles and water. The pebbles are used merely to support the bulb. Use shallow bowls, place a little granulated charcoal in the bottom to keep the water sweet, and cover with a one-inch layer of bird gravel or sand. Set the bulbs on this nearly touching one another, three or more to a bowl, according to size. Fill in with white pebbles, or, if they are not available, more bird gravel. This will prevent the plant from toppling over when in leaf and bloom. Pour in water until it almost reaches the bulbs. Place in a cool spot to root, and grow on in a low temperature. Replenish the water as it evaporates and occasionally change if it shows any signs of getting stale.

When buying Chinese Lily bulbs remember that the largest sizes will give the best results.

The Paper-White Narcissus (*N. Tazetta papyraceus*), with snow-white, starry blossoms borne in good-sized trusses on long strong stems, is one of the most desirable varieties for indoor forcing. The bulbs are of easy culture and can often be grown successfully in bowls of water with moss or pebbles. Florists grow the Narcissus extensively for cut flowers and, for flowering in pots at Easter time, the bi-color (*polyanthus*) forms of the Tazetta Narcissus, known also as Roman Narcissus. The variety *grandiflora* with larger trusses and greater individual bloom is rapidly su-perseding the earlier forms.

Boston Fern

Nephrolepis exaltata bostoniensis

Many people believe it impossible to grow Ferns in the house or in the window garden. Of some rare varieties this is all too true, but there are perhaps a couple of dozen Ferns that may be grown, and their finely cut fronds will have a graceful, airy effect possessed by few other plants.

The popular Sword Fern (*N. exaltata,*) now almost entirely superseded by the newer variety, *bostoniensis,* should be found quite satisfactory, will even stand some neglect and still recover if properly attended to. The fronds of a large Boston will be two to three feet long, two to three inches across, and of a rich green color. As a potting mixture rich loam and manure are required with a little sand. Water must be provided regularly in considerable quantities. Long cord-like runners or stolons are produced from the base of the plant by which all Sword Ferns are propagated. New forms in great numbers have been produced from the Boston, but few are desirable as house plants. There are several attractive plumose forms with fronds a foot or so long and quite broad that are available for indoor use, and *Piersoni* and *Barrowsi* are both well recommended.

Guernsey Lily

Nerine sarniensis

The Guernsey Lilies are a genus of small, ornamental, bulbous plants with deciduous foliage. *N. sarniensis,* with attractive shades from salmon to scarlet and glowing crimson, is late-flowering with blossoms somewhat similar to but smaller than Amaryllis. The flowers appear in a dense umbel before the leaves in late autumn or early winter. The Guernsey Lily will well reward the amateur's care and attention. Pot the bulbs in three- or four-inch pots, one bulb to a pot, with good rich soil and give no water till the flower spike begins to show life. After the leaves appear, supply water in good quantity till the foliage begins to turn yellow. Then cut down and rest the bulbs until time to start growth for another winter. Nerines succeed best in a winter temperature of about fifty-five degrees.

Sweet Olive

Olea fragrans

The small white flowers of the Sweet Olive are produced all through winter and should scent a room or greenhouse with delightful perfume. The plant is evergreen, of bushy habit, and with holly-like, somewhat leathery leaves that withstand well the hazards of indoor conditions. Though easy to grow and to take care of, the Sweet Olive is not always easy to propagate. Slips with a heel (a portion of the old stem) should be taken and inserted in sand under a bell glass in a temperature of sixty-five degrees. Soil should consist of loam, peat, and sand in almost equal portions. The American Olive, related to the Olive of commerce, is hardy in the South and in the North is often found in conservatories.

Oxalis

Oxalis Bowiei

Oxalis has the reputation of being one of the easiest plants to grow and should be in all ways satisfactory. This Oxalis is tuberous rooted with trifoliate leaves and large rosy-red flowers which are often produced all through the winter. The leaves are large, fleshy, bright green in color. Bulbs should be started in early spring in light sandy soil and kept moist and shady until it is desired to bring them out for flowering. Some species do better if rested after their season of bloom; others contrive to grow and to blossom almost throughout the year. There are many other desirable winter-flowering Oxalis, including the charming Grand Duchess group.

Screw Pine

Pandanus utilis, P. Veitchi

The Screw Pine, very popular and thoroughly successful in house culture, obtains its name from the fact that the leaves are arranged along the stem in spirals. *P. utilis* is stronger growing than *Veitchi*, but the latter is very attractive, the leaves being light shiny green with broad pure white stripes, recurving gracefully and set with formidable spines along the edges and midrib. While still small the Screw Pines are valuable as table decorations. They need rich but carefully drained soil which must not be packed too closely about the roots. The Screw Pines are more or less subject to spot caused by small insects burrowing under the epidermis of the leaf for which there seems to be no remedy. Over-watering tends to induce an attack of this insect and should be avoided. The plants sucker freely, making it a matter of no difficulty to obtain new stock. A recent Screw Pine with yellow instead of white stripes and with its winter growth a deep gold, *P. Sanderi*, promises to be a very successful variation.

Lady Washington Geranium

Pelargonium domesticum

A corner window of well-grown Geraniums—the familiar whites and pinks with a dash of more vivid scarlet or salmon—will make a charming winter picture. The Geranium is the cheapest and surest of bloom of the plants of winter. Cuttings of many varieties made in spring should flower from Christmas on. The Lady Washington has not so many flowers in a truss as has the common Geranium, but the trusses are very large and effective, the flowers usually with a white ground marked or blotched with red or purple. Make cuttings in spring and keep outdoors over summer, during which they should be watered frequently and tips that show a tendency to become straggly pinched back. On the approach of winter bring the plants indoors. They should bloom in March or April. As soon as Lady Washingtons are well established in their flowering pots, manure water should be supplied regularly until flowering season. If the red spider or the aphides appear, syringe with one of the numerous tobacco extracts diluted with water. Slight shade will prolong the blooming season.

Peperomia

Peperomia argyreia

Peperomia is a dwarf foliage plant of easy culture and neat habit, indispensable for edgings in the greenhouse and for indoor floral embellishment. The attractive leaves are thick and fleshy, bright green, banded or marbled white; the reddish leaf stalks are attached to the under side of the leaf blade. Peperomia is easily increased by division and will grow in light and sandy soil if necessary. A minimum temperature of fifty degrees is essential, and there should be abundance of water about the roots; if these not over-difficult requirements can be met, there should be no trouble in growing this useful little plant.

Night-Blooming Cereus

Phyllocactus, Hylocereus, and others

The Night-blooming Cereus is of easy growth in a sunny' window and the flowers, white, fragrant, sometimes a foot long, are among the most charming of those commonly produced indoors. When planted in a greenhouse and encouraged to climb, the plant often attains a height of fifteen or twenty feet, becoming a fragrant mass of bloom; but where so much space cannot be afforded, a small plant two or three feet high in an eight-inch pot will provide a more modest display. The Phyllocactus family is easily increased by means of cuttings which, after taking, are usually allowed to lie a day or two before being inserted in sandy soil. Young, just-ripened shoots are best, though any piece of the stem provided with a bud will generally grow.

Spruce

Picea excelsa, P. pungens

The highly ornamental and attractive Spruces are so frequently planted about suburban homes and more extensive estates, for screens and for windbreaks and for specimens, that they may well be included within the modest limits of this volume. The Spruces are pyramidal, with four-angled leaves, sharp pointed and distributed spirally along the shoot, and pendant cones of which there is an annual crop.

The Norway Spruce (*P. excelsa*) is the familiar Spruce of dooryards with long cones hanging on the topmost branches and lower limbs drooping to the ground. It may be sheared to produce a fine hedge and for this purpose young trees should be set out so that their branches will just touch. Dwarf Spruces, very slow growing, are offered for garden use and there are varieties with golden foliage and with foliage that droops far more than type.

The Colorado Blue Spruce (*P. pungens*) is a cool, crisp-looking tree, rapid growing, and in its youth very symmetrical. The Spruces as a family like deep, moist, sandy soil; *pungens*, however, will do very well on soil quite poor and dry. The leaves of the type are deep green; the varieties most commonly planted are those with leaves of steely blue. The Colorado Spruce is one of the hardiest of Evergreens.

The very blue form grown for lawn decoration is *P. pungens Kosteri*.

Pine

Pinus strobus, P. rigida, P. resinosa, etc.

One half of the eighty known species of Pines grow in North America. Singly, or arranged in groups in small groves, Pines are to be seen with more or less frequency in home grounds serving as shelter and windbreaks, as shade and ornamental trees. Their winter beauty and usefulness single them out above others and make them beloved of home-makers both rich and poor. Within our narrow limits we can do no more than indicate a few of the more commonly planted sorts.

The White Pine (*P. strobus*) thrives anywhere except on wet clay subsoil and is our most useful Conifer for general planting. As a forest tree it has been known to attain a height of two hundred and fifty feet with a trunk seven feet in diameter at the base. The needles are light green and silvery, arranged in clusters of five.

The Pitch Pine (*P. rigida*) will not grow as high: eighty feet is about the standard for full-grown trees. The Pitch Pine is hardy, of very rapid growth, of symmetrical habit with spreading horizontal branches. This is one of the few Evergreens that will withstand ocean breezes and the effects of salt spray.

The Red Pine (*P. resinosa*) is a northern Conifer, its range being from Newfoundland to Pennsylvania and from Manitoba to Minnesota. The Red Pine stands trimming well and is a favorite for garden use. The bark is red and the light green leaves are arranged in pairs. Poor sandy soil and dry rocky hillsides offer no impediment to the growth of this sturdy tree which will look especially picturesque in ripe old age.

The dwarf Mountain Pine (*P. montana Mughus*) makes an almost globular bush ten feet high. The leaves are bright green, particularly attractive in spring when new growth is starting. This dwarf is frequently massed at entrances and along roadbeds and terraces. Resistance to cold and readiness with which it stands being transplanted are additional though scarcely needed recommendations.

There are also foreign Pines—Austrian, Swiss, Japanese —many of which would be more frequently planted if they were better known.

Stevia

Piqueria trinerva

The light graceful Stevia is invaluable for cutting and quite dependable in coming into bloom within estimated

limits. It is the most fragrant white flower you can be
sure of for Christmas, and by arranging plants in succession you may obtain bloom practically all through the
winter. Take cuttings after the plant is done flowering
(in January usually) and shift to larger pots as the young
plants develop. Plunge outdoors in ashes over summer.
It is important that the plants be turned occasionally and
the ends pinched out to induce symmetrical growth. With
the autumn chills bring Stevia inside and store in a cool
spot till you are ready to force them into bloom. A winter
temperature around fifty degrees is thought to be best for
this very attractive flower. There is a splendid variegated form and a pretty dwarf, *nana*.

Primrose

Primula obconica, P. Sieboldi, P. sinensis, etc.

Many of the Primroses are suitable for indoor culture in
small houses, though one will be always handicapped in
starting the young plants without the aid of a greenhouse.
Primroses are early, gay, neat, profuse in flowering, a joy
and a delight to the lover of flowers.

P. obconica, particularly to be recommended in var.
grandiflora, is among the most useful of all Primroses.
Large single flowers are borne in clusters on the tops of
stems four to ten inches high, individual flowers being
often an inch and a half across. The type color is lilac,
with crimson, white, pink, and rose-colored variations offered. The leaves are almost round, forming a rosette
supporting the flower stalk. The hairs on the leaves are
irritating or poisonous to some people, producing a rash
somewhat like that caused by Poison Ivy, which has caused

this Primrose to be planted less frequently than it should be on its undeniable merits. *P. obconica* will grow in greater range of temperature than most indoor plants, and the season of bloom is long and brilliant.

The Chinese Primrose (*P. sinensis*), another desirable indoor species but not one to be raised from seed except in a greenhouse, needs a temperature between fifty and sixty degrees at the time of flowering. The *stellata* forms are more graceful than the large-flowered sorts.

P. malacoides bears its small pink flowers in spring on a long loose spike. *P. Sieboldi* is beautiful, free-blooming, with large, variously colored, deeply cut flowers. *P. floribunda* yellow; *P. Forbesi* lilac with yellow eye; and *P. kewensis* a yellow hybrid, all have their admirers.

Seeds for Primulas are sown from January to March and by May the seedlings should be ready for thumb pots. After the middle of September the night temperature had best be kept about fifty degrees. In the various repottings do not press in too closely about the roots or cover the crowns of the plants. Soil should be quite heavy for *P. obconica*, three parts loam and one part cow manure, but need not be as heavy for *P. sinensis* and for many of the hybrids.

Spider Fern

Pteris cretica

The Spider Ferns are among the best small Ferns for the home, for window gardens, and particularly for table decoration. *P. cretica*, one of the safest of Pteris to try, grows nearly a foot high with straw-colored stalks and dark green foliage plain, or in some varieties with white markings. It has the further advantage that it will grow with a minimum of light and is therefore available for shaded windows. Good drainage is essential and the plants are greatly benefited by an occasional spraying with clear water. Loam, leaf soil, and well-decayed manure make the needed potting mixture, and propagation is to be effected by means of spores or by division of the old plants.

Another excellent Spider Fern is *P. serrulata*, not so strong a grower, however; it has brown stalks and the edges of the pinnae are sharply saw-edged. *P. argyraea* is stronger, growing with a broad white band down the middle of each division of the frond.

Calla Lily

Richardia aethiopica, R. Elliottana

The pure white flowers of the Calla Lily rising amid vigorous dark green foliage are among the most charming of indoor flower exhibits. The Calla retains its popularity year after year even though it is sometimes grievously disappointing as to bloom. Calla needs very rich soil—loam and well-decayed manure in almost equal parts. Bulbs that are rested during the summer are thought to respond better to winter forcing than those kept in light and heat the year round. Bulbs should be brought into growth again in September. One good watering should be sufficient at the start. When the plants are well under way, they will need watering copiously till the end of the flowering season. A winter temperature always approximately sixty degrees is strongly recommended.

The yellow Calla (*R. Elliottiana*), similar to the more common Calla except that the flowers are bright yellow

and the leaves spotted white, will make rapid growth if
brought into light and heat in early spring. Plants may
come into vigorous bloom within ten or twelve weeks after
growth is under way. Culture is similar to that of the
white Lily.

Pussy Willow

Salix discolor

If you wish to cheat the winter and produce the signs of
spring while wind and storm still rage outside, bring indoors some Pussy Willow cuttings in December or January
and place them in water in a warm room. The Pussy
Willow, gathered in armfuls by children of all ages over
the wide stretch of country in which the Bog Willow flourishes, heads the long procession of flowering shrubs and
trees that lasts through the spring to the edge of midsummer. The pollen-bearing and seed-bearing catkins are
different in appearance and are produced on separate
trees; the pollen-bearing are fluffy yellow, the seed-
producing silky and gray. The cultivation of Willows is
simple. A twig stuck into moist soil will grow to be a tree.
When Willows are set out in damp situations their roots
drain and greatly improve the land. The numerous members of the Willow family offer many varieties, attractive
in form and foliage and well suited to the purposes of garden embellishment.

Bowstring Hemp

Sansevieria thyrsiflora

Bowstring Hemp has very stiff, erect, white-spotted
foliage. Their general appearance is attractive and their

toughness enables them to regard with indifference the adverse conditions with which all indoor plants have to contend. Bowstrings were formerly made from a fiber obtained from the leaves of this Sansevieria. *S. zeylanica,* equally as well known and equally as tough, offers striking foliage variation. *S. zeylanica* is light green with many traverse markings of grayish white, and the leaves stand up as straight as small sticks. There is also a variety with round leaves (*S. cylindrica*) not so frequently met with in cultivation. Sansevierias will do well in all sorts of soils, in sun or shade, but preferably in sun with plenty of water. They are easily propagated from leaf cuttings.

Mother-of-Thousands

Saxifraga sarmentosa

Many admirers who have grown Mother-of-Thousands, Strawberry Geranium, Aaron's Beard—the names all apply to the one plant—for years would hardly know how to fill up a window box or hanging basket were this prettily variegated foliage plant not available. This charming Saxifrage forms a rosette of round leaves, light green variegated with silver above and reddish on the under side. The leaves are never more than eight inches high; the flower stalk rises a foot or a foot and a half high, producing whitish flowers in loose panicles. From the rosette of leaves come runners which, as they touch moist soil, root and produce new plants. When a young plant acquires a half-dozen leaves, it may be broken off from the parent and started on its own career. Rich, sandy vegetable soil is to be selected, if there be a choice, and a little shade against the rays of the midsummer sun is highly desirable. Mother-of-Thousands may be planted outdoors and will survive mild winters in the vicinity of New York.

Gloxinia

Sinningia speciosa

Gloxinias, as these plants are called by gardeners, have thick, fleshy leaves and large, showy, bell-shaped flowers of very rich coloration, dotted or blotched on either dark or light ground. Gloxinias are delicate, requiring light soil and careful watering that will be well repaid in the delicacy and softness of both leaf and flower. The plants bloom in early spring and summer and should be kept cool and shaded at that time. Seeds are fine and may be sown and treated as are Begonias; or tubers, or possibly young plants, may be obtained from florists. If tubers are bought, they should be started in a warm spot about midwinter or earlier. Gentle sprayings of the foliage will be found very beneficial.

Sparaxis

Sparaxis tricolor

Sparaxis bulbs are not readily obtainable but the charm of the wonderful color effects to be found in the flowers is most alluring. The plants grow six to twelve inches high and the flowers are produced in clusters on slender stalks in somewhat the same manner as those of Ixia. The flowers are often two inches in diameter and offer red, purple, and orange blotched or streaked on white combinations that are unusual and very attractive. They do well in a temperature that does not fall below a minimum of fifty-five degrees at night and are therefore available for the indoor winter garden. Bulbs should be potted in the autumn in good rich soil with some sand and the addition of a little bonemeal. Keep cool and dark until it is time to bring them out for flowering; then they will need copious supplies of water and the sunniest position available. If given good care they are quite likely to be successful a second season.

Yew

Taxus baccata, T. cuspidata, T. canadensis

The historic English Yew with its very dark glossy foliage, once extensively planted, has been proved to be not adaptable to our climate except in favored spots of the Middle South. We have available, however, *T. canadensis*, the native Yew, a charming, low-spreading, evergreen bush, extremely hardy and invaluable for carpeting purposes in colder climates and for forming undergrowth in the shade of high trees. Also, the richly hued, red-berried, thoroughly reliable Japanese Yew (*T. cuspidata*) which is being very largely planted nowadays. The dwarf Japanese Yew will grow ten feet high with a spread of several feet and with crisp, dark green foliage, but is most popular in its dwarfer form called *brevifolia*. The leaves are arranged flat in two ranks; the flowers are insignificant but the red berries and bark are superlative features of this shrub.

Yews succeed best in deep, moist, well-drained soil. Cuttings may be taken in the autumn and kept over winter in a frame or cool greenhouse. The Yews are slow growing and it is not advisable to try to raise from seed.

Arborvitae

Thuja occidentalis

The flat leaf spray sets off the Arborvitae from other
Evergreens and under its common but unfortunately applied name of White Cedar, this native tree is known
over a wide stretch of territory. Slow growth and compact habit are points in favor for garden use. The
Arborvitae is hardy, will stand severe pruning and late
transplanting, and is easily propagated from seed. Well-
grown specimens will develop into symmetrical trees
sixty feet or more high and there are dwarf garden forms
that never grow higher than four or five feet. Foliage is
brownish green, becoming darker with winter. There
are very many varieties. The Siberian Arborvitae (*T.
occidentalis Wareana*) is narrower, denser, better colored
in winter than the standard type. Among the great
number of improved garden forms available, perhaps
the favorite is George Peabody, orange-yellow, and very
desirable for bedding purposes.

Wandering Jew

Tradescantia fluminensis

The name Wandering Jew has been applied to many
trailing plants of vigorous nature. *Tradescantia fluminen-
sis*, perhaps the best known of those to which the name
has been applied, is an old-time favorite for hanging pots
and baskets. The type has shiny green leaves, but the
variegated forms—yellow, or white striped, or tinged
pink—are those most commonly seen. The stem and

leaves are succulent. The plant grows vigorously, as might be anticipated, in poor soils and in indifferent light. In the greenhouse this Spiderwort will be often found covering bare ground under benches. It is important to remember that variegated forms must be grown where they will receive a fair amount of light or they will tend to revert to the green-leaved type.

Zebrina pendula is another trailing plant to which the same name is frequently applied. The leaves are red above and purple below, with silver bands along the midrib. Pieces about four inches long stuck in the edges of a hanging basket quickly root and in no time at all form a mass of foliage sufficient to obscure the basket.

Hemlock

Tsuga canadensis

The Hemlock, partaking of the general character of the Norway Spruce but more graceful, feathery, and with brighter color, is one of the most desirable of ornamental Evergreens available for garden use. The Hemlock lifts its broad, pyramidal trunk and dark green, spray-like foliage high into the air, in favorable circumstances as high as sixty to a hundred feet. For domestic use this Conifer should not be planted where it will receive full exposure to heavy winds or salt spray. Hemlock stands the trimming shears very well and will make an excellent hedge. A rather moist soil seems to be about the only cultural requirement. Propagation is effected in winter by means of cuttings placed in a cool greenhouse or from seed which should be sown as soon as gathered. The Carolina Hemlock (*T. caroliniana*) is lighter and not so dense in foliage.

Veronica

Veronica speciosa

Shrubby Veronicas, attractive both in foliage and in bloom, are available for window boxes and with some protection will survive moderate winters out of doors. The flowers are at first reddish purple changing slowly to deep blue-purple, in long axillary spikes or racemes. For indoor culture soil should be rich, fibrous, sandy. A half-shady position is desirable for the summer months. Better-formed plants will be produced if the young shoots are kept continually pinched back. Cuttings may be inserted in sand in a greenhouse at any season of the year. The Veronicas are a large family, included among which are several of the most colorful of our garden flowers.

Crab Cactus

Zygocactus truncatus

This is the old-fashioned Epiphyllum or Christmas Cactus. The commonest Cactus for the window garden and generally most satisfactory with its profuse, brilliant, ruby-red or violet-red blossoms. The plants may be grown on their own roots or grafted on some other Cactus The young stems are flat, resembling the claws of a crab, but as they grow older, they become round and woody. Crab Cactus is useful in suspended pots or baskets as the branches hang downward. The plant delights in sunshine and dry air, and its leathery texture renders it resistant to dust and the fumes of gas. The problem of propagation is not bothersome, as bits of stem root readily.

Too much water should not be given this lover of dry soil, especially in winter. A good soil mixture will consist of sandy loam three parts, leaf mold one part, and a liberal sprinkling of old mortar to make the combination porous. During summer the plants should be placed outdoors in sunshine.

THE END

COLOR KEY

(See General Index for reference to pages)

BLUE TO PURPLE FLOWERS

Aconite
Aconite, Autumn
Agapanthus
Ageratum
Amethyst
Aster, Alpine
Aster, Stokes'
Barrenwort
Basket Flower
Bellflower, Carpathian
Bellflower, Chinese
Bellflower, Creeping
Bellflower, Great
Blazing Star
Bluebell, Common English
Bluebell, Virginia
Clarkia
Chamomile, False
Columbine, Rocky Mountain
Cupid's Dart
Daisy, Swan River
Dead Nettle
Delphinium, Hardy
Flox, Perennial
Forget-me-not
Foxglove
Gentian, Alpine
Glory-of-the-Snow
Grape Hyacinth
Guinea-Hen Flower
Heliotrope
Hellebore
Hepatica
Holly, Sea
Honesty
Hyacinth Bean
Hydrangea
Hysop

Immortelles
Indigo, Bastard
Indigo, False
Jacob's Ladder
Larkspur
Lavender
Lilac, Summer
Lobelia
Loosestrife
Love-in-a-Mist
Lupine
Matrimony Vine
Mezereon
Mist Flower
Monk's Pepper Tree
Morning Glory
Peppermint
Periwinkle
Plumbago
Raspberry, Flowering
Rosemary
Saffron, Meadow
Saffron, Spring Meadow
Sage
Salvia
Sea Lavender
Speedwell
Speedwell, Great Virginia
Spiderwort Common,
Spiraea, Blue
Squill, Autumn
Sweet Rocket
Sweet William, Wild
Valerian, Greek
Veronica
Violets
Water Lily, Zanzibar Blue
Wisteria

MAGENTA TO PINK

Alleghany Vine
Azalea
Bleeding Heart
Bouncing Bet
Carnations
Clover, Bush
Crab Apple, Japanese
Cyclamen
Garland Flower

Geranium, Wild
Heaths, Winter Blooming
Honeysuckle, Tartarian
Hydrangea
Judas Tree
Lavatera
Mallow, Swamp
Marigold, Fig
Marjoram, Pot

MAGENTA TO PINK—*Continued*

Millfoil
Mulberry
Pink, Wild
Poppy, Plume
Sea Thrift
Sedum, Showy
Steeplebush
Sweet William

Tamarisk
Tunica
Turtle Head
Valerian
Wax Plant
Weigela
Willow Herb

WHITE AND GREENISH

Achillea, The Pearl
Allspice, Japanese
Anemone, Poppy
Anemone, Snowdrop
Aster, Alpine
Astilbe
Baby's Breath
Barrenwort
Basil
Bladder Nut
Bridal Wreath
Campion, Evening
Candytuft, Evergreen
Cape Jessamine
Cereus, Night Blooming
Chokeberry
Christmas Rose
Cinnamon Vine
Clover, White
Cornel
Daisy, English
Daisy, Moonpenny
Daisy, Shasta
Day Lily
Deutzia
Elder
Everlasting, Pearly
Fair Maids of France
Farewell to Spring
Fetter Bush
Feverfew
Foxglove
Gas Plant
Goat's Beard, True
Goumi
Hawthorn or May
Hellebore
Hemp
Hercules Club
Honesty
Honeysuckle, Bush
Honesuckle, Hall's
Honeysuckle, Japanese
Hyacinth, Giant Summer
Indigo, False
Kerria, White
Leucothoë
Lily, Amazon

Lily, Bermuda Easter
Lily, Calla
Lily, Chinese Sacred
Lily, Gold-banded
Lily-of-the-Valley
Lily-of-the-Valley Tree
London Pride
Love-in-a-Mist
Magnolias
Man-of-the-Earth
Marguerite
Meadow-Rue, Feathered
Mock Orange
Mountain Lady's Mantle
Myrtle
Narcissus, Poet's
New Jersey Tea
Olive, Sweet
Pearl Bush
Pepperbush, Sweet
Poppy, Prickly
Rock Cress
Sage, Silver
Sea Thrift
Shadbush
Shooting Star
Silver Sweet Vine
Snakeroot, White
Snowball
Snowball, Japanese
Snowdrop
Snowdrop Tree
Snowflake
Solomon's Seal
Sour Wood Tree
Stagger Bush
Star-of-Bethlehem
Stevia
Sweet Alyssum
Toad Lily, Japanese
Tobacco, Flowering
Tuberose
Viburnums
Virginia Creeper
Watsonia, White
Wayfaring Tree
White Fringe
Yucca

YELLOW AND ORANGE

Aconite, Winter
Adonis
Allamanda

Artichoke, Jerusalem
Ashberry
Avens, Long Plumed

COLOR KEY

YELLOW AND ORANGE—*Continued*

Barberry, Japanese
Bladder Senna
Blanket Flower
Buckthorn, Sea
Burning Bush
Butterfly Weed
Calceolaria, Shrubby
Canary Bird Flower
Chrysanthemum, Annual
Cinquefoil, Shrubby
Columbine, Golden Spurred
Columbine, Wild
Column Flower
Cone Flower
Crown Imperial
Daisy, African
Daffodils
Dutchman's Pipe
Everlasting
Fair Maids of France
Genista
Globe Flower, Mountain
Gold Tuft
Golden Bell
Golden Chain
Golden Glow
Henry's Lily
Hop, Japanese
Hypericum
Jasmine, Sweet

Jonquil
Lemon Lily
Leopard's Bane
Marguerite, Golden
Marigold
Marigold, Pot
Monkey Flower
Musk Plant
Nasturtium
Oleaster
Pea-tree
Poppy, Horned
Poppy, Iceland
Prickly Pear
Primrose
Primrose, Evening
Rose, Japanese
Senna, Wild
Sneezeweed
Sneezewort
Spice Bush
Stonecrop, Dark Green
Sunflower
Sunflower, False
Tar Weed
Tickseed
Wallflower
Wallflower, Perennial
Witch Hazel
Witch Hazel, Japanese

RED AND INDEFINITES

Almond, Double Flowering
Anemone, Japanese
Bean, Scarlet Runner
Bee Balm
Begonia
Blazing Star
Cactus, Crab
Campion, Rose
Canna
Cardinal Flower
Catchfly, German
Clarkia
Clerodendron
Cockscomb
Coneflower, Purple
Coral Bells
Crown of Thorns
Dragon Head, False
Flamingo Flower
Foxglove
Fuchsia, Cape
Geranium

Geranium, Lady Washington
Giant Reed
Heath
Honeysuckle, French
Laurel, Mountain
Lily, Guernsey
Lily-of-the-Palace
Mallow, Musk
Maltese Cross
Manettia
Mountain Fleece
Oxalis
Peach, Flowering
Poinsettia
Poppy, Corn
Poppy, Oriental
Quince, Japanese
Red-Hot Poker
Salvia
Shooting Star
Strawberry Shrub
Trumpet Vine

IN VARIETY

Anemone, Poppy-Flowered
Aster
Aster, China
Azalea
Balsam, Garden
Beard Tongue

Begonias
Butterfly Flower
Calceolaria
Camellia
Canterbury Bell
Carnations

300   COLOR KEY

IN VARIETY—*Continued*

Chrysanthemum
Cineraria
Clematis
Cornflower
Cosmos
Crocus
Crocus, Autumn
Dahlia
Four o'Clock
Freesia
Fuchsia
Gladiolus
Globe Amaranth
Gloxinia
Hollyhock
Hyacinths
Iris
Ixia
Lantanas
Lilacs
Lilies
Love-Lies-Bleeding
Mignonette
Moss Pink
Pansy

Pea, Perennial
Peas, Sweet
Peony, Chinese
Peony, Tree
Petunia
Phlox, Perennial and Annual
Poppy, California
Portulaca
Primrose
Pyrethrum
Rhododendron
Rose of Sharon
Roses
Salpiglossis
Saxifrage
Scabiosa
Snapdragon
Sparaxis
Stock
Sweet Sultan
Sword Flower
Tulips
Verbena
Wishbone Flower
Zinnia

GENERAL INDEX OF NAMES

301

GENERAL INDEX OF NAMES

GENERAL INDEX OF NAMES 311